Vocational and Transition Services for Adolescents With Emotional and Behavioral Disorders

Strategies and Best Practices

Michael Bullis & H. D. Fredericks

Editors

Co-published by

Research Press
2612 North Mattis Avenue
Champaign, Illinois 61822
(800) 519-2707
www.researchpress.com

**Behavioral Institute
for Children and Adolescents**
1153 Benton Way
Arden Hills, Minnesota 55112
(651) 484-5510

Copyright © 2002 by Michael Bullis and H. D. Fredericks
All rights reserved.
Printed in the United States of America.

5 4 3 2 1   01 02 03 04 05

Copies of this book may be ordered from Research Press at the address given on
the title page.

Composition by Jeff Helgesen
Cover design by Linda Brown, Positive I.D. Graphic Design, Inc.
Printed by McNaughton & Gunn, Inc.

ISBN 0–87822–465–3
Library of Congress Control Number 00–109596

Contents

Chapter 7: Tracking Student Progress   123

Vicki Nishioka

Chapter 8: Job-Related Social Skills Training   139

Vicki Nishioka and Michael Bullis

Chapter 11: Gathering Longitudinal Information on Transition Adjustment 185

Michael Bullis

Figures

Preface

This book is based on two primary lines of work that Bud Fredericks and I worked on and directed from 1985 through 1995 while we both were at the Teaching Research Division of what was then Western Oregon State College, now Western Oregon University. The Sprague project was funded through various agencies in the state of Oregon and served adolescents with emotional and behavioral disorders who had been placed in foster care and other supportive living arrangements without success. These persons subsequently were referred to Bud and his staff at Teaching Research, then to the Sprague project, which included comprehensive living, educational, and vocational services. The second project, Job Designs, was funded through a series of federal grants and was located at a residential treatment center for adolescents who had been removed from their natural homes and who often exhibited antisocial behaviors. The primary focus of Job Designs was on securing and supporting these adolescents in the competitive workplace. In addition to these two programs, we added chapters from our colleague and good friend Michael Benz, on developing school and community partnerships, and a chapter from Julie Bulen on consulting with schools to develop alternative secondary education programs for youth with emotional and behavioral disorders.

It is fitting that we acknowledge Teaching Research, inasmuch as the support and flexibility we were afforded by that agency allowed us to pursue our interests and contributed greatly to the development of the programs we describe here. As things happen, however, Bud retired from Teaching Research in 1995, and at roughly the same time I accepted a position at the University of Oregon.

I must admit that I am uncomfortable in being listed as the first author. Bud Fredericks was the primary architect of the Sprague project and the first version of Job Designs (the project received two other grant awards under my direction). Bud is one of the true giants of the special education field, and his work has shaped our present educational and social service system, as well as affected in a positive way the lives of thousands of people with disabilities. After he retired he graciously told me to take the lead on the book, a gesture in keeping with his style. I believe that one of the greatest gifts I have been given is the opportunity to work closely with Bud over the years. He has taught me more than I can recount about the subject of this book, as well as about being a better professional and human being. We all need our heroes—Bud is mine.

At some point (memory fails as to exactly what point) we decided to try to describe how the programs were structured and what it was that our staff did with and for the young people with whom they worked.

This intent was the genesis of this book. We also wanted to involve the staff who actually did the work as the primary authors in order to make the text as realistic and pragmatic as possible. As they—and we—worked on the Sprague and Job Designs projects, as well as others, and our own life events sometimes interrupted our work, this book moved forward in fits and starts.

The book is composed of chapters that accurately reflect the major activities our staff engaged in when working with adolescents identified as at risk, emotionally or behaviorally disordered, socially maladjusted, or mentally ill (as described in chapter 1, the terms used with this broad population are quite numerous). Within each chapter, we have presented and described major responsibilities and service activities. To illustrate key points we have presented case examples (all names that are used are fictitious) and examples of forms we have developed and used over the years. Throughout, we have tried to be practical and direct in our presentation in the hope that people in the "real world" will actually use this book to work with adolescents in service settings.

I would be remiss not to thank our two project consultants who helped us over the years: the late Robert Gaylord-Ross and Gene Edgar. It was an honor and pleasure to work with these close friends and colleagues. I also want to thank Cheryl Davis and Matt Ramsey for their exceptional work in editing and formatting the first draft of this document. Between then and now, Drs. Sheldon Braatan and Eleanor Guetzloe of the Behavioral Institute for Children and Adolescents, an organization with which I have worked for a number of years, took this manuscript to Research Press. Finally, Karen Steiner at Research Press worked hard to make the final version of this book as readable and "user friendly" as possible. Any errors, however, are mine alone.

This document and the work it represents are dedicated to the many professionals with whom we worked, and to the adolescents in our projects and their families.

—MICHAEL BULLIS

bullism@oregon.
uoregon.edu

CHAPTER 1

Introduction and Overview

Constance Lehman

For the past 25 years concern has been expressed about the lack of appropriate and effective services for the children and adolescents to whom we refer in this book as having emotional and behavioral disorders (EBD; Joint Commission on the Mental Health of Children, 1969; Knitzer, 1982; President's Commission on Mental Health, 1978). This population truly is quite broad and encompasses persons called emotionally disturbed, mentally ill, socially maladjusted, antisocial, criminal, and deviant—to name but a few titles.

For a variety of reasons it has been difficult to provide effective support to this population. Specifically, the diversity of the emotional and behavioral characteristics exhibited by these individuals presents a challenge, and interrelated environmental factors complicate the process of distinguishing individual characteristics that require specialized intervention from family and community variables that influence emotional and behavioral responses. In addition, there is growing acknowledgment among professionals and parents that perhaps the greatest barrier to providing effective support to children and adolescents with EBD is the fragmented nature of the categorical service delivery systems of the education, social services, juvenile justice, mental health, and health fields (Nelson & Pearson, 1991). To a large extent, these services have become institutionalized and bureaucratized, making it difficult at best to support individual children and their families in a coordinated and effective manner.

During the past decade federal initiatives, combined with state and local program planning and implementation, have begun to affect the way in which services are delivered to adolescents with emotional and behavioral disorders. A gradual shift is occurring from the categorical approach to the provision of services to these persons and their families to an integrated, coordinated system of support at the local level. This shift to an ecological orientation to understanding the etiology of emotional and behavioral disabilities and support of individuals based on each person's characteristics and circumstances relies on individualized assessment and systematic, coordinated support to meet goals and objectives determined by these adolescents and their families.

For the majority of adolescents transitioning from school to the responsibilities of adult life, comprehensive support includes community-based vocational training and employment opportunities combined with provision of effective related services from community resources. This combination of services is necessary to increase the chances that these individuals will be able to live productive and fulfilling lives in their communities. The purpose of this book, then, is to present a community-based vocational placement and training model. In this model the role of the service coordinator is emphasized to ensure that adolescents receive comprehensive support that enhances their ability to succeed at work and that their unique needs are addressed in a timely and appropriate manner.

This chapter provides a frame of reference by defining the population of youth who are considered emotionally or behaviorally disturbed. It includes an estimate of the prevalence of emotional or behavioral disorders and focuses on the interrelated child, family, and environmental factors that contribute to poor outcomes for this heterogeneous group in transitions to education, work, independent living, and social settings. The discussion builds the rationale for developing and implementing individualized support systems that provide services appropriate to the individual and the individual's unique life circumstances.

To provide a context for the recommended service delivery model, this chapter includes overviews of two programs using this community-based system of support, followed by case examples of students who have benefited from this approach. The chapter concludes by outlining each succeeding chapter.

POPULATION

In order to talk coherently about adolescents with emotional and behavioral disorders, it is important to define who is described by that term. This section begins by giving the current and proposed federal special education definitions for emotional and behavioral disorders. These definitions are followed by discussion of the prevalence of emotional and behavioral disorders. An overview of the complex nature of these disorders follows.

Perhaps the most common label for this population in the public schools is the term *seriously emotionally disturbed (SED),* which has been changed to *emotionally disturbed (ED)* in the most recent amendments of the Individuals With Disabilities Education Act. This term refers to those students eligible for special education services and whose inability to learn is due to emotional characteristics. We should note that it is entirely possible for students labeled as ED by the schools not be considered as having an emotional condition or mental illness according to the medical or social service community and the guidelines used by those agencies. Further, students with sporadic school attendance patterns or who move frequently but who manifest extreme behavioral and emotional problems may not have gone through the administrative process to acquire such a label in the school setting.

The definition of ED reads as follows (IDEA 1997, Section 121a.5):

> *(i) The term means a condition exhibiting one or more of the following characteristics over a long period of time to a marked degree, which adversely affects educational performance:*
>
> > *(A) An inability to learn which cannot be explained by intellectual, sensory, or health factors.*
> >
> > *(B) An inability to build or maintain satisfactory interpersonal relationships with peers and teachers.*
> >
> > *(C) Inappropriate types of behavior or feelings under normal circumstances.*
> >
> > *(D) A general, pervasive mood of unhappiness or depression; or*
> >
> > *(E) A tendency to develop physical symptoms or fears associated with personal or school problems.*
>
> *(ii) The term includes children who are schizophrenic. The term does not include children who are socially maladjusted, unless it is determined that they are seriously emotionally disturbed.*

Many professionals (e. g., Bower, 1982; Kauffman, 1989) have been critical of this federal definition. The interpretation of the definition differs from state to state—and even from site to site within states. Therefore, there is no uniform label for these students from state to state or even from city to city within a particular state. Consequently, it is difficult to generalize the results of empirical studies conducted in one region or another, or to talk meaningfully about adolescents with these disorders (Kavale, Forness, & Alper, 1986).

Because of the problems in the federal terminology and classification, in this book we refer to individuals as having *emotional and behavioral disorders* (EBD), a term that is gaining acceptance in special education and that we use to refer to the broad population of adolescents with emotional *and* behavioral challenges (Forness, 1988; Forness, Kavale, & Lopez, 1993; Forness & Knitzer, 1992).

In addition, many children and adolescents with these disorders may also have specific learning disabilities (LD). In a survey of 100 families in Oregon with children who had emotional or behavioral disorders, Lehman (1996) found that nearly half of the children and youth with Attention Deficit Hyperactivity Disorder (ADHD) and Attention Deficit Disorder (ADD) also were diagnosed with LD. Nearly 40 percent of youth with the label ED also had learning disabilities. Adolescents with EBD may also carry mental illness diagnostic labels. These include the categories of disruptive behavior disorders, anxiety disorders, and psychotic disorders, as well as a number of other categories identified in the fourth edition of the *Diagnostic and Statistical Manual of Mental Disorders* (DSM-IV; American Psychiatric Association, 1994).

The prevalence of EBD in children and adolescents is difficult to ascertain, largely because of the lack of a common definition of emotional or behavioral disorders across disciplines and the inadequacies of current assessment and diagnostic instruments in identifying emotional or behavioral disorders. The identification process becomes even more complicated when individual child and family characteristics and environmental factors that influence behavior are considered (Farrington, 1987; Institute of Medicine, 1989; Loeber, 1991). In spite of these difficulties, there is general agreement that 5 percent is a very conservative estimate of prevalence of these disorders in children and adolescents, and estimates of approximately 12 percent may be closer to the actual rate (United States Congress, Office of Technology Assessment, 1986). There is general agreement across disciplines that the majority of these children and adolescents require a range of services that cannot be met by categorical systems in isolation and that an integrated system of support must be available, in many cases, well into adulthood (Nelson & Pearson, 1991). For the past 20 years, federal and state policies and programs have increasingly reflected a growing consensus among professionals and family advocacy groups that to improve home, school, and community adjustment for this population, community-based systems of supports that rely on systematic, person-centered and family-focused service coordination are more successful than categorical approaches (Burchard, Burchard, Sewell, & VanDenberg, 1993; Illback, 1993; Jordan & Ichinose, 1992).

Within a community-based system of support, it becomes essential to understand differences in child and adolescent developmental characteristics and the types of support needed at specific stages of development. The population of interest in this book is adolescents prior to transitioning from school to adult life. To increase opportunities for making a successful transition to adult life, the types of support this age group needs generally include (a) academic assistance, (b) social skills training, (c) independent living skills, and (d) systematic vocational training and employment experiences.

TRANSITION EXPERIENCES

The realities of the current economic situation make successful transition to employment difficult in general for adolescents. Various other obstacles, however, uniquely faced by adolescents with EBD, further bar their chances for transition success. These additional obstacles include (a) lack of educational participation; (b) higher than average unemployment after leaving school; and (c) lack of social skills required to maintain work, peer, and family relationships. The dropout rate for adolescents with EBD is higher than for any other disability category and nearly twice the rate for adolescents as a whole, including those with and without disabilities (Weber, 1987). For adolescents with EBD that rate is estimated to be greater than 50 percent (Wagner, 1991), as compared with 25 percent for the general population (Hess, 1986; Rumberger, 1987). Most adolescents with EBD do not go on to postsecondary programs (Neel, Meadows, Levine, & Edgar, 1988). Neel et al. collected employment and continuing education data for 160 young adults. Of the group sampled, only 17 percent were attending some form of postsecondary education, and 31 percent were unengaged (not working or attending school). In addition, studies conducted by Wagner and Shaver (1989) and Kortering and Edgar (1988) have shown around a 50 percent unemployment rate for students with EBD after leaving school. An analysis by Marder (1992) suggests that, 4 years after high school, the unemployment rate for this population is 58 percent. Finally, the propensity for this population to engage in antisocial and criminal behaviors adds to their difficulties in transitioning from school to meaningful work.

A number of other factors contribute to problems in transition achievement for this population. Among these factors are (a) low acceptance by peers, (b) aggressive behavior, (c) drug and alcohol abuse, (d) stealing, and (e) lying. Social issues such as low acceptance by peers and inappropriate social skills may predict dropping out of school and criminality (Parker & Asher, 1987) and additionally may contribute to low self-esteem and negative feelings toward mainstream society. Bullis and Gaylord-Ross (1991) report that many studies indicate that EBD during adolescent and adult years is related to deficits in social skills (Dishion, Loeber, Strouthamer-Loeber, & Patterson, 1984; Freedman, Donahoe, Rosenthal, Schlundt, & McFall, 1978; Gaffney & McFall, 1981; Hazel, Schumaker, Sherman, & Sheldon-Wildgen, 1982); social cognition (Dodge, 1980); and social problem solving thinking (Chandler, 1973; Kendall, Deardorff, & Finch, 1977; Levinson & Neuninger, 1971; Platt, Scura, & Hannon, 1973; Platt, Spivack, Altman, & Altman, 1974; Slaby & Guerra, 1988). These findings support the teaching of appropriate social and problem-solving skills to adolescents with EBD, focused on the context of real-life experiences.

The need to address the transition to independent living for adolescents with EBD systematically goes beyond the moral responsibility inherent in the educational system. The costs to society of not providing this population with effective support structures are apparent in every community. The high dropout rate and its association with an individual's increased likelihood to engage in criminal activity (Kunisawa, 1988; Levin, 1982) and to live in poverty (Hess, 1986) necessitate an increase in resources to support the juvenile and adult correction systems and public assistance programs. According to Levin (1982), male dropouts between the ages of 25 and 30 cost society $237 billion in lost earnings, $71 billion in lost revenue, $3 billion in welfare expenditures, and $3 billion in crime prevention services. Costs related to criminal acts by this group total hundreds of millions of dollars per year (Goldstein & Glick, 1987). Additionally, costs to the victims of these crimes, the expense of service provision, and family turmoil are uncountable. To forestall this cycle of antisocial, nonpurposeful behavior, there is an urgent need to offer systematic job development and training and support to this population.

SERVICE COORDINATION

During the past two decades professionals across the service systems have increasingly acknowledged that, when specialized assistance is needed from more than one of the categorical systems, the categorical approach to service delivery is ineffective and inefficient in producing positive outcomes for individuals with EBD and their families. Therefore, although it is important to recognize the pragmatic value of eligibility criteria and diagnostic labels, effective service provision for this diverse population may depend more on the provision of systematic service coordination focused on the strengths and needs of each individual youth than it does on the diagnostic category in which the individual "fits" (Lehman, 1996).

Federal policies initiated in the fields of education, juvenile justice, mental health, and child welfare have enabled the creation of collaborative community-based integrated services for adolescents with EBD, in which service coordination is fundamental to program implementation (Nelson & Pearson, 1991). One of the guiding principles of community-based coordinated systems of support for this population is that service provision is individual centered and family focused (Stroul & Friedman, 1986). In other words, support is provided on a person-by-person and family-by-family basis. The emphasis is on individualized support that matches the developmental needs of the adolescent within the context of the home and community environment. This orientation can be called an "ecological approach."

We operationalize this theoretical approach through the use of the transition specialist (TS). Transition specialists typically are individuals who have experience in providing vocational services to adolescents and adults with disabilities—not necessarily to persons with EBD. They may or may not have a college degree; it has been our experience that there is no substitute for job development and placement experience. These staff work closely with a group of 12 to 15 persons to (a) develop jobs, (b) provide job placement and support, (c) assist in service management activities, and (d) serve as advocates. The relatively low ratio of students to staff is one of the reasons for our success, and caseloads much larger than these parameters are *strongly* discouraged.

COMMUNITY-BASED PROGRAMS

The movement toward pragmatic programs of training and support for the EBD population has been encouraged and, in many instances, made possible by federal legislation. The federal transition initiative authored by Madeleine Will, then Assistant Secretary of the Office of Special Education and Rehabilitative Services (OSERS), emerged in 1984. This transition model described the types of services needed to facilitate the transition from school to work for students with disabilities. Paralleling the transition initiative were the Rehabilitation Act amendments spelled out in Public Law 99–506, enacted in 1986. These amendments expanded the supported employment initiatives to include individuals with learning disabilities and emotional and behavioral disorders. Coupled with the expansion of services was the availability of federal dollars, through the Rehabilitation Services Administration (RSA), for research and demonstration projects designed to provide supported employment to the newly included populations and to develop program strategies that would be evaluated for their effectiveness.

The underlying philosophy for developing and implementing community-based vocational and transition programs for adolescents with EBD is that these persons have the right to live and work in their communities. The goal of these programs is to increase this population's chance for successful integration into their communities as adults through comprehensive vocational and functional skills training in both school and community settings. The challenge for educators is to develop and implement programs that tap into existing resources while providing a support structure that meets the varied needs of this diverse and complex group.

This book, then, provides suggestions for ways in which to develop and implement such transition programs. The recommendations we make are based on two projects that operated through the Teaching Research division of what during the time of service was Western Oregon State College and now is Western Oregon University: the Sprague High School Program and Job Designs.

Sprague High School Program

The Sprague High School Program served adolescents with EBD at Sprague High School in Salem, Oregon, for 13 years (Nishioka-Evans, 1987). This program supported students ages 13 to 21 whose behaviors could not be controlled in their own homes. Most students resided in residential care programs operated by Teaching Research. There were two main residences, a group home and a supervised apartment complex, with a few students living in foster care or, on occasion, with their natural parents. All were identified as having EBD with cognitive disabilities (e.g., mild and moderate mental retardation). The behaviors students exhibited reflected severe psychopathology, such as schizophrenia, bipolar disorder, conduct disorder, antisocial personality, oppositional defiant disorder, and pedophilia. Histories of antisocial behaviors—for example, assault, burglary, sex abuse, and prostitution—had frequently sabotaged previous attempts to support these individuals in both the school and home environments.

The program incorporated school, vocational, and residential components. The core of the school program was a functional curriculum (Fredericks & Nishioka-Evans, 1987). The foundation for the model's success was the maintenance of a positive learning environment. This instructional model emphasized practical learning grounded in the requirements of working and living in the community, as well as use of a task-analytic, behavioral teaching approach. Instruction was provided in three major content areas: (a) independent living, (b) social interaction, and (c) vocational skills. Particular attention was paid to preparing students for the living and work settings they would move to upon leaving the program and to involving all appropriate service agencies and resources in the eventual movement of the student to another setting. The TS, responsible for assuring that each student's vocational goals were met, provided job development, placement, and monitoring, along with case management services, because issues not related to work often impact work performance. The students learned independent living skills in actual residences; practiced vocational skills in community-based work settings; and practiced correct social behaviors for community integration in the work, residential, and school environments in which these social behaviors naturally occur.

In line with this community-based instructional philosophy, a five-phase system for providing each student with concrete behavioral and skill expectations was employed. The phased format of this system emphasized increasing the student's level of responsibility to self-manage his or her own behavior. Each higher phase was more demanding than the last; movement through the system progressed from closely supervised training in unpaid work to unsupervised and paid work in competitive jobs. As a direct result of our experiences in the Sprague program, we developed the Job Designs program.

Job Designs

Job Designs was a collaborative effort between a residential treatment center for children and adolescents with EBD and Teaching Research (Bullis, 1992b; Bullis & Cheney, 1999; Bullis, Fredericks, Lehman, Paris, Corbitt, & Johnson, 1994; Fredericks & Bullis, 1989). Students in the program ranged in age from 16 to 21. Places of residence included the residential treatment center, group homes, the homes of parents/guardians, and independent living settings. The behavioral characteristics of the population served paralleled those of the Sprague participants. One distinct difference was that the majority of Job Designs participants were of average or above-average cognitive ability. Students participating in Job Designs attended either one of two public high schools or the on-campus school. In addition, some were home tutored, had dropped out, or had graduated from high school. The structure for coordinating support and transition services and for providing consistent intervention strategies was often not school centered.

The minimum age for referral to Job Designs was 16, with most students referred at 17 years of age. The majority of persons in the program were expected to live on their own within 1 to 2 years. An important task of the TS was to address the transition needs of students. Activities to teach independent living and social problem solving skills began immediately. Whenever possible, program staff kept in contact with students for 6 months to 1 year after they left the program to provide support during the transition to independent living.

Case Examples

Students in both the Sprague program and the Job Designs effort had family and personal histories that had severe negative impact upon their self-esteem and ability to perform positively in life. The following case examples illustrate how the model presented in this book positively affected the lives of youth with EBD.

When Charles was referred to the Job Designs program, he was living in a cottage at a residential treatment center for children and adolescents with EBD. He had been physically and sexually abused as a child, lived in a number of foster homes, and had a history of alcohol and drug abuse, and physical aggression when upset with others. As a result of numerous violent attacks against his mother, he was placed in foster care settings. His behavior while in foster care continued to be violent (i.e., fighting with peers and continued abuse of drugs and alcohol). On the basis of these uncontrolled behaviors, Charles was placed in residential treatment. In addition to behavioral issues, Charles exhibited learning disabilities in reading and math, and had experienced difficulty in school throughout his childhood.

At the time of follow-up, Charles was 18 years old. He had been successfully employed for a small building supply company for the past 9 months. He had been hired as a paid employee to load and unload trucks, make deliveries, and organize the inventory. Charles learned his job tasks from his supervisor and co-workers. He received social skills training from the TS on a one-to-one basis and through the program's vocational support group. In addition, the TS provided service coordination by monitoring Charles's attendance and progress in his drug and alcohol treatment group and his management of independent living responsibilities such as payment of rent and utilities. The TS monitored the worksite through weekly phone calls or face-to-face conferences with Charles's supervisor.

That Charles held a job for 9 months represented a breakthrough in his life. In addition to maintaining his work performance, he worked through conflicts with co-workers by using problem-solving skills learned and practiced with the TS and his peers in the vocational support group. As a result of the assistance Charles received from Job Designs staff, his employer, and his peers, Charles learned how to get and keep a job, alternative ways to deal with problems at work and with peers, and how to live independently in the community. During the transition to independent living, the TS communicated with Charles's counselor at the county mental health department, Children's Services Division caseworker, and juvenile probation officer to assure that

Charles would continue to be supported upon leaving the Job Designs program.

Susan was originally referred to the Sprague High School Program by children's services. Susan's family had a history of problems, including her mother's abuse of drugs and alcohol. She lived with her father prior to being placed in foster care and in a large state mental hospital's adolescent unit. She had learning disabilities in the areas of language and math. Norm-referenced tests showed her to exhibit borderline mental retardation. Susan also had a seizure disorder controlled by medication as well as a history of noncompliance with requests by teachers and employers, clinical depression, and self-injurious behavior. When referred, she had no friends or supportive acquaintances.

The Sprague program worked well for Susan in a number of ways. The functional curriculum taught her practical skills, such as how to find and maintain an apartment; budget money; solve communication problems with friends, employers, and co-workers; and learn and maintain personal hygiene and grooming. Susan learned independent living skills, vocational skills, and communication and social skills in school, in the residential setting, and at her community job. Sprague's residential component offered Susan a peer support network and a structured "home setting" in which she practiced social and problem-solving skills. The community-based vocational component provided Susan vocational training and work experience. The Sprague program furnished opportunities for building self-esteem along with a coordinated structure of support across the domains of home, school, and work.

After her graduation from the program Susan moved in with her father, worked at a pizza parlor, and enrolled at the local community college on a part-time basis. She required little monitoring on the job. The TS initiated Susan's enrollment in the community college and referral to the county mental health services and local office of vocational rehabilitation. In addition, she continued to monitor Susan's progress and provide assistance in planning long-range educational and career goals. She met with Susan on a regular basis and assisted her in maintaining a social network. Susan's father, owner of a small business, began employing students with EBD participating in other vocational projects operated throughout the schools and community programs in the locale.

SUMMARY AND CHAPTER OVERVIEW

The programs described in this book provide practical support to individuals like Charles and Susan. This support includes service coordination; job development, placement, and monitoring; social skills training; and instruction in independent living skills to make transition to adult life more successful. An important part of the transition process is referral to agencies such as the local office of vocational rehabilitation, Social Security Administration, local community college or career training program, and individual or group counseling services.

The purpose of this book, then, is twofold (a) to point out key procedures and characteristics important to community-based vocational programs for adolescents with EBD and (b) to provide a blueprint of the components of a successful program. Throughout the book, we include samples of the numerous forms we used in managing the program. Blank copies of these forms are gathered in Appendix A; any of these may be photocopied for noncommercial use in running a similar program, or you may wish to use them as a starting place for developing your own materials. The chapters following this introduction describe the key elements in implementing a successful community-based vocational program in general and for the EBD population in particular.

Chapter 2: Building School and Community Partnerships. Adolescents with EBD present varied and multiple service delivery needs. Accordingly, various service agencies outside the school setting should be involved in service delivery efforts. However, it often is difficult to build and manage the interconnections among these disparate groups. This chapter details steps for developing this system of services.

Chapter 3: Intake and Preplacement. The intake and preplacement process encompasses all procedures that occur with a student prior to job placement (e.g., student referral, student interview, contacts with school and agency personnel and parents/guardians). These information-gathering steps provide an abundance of data that allow program staff to assess the student's strengths and needs.

Chapter 4: Job Development and Placement. The job placement process involves the careful appraisal of worksites, including employers and co-workers, actual job tasks, opportunities for learning and personal growth, and physical settings. These factors must be carefully measured against student strengths and needs. This chapter gives examples of job matching and procedures for preparing students for interviews, the interview process, and actions to take after a student is hired (e.g., scheduling, transportation, clothing purchases).

Chapter 5: Job Training and Support. It is the responsibility of program staff to recognize changes in work performance and intervene in a timely manner to assist students in keeping their jobs. Issues affecting job performance can be work related or not. This chapter describes procedures for collecting work and nonwork data, interpreting that data, and providing appropriate interventions.

Chapter 6: Behavioral Interventions. This chapter provides detailed information regarding implementation of informal and formal behavioral intervention strategies that have been effective with students with a wide range of behavioral problems.

Chapter 7: Tracking Student Progress. As the need for accountability becomes more apparent in school and social programs, it is essential for programs to demonstrate a positive impact on their participants. This chapter describes procedures for documenting student gains in the areas of skill acquisition and behavior. The methods described include employer and staff evaluations of students, evaluation of job-related social skills, and collection of work data. Examples are given on how to adapt intervention strategies for particular individuals.

Chapter 8: Job-Related Social Skills Training. Difficulty in getting along with others has caused isolation and failure in many instances, including work settings. This chapter describes a social skills training approach that helps students learn prosocial and problem-solving behaviors that are effective at work, home, and school, as well as in other community settings.

Chapter 9: Vocational Support Groups. One forum for providing program participants with additional support is the vocational support group. This structured peer group provides both a social network for students and opportunities for training in independent living skills, problem solving, and job-oriented requirements (e.g., resume writing, job search techniques).

Chapter 10: Providing Consultation and Technical Assistance. In our experience, it is easier to talk about how vocational transition programs should be structured and quite another to implement such programs in schools. Through several staff and program development projects, we have gained insight into the ways in which the precepts presented in this book can be realized in the school context. This chapter describes them.

Chapter 11: Gathering Longitudinal Information on Transition Adjustment. All too often, little attention is paid to evaluating the impact of programs of this type on the students who are served, their families, school personnel and programs, employers, and community service agencies. In this era of fiscal austerity it is critical for evidence to be amassed from multiple sources to document the positive effects of these programs and their services.

It is our hope that this book will enable professionals to develop and implement community-based vocational and transition programs that have a positive impact on individuals with EBD while creating an atmosphere of community participation and support for these students as they make the difficult transition to adult life.

CHAPTER 2

Building School and Community Partnerships

Michael R. Benz

The concept of school and community partnerships is embedded in current legislation and represents a "best practice" marker for all adolescents, especially for adolescents with disabilities and those with emotional and behavioral disorders (EBD). Strong school and community partnerships provide the foundation for effective transition services. This is especially true for adolescents and young adults with EBD for the reasons highlighted in chapter 1 of this book. The high-risk behaviors exhibited by many adolescents with EBD are interrelated and tend to cluster together. Moreover, emotional and behavioral disabilities do not simply "go away" once students leave school and enter the community. Responding to these multiple, long-term needs will require effective multiagency collaborations. Providing comprehensive, effective vocational and transition services for youth with EBD also requires coordinated services from schools and a variety of community resources (e.g., social services, vocational rehabilitation, juvenile justice, mental health). Unfortunately, the fragmented nature of the service delivery system in most communities is often the greatest barrier to providing effective support to adolescents with EBD.

Two related yet distinctly different reasons exist for building partnerships between schools and community agencies: (a) to secure the community resources needed to help *an individual student* accomplish the transition goals he or she has identified (e.g., referral to vocational rehabilitation) and (b) to improve the capacity of schools and communities to provide services and resources that will enhance the transition of *all students* with disabilities—for example, developing guidelines for integrating procedures for Individualized Education Programs (IEPs) and Individualized Written Rehabilitation Plans (IWRPs; Benz, Lindstrom, & Halpern, 1995). The other chapters in this book describe procedures for securing community resources to help individual students accomplish their vocational and transition goals. This chapter focuses on strategies for building the capacity of schools and communities to support the vocational and transition needs of all youth with disabilities, including youth with EBD. Specifically, this chapter (a) reviews issues and barriers that prevent schools and community agencies from working together more effectively in support of adolescents in transition and (b) describes an approach for building and sustaining effective school and community partnerships.

COLLABORATION ISSUES AND BARRIERS

Schools and community agencies do not naturally or easily work together well. Unfortunately, community agencies do not always work well together either. Why is this? The most common areas of difficulty are listed in Figure 2.1.

Most of the issues separating schools and community agencies, and community agencies from one another, stem from the different purposes and mandates that govern their activities. This is an issue of *entitlement* versus *eligibility*. Children in the United States are entitled to a public education. The idea that education should be publicly funded and universally available is so strongly held in our country it goes without question. The passage of the Education for All Handicapped Children Act (Public Law 94–142) in 1975—now titled the Individuals With Disabilities Education Act—extended this fundamental right to a free and appropriate public education to all children and adolescents with disabilities. No comparable mandate exists for adult services. Adult services (e.g., vocational rehabilitation, mental health, higher education) are eligibility driven. As such, adult service agencies differ from schools and from one another in two fundamentally important ways: access and availability. Individuals wanting to access adult services must go through a process whereby they are determined eligible for the services the agency provides. Individuals determined ineligible cannot receive services. Most adult agencies have been established by federal or state legislation to provide a prescribed pattern of services (e.g., vocational services, educational services) or to serve a particular population (e.g., people with psychiatric disabilities, out-of-school teen parents, substance abusers). Differences in legislated mandates usually result in different eligibility criteria across agencies in the community. Unfortunately, most people who require services from community agencies do not fit neatly into such boxes. This is especially troublesome for adolescents and young adults with EBD, whose needs often dictate multiple agency involvement.

The fact that adult agencies are eligibility driven also means that, unlike public schools, services from these adult agencies are *not* universally available. Lack of availability can occur in two ways. First, a particular agency may not be located in a specific area. This may be especially likely in some rural communities. Second, an agency may be located in the community but unable to serve additional people due to funding limitations. Again, because there is no entitlement to adult services, the number of individuals who can receive services is limited

Figure 2.1
School/Community Collaboration Issues and Barriers

1. Eligibility for services

   • Entitlement versus eligibility

   • Narrow focus of services/target population

   • Different eligibility criteria

2. Location and availability of adult services

3. Communication/coordination among agencies

4. Consequences for youth with EBD

   • Knowledge of available services

   • Ability to access relevant services

   • Support to benefit from services

by the amount of funding provided. Typically, agencies respond in one of two ways when funding limitations occur. Sometimes individuals are put on waiting lists with the hope of receiving services in the future. Sometimes agencies change their eligibility criteria (e.g., colleges raise standards for admission) or their priority for services (e.g., vocational rehabilitation agencies focus on individuals with the most severe disabilities). Either way, the functional effect is the same—services are denied to some individuals who need them.

These issues have direct implications for building effective school and community partnerships. Effective partnerships require regular communication and coordination. This can be difficult when schools and various community agencies operate under such different mandates and when they differ so greatly in their eligibility criteria, accessibility, and availability. The consequences for adolescents with EBD and their families are enormous. When communication and coordination across schools and community agencies, and among different adult service agencies in the community, are limited or nonexistent, the burden of knowing what transition resources exist in the community, identifying and accessing relevant agency resources, and successfully using these resources falls completely upon adolescents with EBD and their families. Given this set of circumstances, it should not be surprising that follow-up and follow-along research shows consistently that young adults with EBD rarely access adult services such as vocational rehabilitation during the transition years (Kortering & Edgar, 1988; Valdes, Williamson, & Wagner, 1990). The next section describes an approach for structuring more effective school and community partnerships to support transition-age adolescents with EBD and their families.

Mobilizing local community resources through partnership-building activities has been a high priority in special education for several years (Johnson & Rusch, 1993), and it has received considerable attention in many of the State Transition Systems Change Projects that have been funded and implemented across the country in the recent past (National Transition Network, 1996–1997). Almost always these efforts have taken place at the local community level, and almost always they have taken the form of establishing a team of relevant stakeholders and a process for guiding and supporting their activities. These teams have been called "community transition teams," "core transition teams," and "interagency transition councils," among other names (Halpern, Benz, & Lindstrom, 1992; Izzo, 1994; Lindsey & Blalock, 1993).

Despite differences in names, these approaches have many similarities. These similarities, and the lessons that have been learned from these approaches, form the framework for building effective school/community partnerships. First, the instrument for change should be a local community transition team. Two aspects of this statement are worth highlighting: *local community* and *team*. The focus of change and improvement should be the local community. Students leave a local high school and enter a local community. The success students experience will in part be a result of the services and resources available in a specific high school and community. The instrument for change should be a team of key people concerned about the transition of students with disabilities in general and adolescents with EBD specifically. By definition, transition is a process that involves schools, families, and communities. Ensuring that adequate services and resources are available to support students during the transition years must therefore be the responsibility of all of these key groups.

Second, local teams should use a systematic process to guide their activities. A basic four-step "management-by-objectives" approach can be useful for this purpose:

1. Establish a local community transition team.

2. Assess local program improvement needs.

3. Develop and implement an action plan.

4. Evaluate accomplishments and repeat the cycle.

These four steps are presented and described briefly in the remainder of this chapter. Readers interested in developing a local community transition team as a means to improve transition services for youth may wish to consult Blalock and Benz (1999), which describes these four steps in much greater detail.

Before reading the procedures next outlined, take a moment to read the vignette in Figure 2.2, which details a local transition team's program improvement efforts over the course of 3 years. This local transition team's experiences illustrate the kinds of program capacity changes that can occur on behalf of youth, specifically illustrating the ways in which a team's activities relate to one another within any given year and the ways in which activities build cumulatively on one another to create change over time. Two areas of activity are described, both of which address this team's general concern for improving transition services within its community: developing transition planning procedures and increasing family involvement in transition.

Step 1: Establish a Local Community Transition Team

Build a Representative Team

The primary purpose of team building is to establish a strong, cohesive team that represents the community. The initial development of a transition team usually involves two activities: (a) establishing an appropriate geographical and political framework for the team and (b) identifying people who are willing and able to serve as team members.

The manner in which you define the basic geographical and organizational boundaries of your transition team will have a tremendous impact on its ultimate success in your community. Therefore, you should undertake this step with very careful consideration. Each team will develop a unique framework for establishing team boundaries and for meeting the needs of its local community. For example, some rural areas might form both local (town or district) and regional (possibly county) transition teams so that all local areas can benefit from one another's successes and resources. Team membership may also show great variation according to the needs of the community. The size and location of your community is relevant in several ways to how your team may be structured. Factors include (a) the available pool of applicants; (b) competition for resources; (c) logistics imposed by the distances between agencies, families, or organizations you wish to include; and (d) the number of school districts with secondary special education programs.

With regard to identifying potential team members, teams should include the full array of people who are concerned about secondary special education and transition programs in their communities. This array of team members includes representatives from four groups: (a) adolescents with disabilities and their families; (b) school personnel (e.g., teachers, administrators, counselors, school-to-work staff); (c) adult services personnel (e.g., vocational rehabilitation, mental health, community college); and (d) community representatives (e.g., employers, chamber of commerce, ministerial association). Once teams are established, team building becomes an ongoing process in which members examine their local community regularly to determine who is needed to represent the community adequately.

Set the Team Up for Success

The initial meetings of your team can place you en route to productivity if you employ a few basic strategies—specifically, holding meetings in

Figure 2.2

A Community Transition Team's Improvement Efforts Over Time

Developing Transition Planning Procedures

Transition planning for students with disabilities was a priority for many local community teams even before the legislative mandates in the Individuals With Disabilities Education Act (IDEA; Public Law 101–476) were put into place. This local transition team focused its attention on this area over a 5-year period, beginning with the development of a written transition planning document and culminating with ongoing procedures to use specially trained school district personnel to engage in a transition planning process with some very difficult students.

During the first year, a small subcommittee of school personnel worked with family members and adult agency representatives to create an Individualized Transition Plan (ITP) form and procedures that would reflect a philosophical emphasis on preparing students for life after high school. Over the course of the school year, this new process was field tested by a few teachers with a few students. The following year, Public Law 101–476 passed, and transition planning was mandated. Now the school district was convinced of the need to develop transition goals for all students with IEPs. To assist in this process, the community transition team applied for a cooperative personnel planning grant from the Oregon Department of Education. The grant was used to support inservice training for a group of secondary special education teachers. The training had two components: (a) the new transition services component of IDEA and (b) the new transition planning documents developed by the team. As a result of this inservice training, the original ITP forms and procedures were modified to meet the requirements of the new legislation. Over the course of the next 2 years, all of the district's certified special education staff (over 200 people) were trained to use the new transition planning forms and procedures.

Now all the special education teachers in the district had a set of written procedures and a form to guide them in their transition-planning efforts. However, the transition team felt that more needed to be done to ensure that all students had the benefit of these procedures. The final step was to apply for another grant to train a group of "transition facilitators" (both teachers and support staff), who would work with students and families to assist them in the planning process. Their mission was to find students who were really struggling with (or who may have dropped out of) the existing school system and to develop a relationship with these students and their families. These facilitators helped to "hook students up" with needed services and facilitate a process for developing a "person-centered" transition plan.

Increasing Family Involvement in Transition

During this same time frame, another subcommittee of the transition team focused its efforts on increasing family involvement in the transition process. This issue was ranked near the top of the transition team's formal needs assessment, based on the belief that families needed more information to support students with disabilities during the transition years. With that goal in mind, the team decided to schedule several events to educate family members about the transition process and possible transition resources.

During the first year of plan implementation, the team hosted a Transition Fair. The fair followed the format of a home and garden show, with various adult service agency representatives setting up information tables around the school gym. Parents (and students) could wander around the room, collect materials, and ask questions about possible post-school resources. This fair was a good way to provide introductory information to a lot of people at the same time. However, some parents wanted more in-depth information and a forum for sharing their concerns. To fill that need, Parent Coffees were designed. These were evening meetings (complete with pie and coffee), each organized around a specific transition topic—for example, applying for Social Security benefits or postsecondary education options. At each meeting, a guest speaker from the community presented information, and school staff were available to answer questions and discuss how these resources might affect specific students.

The coffees were a great success! In fact, the team decided to hold them once a month over the following school year. Yet the team was not totally satisfied. The next step in accomplishing their overall goal of increasing parent involvement in transition was to develop a class for parents of students with disabilities. This class, titled "A Parent's Survival Kit," was developed jointly and team-taught by a high school special education teacher and a local vocational rehabilitation counselor who volunteered her time in the evening. The class was revised based on parent input, continues to be offered as an ongoing course at the local community college, and involves staff from several high schools, the community college, and adult service agencies. The class has been a wonderful opportunity for parents to get information and help prepare their students for the transition from school to the community. As one parent commented, "One of the things that helped me though this [transition] process was talking to other parents who have children with disabilities. Another was having professionals who could describe the whole picture and offer educated advice."

Note. From "Mobilizing Local Communities to Improve Transition Services" by M. R. Benz, L. Lindstrom, and A. S. Halpern, 1995, *Career Development for Exceptional Individuals, 18,* pp. 21–32. Adapted by permission.

locations that are "open" to all potential members and establishing a positive framework for change through a mission statement.

A review of several factors is helpful in determining where to hold meetings so many will attend, particularly many who represent the community's key stakeholder groups. First, cultural, ethnic, economic, and geographic differences promote more separation than we might like in many communities. Hold the meetings at a place that invites all groups to participate, such as a community center or restaurant. It is risky to assume that the school will necessarily be perceived as a friendly place, due to its institutional nature, no matter how friendly the school staff have tried to be. This may be especially true for youth with EBD and their families. The same perception may hold true for the city hall or a bank. It is essential, of course, to ensure the physical accessibility of meeting sites regardless of where they are held. Also, select a site that is central to the geographic region covered by your team to maximize attendance. A related strategy is to agree to rotate around the region so that all geographic subgroups have a chance to "host" a meeting, thereby increasing ownership of the team's activities. An advantage to rotating is that schools, employers, and adult agencies have a chance to show physical features and even specific activities of their programs or operations to team members.

Improving transition services and programs through a local team's efforts, in concert with efforts at the student and school-building levels, is most likely when team members have shown an interest in change and a willingness to pursue change. Spending some time evaluating at least a *core* group's commitment to change would be wise before wasting people's time or an agency's money on setting up a community transition team. If support for change exists, then the team's activities will help bring many others on board and exert the external pressure often needed to move bureaucracies to advance. Often, local transition teams have found that developing a mission statement to guide the team's efforts can serve as a means to discuss team members' commitment to change. Through these discussions, team members are able to create a shared vision that can serve as a cornerstone for future activities and a means to evaluate the team's focus and effectiveness. Blalock and Benz (1999) have suggested that a mission statement for a local transition team should be (a) clear, jargon free, and understandable; (b) concise enough for everyone to remember and use; and (c) compelling, powerful, and urgent. Mission statements that meet these criteria can be vital tools for inspiring and energizing the team and the broader community. Everyone understands where the group is going and how he or she fits in.

Step 2: Assess Local Program Improvement Needs

The primary purpose of needs assessment is to allow team members a collective opportunity to examine the current status of secondary special education, transition, and adult service programs and resources in the community. The needs assessment process basically addresses the overall question "How are we (the school and the community) doing in our job to help students with disabilities prepare for a satisfactory life as young adults?" The answer to this basic question leads to a greater awareness of program changes needed to achieve this broad goal. Ideally, this is a process in which team members can hear the perspectives of different groups (e.g., school personnel can hear the concerns of parents and employers) and then arrive at a general consensus about the highest priorities for improvement.

The needs assessment process used most commonly by local transition teams includes two major components: (a) identifying 8 to 10 program improvement goals and (b) selecting 3 to 5 top-priority goals. Each of these components usually is completed in the context of a team meeting.

Identify 8 to 10 Program Improvement Goals

The purpose of this first component of the needs assessment process is to help team members identify a finite list of program improvement goals. This is not as easy as it may seem. In most communities many aspects of secondary school curricula and programs, transition services, and adult agency and community resources *could* be improved to serve youth with EBD and other disabilities and their families better. Moreover, there are many perspectives on which aspects of the school and community are most in need of improvement, and many of these perspectives will be represented on your team (e.g., parents, students/school leavers, school and adult agency staff, and community representatives). The challenge is to identify a concrete, finite, feasible

provement goals that incorporate the perspectives of
...olders.

...nz (1999) describe a generic process for goal identifica-
...ominal group process approach toward program plan-
...Delbecq, Van de Ven, and Gustafson (1975). This
...d in Figure 2.3, assumes that your local team has
...bers during the needs assessment phase. The steps
...bgroups of members in order to encourage greater
... If your team has 10 or fewer members, you may
...e structured discussion process as an entire team.
...sing the same general process described in Figure 2.3
...p activities. The outcome of the nominal group
...buld be 8 to 10 program improvement goals that the
...ussed and, by voting, agreed are important for
enhancing the capacity of schools and communities to serve the transition needs of youth with disabilities and their families, particularly youth
with EBD.

Select 3 to 5 Top-Priority Goals

At this point in the needs assessment process, your team will have
identified 8 to 10 goals that have emerged as important areas in need of
improvement. Your team cannot address all of these goals in one year,
of course. The purpose of this step in the needs assessment process is to
identify a smaller number of goals that will structure your team's plan
during the upcoming year. Teams accomplish this process in a goal-
setting meeting, where the team members discuss all 8 to 10 goals to
identify a subset of 3 to 5 top-priority goals. Use the following three
steps to identify your team's highest priority goals.

First, engage team members in a structured discussion of each of
the 8 to 10 goals, using the major selection factors of *support, feasibility,* and *impact.* Underlying the *support* factor is the critical importance
of selecting goals that will encourage the interest and involvement of a
majority of team members, whether they represent the interests of parents, schools, adult service agencies, or the community in general.
Attending to the issue of *feasibility* will increase the likelihood that
your team will be able to complete the selected goals successfully.
Thinking about the desired *impact* of the selected goals will sharpen
the focus on identifying those goals that hold the greatest immediate
potential for affecting the lives of the adolescents and young adults
with disabilities in your community. Discussing the entire set of 8 to 10
goals from the perspective of these three selection criteria can help create a common frame of reference for team members to use in selecting
the highest priority goals for the upcoming year. One note of caution:
Allow for discussion, but keep the group focused on the task of prioritiz-
ing goals based on the selection criteria. Past experience has shown
that during this part of the meeting some team members can drift into
problem-solving discussions instead of focusing their attention on the
selection of goals. If this occurs, gently bring the team back to the topic.

Figure 2.3
Summary of Steps in the Nominal Group Process

1. Depending upon the size of your team, divide the team into subgroups of six to eight members each, ensuring as much as possible that each subgroup remains representative of the team overall (e.g., don't have all school staff in one subgroup and all parents in another subgroup). This encourages greater variability in the goals identified by each subgroup. Ask one member from each subgroup to serve as a facilitator.

2. Provide each team member with paper or 3 × 5 index cards. Instruct group members to "List the things you would like to see improved in the schools or in the community in order to help youth transition successfully from school to the community. As best you can, try to write these things as positive goal statements that we could work on as a team (e.g., 'Provide students more job experience in high school' or 'Provide families more information about community resources')." Instruct team members that they are to do this step independently and without speaking to other team members in their group. Give them 20 to 30 minutes to complete this step.

3. At the end of the allotted time, provide each subgroup with a large sheet of poster paper, marking pens, and masking tape, and ask the subgroup facilitator to serve as recorder for his or her group. Within each subgroup, ask team members one at a time to give one goal statement from the list of goals they created. As each team member reports his or her goal, the facilitator records the goal on the poster paper exactly as the team member reported it. Continue this round-robin process of having one team member report on one goal until all team members have reported on all goals they created. If team members have created similar goals, these may be designated by check marks rather than writing out similar goals. Take only as much time as is necessary to record each member's goals.

4. After all goals are recorded, give each subgroup 20 to 30 minutes to discuss, clarify, and elaborate on the entire list of goals they created. At the end of the 20 to 30 minutes, give the subgroup members additional paper or 3 × 5 index cards and ask them to vote privately on the five goals they feel are most crucial to address. Give subgroups 10 minutes to complete this voting activity. Have subgroup facilitators collect the vote cards and record (with help if necessary) the votes of the subgroup directly on the paper next to the relevant goals. Give subgroup members a break while the votes are being tallied and recorded.

5. Assemble the work of the subgroups, then bring all team members back together. Give each subgroup 5 to 7 minutes to report on the top goals that emerged from their identification, discussion, and voting activities. The specific number of goals you ask subgroups to report on will depend on the number of subgroups. The outcome of this reporting process should be approximately 12 to 15 goal statements, which become the focal point for discussion and voting by the entire team.

6. Give the entire team 20 to 30 minutes to discuss, clarify, and elaborate on the combined list of 12 to 15 goals that have now emerged from the work of the subgroups. Keep the group focused on understanding the purpose and intent of the goal statements. (Sometimes during these discussions, team members drift into generating solutions to the problems that appear on the list as a way of deciding whether a goal is important or worth pursuing.)

7. At the end of the 20 to 30 minutes, give the subgroup members additional paper or 3 × 5 index cards and ask them to vote privately on the five goals they feel are most crucial to address. Give subgroups 10 minutes to complete this voting activity. After the voting is complete, collect the vote cards, and set the time and location for the next needs assessment meeting, in which team members will review the results of the voting and select 3 to 5 top-priority goals to address in the upcoming year.

Second, select the top goals by having each team member vote for his or her top three priorities. Use an overhead transparency or poster paper to record team members' votes. Add the total points to determine the top 3 to 5 goals for the entire team.

Third, once the top 3 to 5 goals have been identified, obtain consensus on these top goals. Ask, "Is there anyone who *can't* live with these goals for the next year?" Allow discussion until team members agree that the top 3 to 5 selected goals are the most important ones for the team to address over the course of the next year.

Step 3: Develop and Implement an Action Plan

The purpose of this step is to translate the team's priorities for improvement into a concrete plan that can be accomplished in a school year. Limiting activities to a school year (or a calendar year) helps ensure that team members will complete their activities and experience success in a timely manner and come to view the community transition team as a useful mechanism for improving transition services and resources.

Develop a Concrete Action Plan

Like most action plans, the plan developed by team members should specify the objectives, activities, timelines, and persons responsible for accomplishing the plan. Two common ways for team members to develop an action plan are through several (typically two to three) team meetings or through an all-day planning workshop. Your team will need to decide which strategy makes most sense given the time constraints of individual team members. If team members can devote a day to planning, this often is most advantageous, both in terms of developing a specific action plan and in building relationships among team members. A sample agenda for a day-long planning workshop as proposed by Blalock and Benz (1999) is included in Figure 2.4.

Using the agenda in Figure 2.4 as a general framework, team members should review the 3 to 5 top-priority goals they selected earlier. Doing so provides a good introduction to the purpose of the planning activities and also allows team members to reaffirm the decisions that have been made. To identify objectives, team members can use the nominal group procedures presented in Figure 2.3. The result of this process will be the identification of one or more concrete objectives for each goal. The number and type of objectives team members choose to address for each goal are decisions completely at the discretion of the

Figure 2.4
Action-Planning Workshop Agenda

Planning workshop 8:30–4:00

8:30 A.M.	Introductions (if new members present).
9:00 A.M.	Overview of the planning workshop. Review transition team purpose and process. Overview of the planning process.
9:30 A.M.	Review top-priority goals selected by the team. Present top-priority goals. Review key discussion points.
10:00 A.M.	Break
10:15 A.M.	First planning session: Identify objectives for each goal. Identify list of possible objectives. Select objective(s) for each goal.
12:00 P.M.	Lunch
1:00 P.M.	Second planning session: Develop each objective. Identify tasks and timelines for first objective. Select a work group for each remaining objective. Identify tasks and timelines for each remaining objective. Reconvene as a group and review all objectives. Identify time and place for next team planning meeting.
4:00 P.M.	Adjourn

Follow-up planning meeting 4:00–6:30

4:00 P.M.	Review and complete plan. Review objectives, tasks, and timelines for each goal. Review time/task calendar, and adjust plan as needed. Identify persons and resources for each objective.
5:30 P.M.	Discuss strategies for implementing the plan. Establish subcommittees and basic operational procedures. Set time and place for next meeting.
6:30 P.M.	Adjourn

team. It is recommended, however, that the total number of chosen objectives be small so the team will be able to manage the workload without overburdening team members.

Once a set of objectives has been identified and chosen for inclusion in the annual plan, team members should develop tasks and timelines for each objective and identify the persons and resources that will be needed to accomplish each objective. Developing a "task analysis" of this kind may come across as an imposing concept to some team members who are not familiar with educational jargon. It is important to demystify the task analysis concept and help all team members feel that they can create a set of logical steps to get from point A to point B. Sample details for one objective included in an annual plan are given in

Figure 2.5. The process of identifying tasks, timelines, persons, and resources should be repeated for each chosen objective until team members have fully developed each objective they will be addressing in their annual action plan.

Implement the Annual Action Plan

The essence of program implementation is the specification and employment of a set of procedures for encouraging and supporting a group of volunteers to accomplish the work of the team's annual plan. It is important to keep in mind that transition teams are groups of individual volunteers. This means, of course, that each team member's own personal priorities will often compete with the team's priorities as captured in the annual plan. When the realities of each member's personal and professional life set in, it will be important to provide team members with structure, guidance, and support to keep them focused on their commitments to the objectives and the tasks specified in the team's annual plan.

Several strategies can help keep team members focused and active as the action plan is implemented. First, it is important to establish a team structure that meets the needs of team members and helps them balance their commitment to the team with their other personal and professional commitments. A supportive team structure can include establishing consistent team meeting procedures (e.g., meeting at times and locations that accommodate team members' needs) and using team meetings effectively (e.g., setting and following an agenda for each meeting that includes a predetermined ending time). Second, most teams choose to distribute the total workload of the plan by breaking into subcommittees to address the specific objectives in the plan. Breaking into subcommittees also has the advantage of allowing team members to volunteer for activities that are closely related to their interests and that match the time they have available for team activities. Finally, most teams appoint a team leader or team co-leaders with responsibility for organizing and monitoring the activities of the subcommittees and team as a whole.

Step 4: Evaluate Accomplishments and Repeat the Cycle

The last step in the process is for team members to evaluate their efforts with respect to impact and outcomes. This evaluation sets the stage for identifying goals and objectives for the next year that build cumulatively on this year's accomplishments.

Program evaluation is a critical component of the community transition team process because it provides the link between program implementation during a current year and program planning for a subsequent year. Spend the time necessary to take stock of your team's efforts and activities. Improving the capacity of your school(s) and community to better support the transition of youth with disabilities is a continual journey, and it is easy for teams to fall into the trap of "do, do, and then do some more." This last phase of the community transition

Figure 2.5
Details of an Action Plan for One Objective

Details of the annual plan

Goal 1: Students with disabilities receive appropriate vocational instruction that prepares them for jobs in their community.

Objective 1.1: Information will be collected on the types of vocational instruction currently provided to students with disabilities.

Subcommittee chair _____ *John Doe* _____

Street _____ *1234 Main Street* _____

City/state/zip _____ *Anywhere, USA*   12345 _____ Phone _*123-555-7890*___

Subcommittee co-chair _____ *Jane Smith* _____

Street _____ *5678 Main Street* _____

City/state/zip _____ *Anywhere, USA*   12345 _____ Phone _*111-555-3333*___

Other team members involved _____ *No* _____

Resources needed to accomplish objective

Personnel? _____ *John and Jane* _____

Duplicating? _____ *Duplicating final products* _____

Postage? _____ *No* _____

Other? _____ *No* _____

Office supplies? _____ *No* _____

Telephone? _____ *Yes — to call teachers* _____

Printing? _____ *No* _____

Other? _____ *No* _____

Tasks and timelines needed to accomplish objective

Task 1: Review forms and procedures used by other transition teams to collect information on vocational instruction.

Desired deadline _____ *11/01/01* _____

Task 2: Develop a plan for collecting information on vocational instruction currently provided to students with disabilities, including (a) the people who will collect the information, (b) the population of students who will be surveyed, (c) the format to be used to collect the information, and (d) the timelines for collecting the information.

Desired deadline _____ *12/01/01* _____

Task 3: Meet with special education and vocational education teachers, and other key team members to discuss the plan and obtain their input and support.

Desired deadline _____ *01/01/02* _____

Task 4: Collect and summarize the information on vocational instruction.

Desired deadline _____ *02/01/02* _____

Task 5: Present the information to appropriate people (e.g., school administration), and obtain support for developing or expanding vocational instruction for students with disabilities.

Desired deadline _____ *02/15/02* _____

team process, evaluation and planning, can provide a short respite along the way to remember how far the team has come and to review the road map for the next leg of the journey.

The community transition team evaluation phase involves two components: (a) evaluating the team's activities and accomplishments and (b) developing an action plan for the next year, using the evaluation information as the foundation for this planning. Your team can complete these activities during the last one or two regularly scheduled meetings of the year, or your team can hold a special combination celebration dinner and team meeting. The disadvantage of the latter option is finding a time when all (or almost all) team members can be present, finding a location for a working dinner, and finding funds to cater the dinner. On the other hand, a dinner meeting provides a special occasion to take stock of the team's progress to date, celebrate the team's hard work and successes, and plan thoughtfully for the next year. Only your team can decide which option offers the most advantages for team members. Figure 2.6 presents a sample agenda for a dinner meeting as proposed by Blalock and Benz (1999).

Regardless of which approach is taken, it is important for team members to have an opportunity to evaluate their accomplishments and to explore thoughtfully the implications of these accomplishments for the program improvement areas they want to target in the next annual plan. As part of the process of evaluating the team's accomplishments, team members also should have the opportunity to evaluate how well the team functioned during the past year. Team members can discuss what worked and what didn't work with regard to how well the team functioned, both in terms of team structure (e.g., subcommittees) and in terms of team operational activities (e.g., team meeting procedures). If you have gotten to this point in the community transition team process, your team obviously has done some things quite well in terms of its functioning. Yet few teams function so well that there is nothing to improve. Keeping both of these perspectives in mind will help your team fine-tune its operations in subsequent years.

SUMMARY

Community transition teams that have followed the basic steps described in this chapter have experienced considerable success in building school and community partnerships focused on improving the transition services and resources available in the community (e.g., Benz et al., 1995). This is good news. Of course, the process is not as easy as it sounds. Team members from the different groups identified (i.e., family members, school personnel, adult services personnel, and community representatives) often do not have a strong history of working well together. As such, they may approach this collaboration opportunity with skepticism. If the community transition team process is to contribute to a strong, effective school/community partnership, it is essential that teams include broad participation from key stakeholders in the

Figure 2.6
Evaluation and Planning Meeting Agenda

4:00 P.M.	Introductions (if new members present).
4:15 P.M.	Overview evaluation and planning meeting.
	Review agenda.
	Review current action plan.
	Identify person(s) to record notes.
4:30 P.M.	Evaluate team accomplishments and activities.
	Describe and discuss accomplishments (e.g., products and/or programs developed, people trained, additional funds acquired).
	Review what worked/what didn't work about team structure and operational activities (e.g., team process questions).
5:30 P.M.	Dinner
6:00 P.M.	Develop action plan for next year.
	Identify new or "carryover" goals and objectives.
	Develop tasks and timelines for each objective.
	Reconvene as a group and review all objectives.
7:30 P.M.	Establish team structure for next year.
	Identify persons and resources for each objective.
	Establish subcommittees and operational procedures.
	Identify person(s) to write summary of team accomplishments.
	Set time and place for next meeting.
8:00 P.M.	Adjourn
	Congratulate one another again for your efforts and successes!

community. If teams are viewed as "something the school is doing," then the partnership is nonexistent. Research suggests that school and adult agency personnel are often the most active on teams because of the close relationship between the team's goals and their ongoing work responsibilities. Conversely, family and community members (e.g., employers) are often the least active members and frequently are the first members to become inactive. The challenge is to create options that allow families and community members to participate meaningfully over time. These strategies must incorporate members' perspectives in the identification of change goals and take advantage of their passions in the accomplishment of goals.

Finally, building effective school and community partnerships requires that change be viewed as a process and not an event. The differences in schools and community agencies described earlier, and among different community agencies, will not be resolved easily. Even under the best conditions, and even with an effective partnership to structure regular communication and collaboration, it will take time to work through these differences. It will take time for families, school and adult agency personnel, and community members to build trust and learn to work together effectively. It will also take time to address the multitude of issues involved in improving transition services and resources for adolescents with disabilities. These issues will take even longer to address fully for adolescents with EBD, given the challenges these young adults face during the transition years.

In short, building effective school and community partnerships requires time and perseverance. In his book *The 7 Habits of Highly Effective People,* Covey (1989) describes this aspect of relationship building as "following the law of the harvest." We close our discussion of school and community partnerships with Covey's thoughts on what it means to follow this law:

> *It simply makes no difference how good the rhetoric is or even how good the intentions are; if there is little or no trust, there is no foundation for permanent success. . . . To focus on technique is like cramming your way through school. You sometimes get by, perhaps even get good grades, but if you don't pay the price day in and day out, you never achieve true mastery of the subjects you study or develop an educated mind. Did you ever consider how ridiculous it would be to try to cram on a farm—to forget to plant in the spring, play all summer and then cram in the fall to bring in the harvest? The price must be paid and the process must be followed. You always reap what you sow; there is no shortcut. This principle is also true, ultimately, in human behavior, in human relationships. (pp. 21–22)*

CHAPTER 3

Intake and Preplacement

Janet Corbitt and Kathleen Paris

This chapter focuses on the intake process, emphasizing actions that should be completed *before* the attempt is made to place the student with emotional and behavioral disorders (EBD) in a job. These activities often take longer than the student or staff would wish, but it has been our experience that the time spent at the front end of the placement and service provision process is invaluable and reaps rewards over time.

POPULATION PARAMETERS

One fundamental is to define clearly the population to whom services will be provided. Our belief is that all people are employable and can become successful and healthy citizens, provided they are afforded appropriate and effective services and supports. Although all referrals—regardless of the severity of disorder—were considered for entrance into our programs, five general stipulations applied:

1. The individual must be formally identified as having an emotional disability *or* be considered at extreme risk for school and personal failure (e.g., have been adjudicated or have an acknowledged substance abuse problem) and be receiving support services from at least one social service agency outside the public school (e.g., public welfare, mental health, corrections).

2. Because of wage and hour regulations governing job placements, individuals referred must be at least 15 years of age.

3. There must be some assurance that the individual will be in the area and accessible to the project for at least 6 months.

4. If the individual presents an extreme risk to the safety of staff or self, reasonable assurance of support services (e.g., detention) from other agencies must be secured.

5. The adolescent—himself or herself—must agree to be involved in the project.

Obviously, variations on these population parameters could be adopted by other programs. Some programs might focus on homeless adolescents, pregnant teenagers, parolees, and so on. In any case, the population served will dictate—at least to some degree—the identity of the project, its funding sources, and the nuances of service provision. It is critical that this identity be clearly stated and that guidelines regarding the target population be followed. In our experience, "stretching" to provide services to persons outside a program's parameters and skill areas is problematic. When staff attempt to work in areas outside their expertise, the services offered can be fragmented and ineffective.

We should note that both the Sprague High School Program and Job Designs served adolescents with extreme and high-risk behaviors, including sex offenders. This specific group was one whose needs we addressed carefully and for whom we took precautions before making placements in community-based jobs or social settings. Although we believe it is possible to serve many of these individuals in the community, we must emphasize that *extreme care* must be taken in placing and monitoring these persons. It is entirely possible that those individuals with lengthy histories or who have been judged to be at risk for offending again may not, and perhaps should not, be served in transition programs except with the most careful monitoring. These decisions should of course be made on an individual basis after reviewing complete information on the individual in question and weighing risks against potential benefits to the student.

OUTREACH TO OTHER AGENCIES

Effective service coordination with community-based agencies—including vocational, postsecondary, recreational, medical, mental health, and housing agencies—is the key to successful vocational placement and transition for adolescents with EBD. Figure 3.1 is a list of the agencies with which we have worked. Once a transition specialist (TS) has identified the services necessary to support a participant in successful community integration, it becomes the responsibility of that individual and his or her TS to locate and contact the appropriate agencies. Maximum responsibility is placed on the individual to take a lead role in this effort; however, in some cases, it is necessary for the TS to take the lead, with the participant assisting in the effort. The dual goals of service coordination are to (a) secure necessary services and (b) offer a context in which the participant can learn to interact effectively with other adults and service providers.

Although establishing formal interagency agreements at an administrative level to effect service coordination has some advantages (see chapter 2), it has been our experience that informal networks through the TS are efficient and effective. The TS often coordinates these multiple services while affording the student as much responsibility and independence as possible and appropriate. The TS's personal relationship with the *individuals* in these agencies is critical. A phone call from

Figure 3.1
Related Service Delivery Agencies

Children's services

This division provided financial resources for the group home and foster care elements of the projects. In addition to providing referrals and group home and foster care funding, this agency often provided funding for work clothing; start-up costs for apartments; stipends for minors preparing to emancipate; and payment of fees for classes in areas of interest, such as electronics or modeling.

County mental health

Referrals were received from the local mental health department. Services provided to students by this division included crisis counseling and drug and alcohol evaluation and treatment.

School district

Whenever possible, program staff worked with the school to design an individual program for students that incorporated work experience and school credit. In addition to receiving credit for work experience, students sometimes were able to receive an English credit for keeping a diary of their work experiences and making a notebook consisting of information needed to fill out basic applications, a current resume, and the dos and don'ts of job searches and interviewing. Project staff participated in the Individual Education Program (IEP) process.

Community college

The community college provided interest and aptitude surveys to students at no charge, offered GED preparation, and served as a work experience site.

Social Security Administration

A portion of our participants received or were eligible to receive Social Security benefits—specifically from Social Security Incentive Programs, such as Plans for Achieving Self-Support (PASS) and Impairment Related Work Expenses (IRWE). These programs allowed eligible individuals to keep their benefits to purchase supplies and services related to getting/keeping a job.

Vocational Rehabilitation

We collaborated closely with the local office for vocational rehabilitation. The partnership was very successful and provided a range of services—for example, work clothing and supplies, assistance with vocational planning, and money for participants to stay in a program designed to teach independent living skills.

Job Training Partnership Act

The local Job Training Partnership Act (JTPA) program proved invaluable to many participants. When a participant was extremely difficult to place, either because of behaviors or because of career goals, we were able to access JTPA funding to pay the individual for hours worked. Our programs provided the job development, training, and on-the-job supervision, and we facilitated compliance with all of the regulations on the part of the employer and participant. JTPA also enrolled many of our participants in the "Learn to Earn" program (in which students are paid for attending their study lab and making progress in academics) and an accredited alternative school.

Figure 3.1
Related Service Delivery Agencies (continued)

Low-cost housing

A low-cost housing agency exists in each county in Oregon. Our relationship with the local branch was that of liaison between the agency and those students who needed assistance to fill out required paperwork and to ensure that the students understood requirements for continued benefits.

Juvenile corrections

Many of our referrals came from the juvenile corrections system. Compliance with the vocational program was sometimes written into the conditions of parole for a student.

Oregon Health Plan

We assisted students in the completion of forms required for acceptance into the Oregon Health Plan, which provided medical and dental benefits for those with qualifying incomes.

Adult and family services

This agency issued food stamps and public assistance to low-income students. Program staff assisted students in the completion of necessary forms and helped them follow through with monthly reporting requirements.

Job Corps

We referred students who wished further specialized training to the Job Corps. The Job Corps program provided a smooth transition from home to independent living and allowed students the opportunity for job training that might otherwise be inaccessible.

Senior and Disabled Services

This agency collaborated with many other agencies to provide treatment and funding necessary for individuals to gain independence. We sought and secured senior mentors for some of our students.

---

a staff person who has taken the time to talk with another staff person and is therefore known is more likely to get results than an anonymous voice on the phone asking for services on behalf of a student. Once a positive relationship has been established, it is easier to generate creative solutions that will meet a particular student's needs. Accordingly, it is important for the TS to contact local agencies; meet regularly with key staff; and identify referral criteria, appropriate contacts, unique terminology, and expectations of the persons they serve (e.g., Are persons automatically dropped if they miss appointments or do not comply with treatment plans?). Although it may not be possible for agency staff to grant all of a student's requests, it is usually possible for them to work together with the TS to generate service alternatives and to identify other sources of support.

Multiple meetings with all of the agencies involved with a student are *very* time consuming. Just scheduling such meetings is difficult because of the numerous commitments of social service agencies. In our experience the amount of delay caused by multiple agency meetings can override the potential benefit of such meetings to the student. When these types of meetings are unavoidable, the TS should contact agency representatives ahead of time to inform them of the purpose of the meeting and their particular role so they can arrive at the meeting prepared to answer specific questions and provide services in a timely way.

INTAKE

Intake is crucial because accurate and comprehensive information on the student and his or her emotional and behavioral characteristics, vocational and life goals and interests, and available supports must be considered in service delivery. Intake activities are conducted by each student's TS. The process is designed to gather the information necessary to identify appropriate worksites for job development and support services. At intake, basic identification, demographic, and vocational information is secured. In addition, at this time the TS, in conjunction with the participant and his or her family, develops an Integrated Service Plan, or ISP, discussed later in this chapter. This plan describes a comprehensive approach to meeting all of the student's social service needs. All contacts and meetings with the student are summarized in the student's case record, maintained by the TS.

Intake Forms

Certain forms may need to be completed when the participant enters the program. First, depending on the program, a release form may be required. A student entering his or her school-based transition program may not need to complete a release to be in that program. On the other hand, in the projects we have conducted, which have been based outside the school and other social service agencies, securing informed consent has been mandatory; those programs would not share information with us unless a form was signed by the student and—if appropriate—by his or her guardian. Generally, obtaining such a form can help you share information quickly with other agencies. As emphasized throughout this book, effective services for this population require the involvement of multiple agencies outside the boundaries of the school. Coordination of this type is fostered by avoiding delays that could be caused by not having an appropriate informed consent form.

All too commonly, persons referred to our programs have had incomplete or scattered demographic information—sometimes in conflicting forms—across different agencies. Also, in some instances agencies have withheld information because of the mistaken impression that we will not accept persons who present certain types of behaviors. In any event, this type of information should be assembled before service provision begins because factors may be uncovered that will influence service provision. For example, a student may have epilepsy and therefore should not be placed near moving equipment, or he or she may be too young to be placed in situations involving power tools. This gathering of information requires careful interviews with the student, his or her family members or guardians, and the referring source. Several contacts may be necessary to complete the demographic profile. As a rule, we will work with an individual *only* if a complete and detailed history has been obtained and we are confident of the placement and service options we can provide. Obviously, safety for the participant, co-workers, and others in the community is paramount, and safety issues must be considered carefully.

It is important to check each student's identification, Social Security number, and work permit. We have worked with students who have lost their Social Security cards and just before job placement claimed no knowledge of their Social Security numbers. In other cases, persons from other countries lacked the correct work documentation. In both these instances it was not possible to complete the placements. We have learned through these experiences that it is essential to check this documentation at the beginning of the program before work placements are attempted. Laws in each state vary with regard to the age at which a work permit is no longer necessary. Be sure to check with your state's labor department to determine this age requirement and what types of jobs are legal for individuals of different ages.

Intake Interviews

The TS working with the student conducts the intake interviews. These contacts promote rapport and allow the TS to gain a "feel" for the individual and his or her service needs. Two interviews are conducted during the intake. We have developed a structured interview protocol that involves asking the individual to rate his or her level of interest in a variety of career areas on a Likert-type scale (see Figure 3.2). Careers rated "1" are targeted first for job development. We also ask questions pertaining to the following areas to gain a clearer perspective on the individual and his or her vocational and social needs and options.

Does the student have hobbies or outside interests? If a student lists music as a hobby, the TS might target CD stores for his or her job development. If a student likes animals, veterinary or farm positions may be good job development choices.

During what days and hours is the student available for work? This is important to know in trying to determine what type of job will suit the individual's schedule and your own. If somebody is available only on evenings and weekends, a job that runs from 8:00 A.M. to 4:00 P.M. can be ruled out.

What scheduling needs to be done to coordinate the student's vocational program, school, work, and home? Students often have rigid schedules involving after-school activities and therapy groups, which may cause them to be unavailable for work on a particular day. A good practice is to make it clear to all team members at the beginning that the TS and the employer must be notified 1 week in advance by school

Figure 3.2
Intake Interview Form

Student _Mike Stevens_   **TS/interviewer** _Jarod_   **Date** _1/11/02_

Address _123 Oak Ave._   **Social security no.** _111-22-3333_   **D.O.B.** _1/11/84_

Anywhere, USA 12345   **Phone** _555-1234_   **Parent/guardian** _B. Stevens_

Does student have a work permit? _____ Yes _√_ No   Work permit no. _____

Student long-range goals

Vocational

_√_ Competitive employment

_____ Supported work

Education

_√_ High school diploma

_____ Community college career classes

_____ College

_√_ Other (_Explain._) _Certified swimming instructor_

_____

Previous vocational training

_____ Application

_____ Interview

_√_ Career awareness

School information

1. After-school activities _Punk band_
2. Favorite classes/activities _History_
3. School/work dislikes _Waking up early to go to school or work_
4. Any physical barriers _None_
5. Hobbies, interests/other skills _Computer games_

Interests

What type of job(s) is the student interested in? Rate preference 1 (high) to 4 (low):

_1_ Art/graphics/photo

_2_ Health care

_2_ Hotel support services

_3_ Auto body/mechanics

_2_ Computers

_1_ Other _Swimming_

_4_ Custodial

_4_ Grounds maintenance

_4_ Farm work

_4_ Construction

_3_ Restaurant work

_3_ Office/clerical

_4_ Manufacturing

_4_ Work with animals

_3_ Work with children

_2_ Retail

Figure 3.2
Intake Interview Form (continued)

Student ___Mike___   Date ___1/11/02___

Previous work experience

Worksite	Dates of employment	Supervisor	Wage	Duties	Reason for termination/comments
Restaurant	2/1/01–present	John Doe	Minimum wage	Busing tables	Still working
Landscaping	6/1/00–9/1/00	Sue Smith	Minimum wage	Spreading dirt and bark mulch	Seasonal

or residential personnel if the participant will not be available during regularly scheduled hours.

What are the student's transportation needs? Will these needs vary during the day? The student and the TS must consider transportation options before placement, including walking, bicycling, taking public transportation, and getting rides with a family member or social service staff member. Whenever possible, independence in transportation should be mandated. If public transportation is the most appropriate option, program staff can teach the student to use a bus schedule and access bus service.

Is the student willing to participate in a work experience position as opposed to working for pay? As discussed in chapter 5, we follow a vocational phase system, which involves increasing responsibility and movement from unpaid to paid work. We have found that moving into a paid position is a powerful motivator for many students and that most are willing to prove themselves in an unpaid placement to earn their way into a paying job. However, some participants will not consider an unpaid placement for any reason. In such instances, it is important to state clearly why unpaid placements are important and then develop an agreement—if need be, in the form of a written contract—that states the criteria for moving to a paid position.

What types of jobs is the student not interested in? Often adolescents have very specific ideas about where they would like to work and—equally important—where they would *not* like to work. A job that is of interest to the student offers a better chance of success.

Does the student have any physical limitations or take any medications that would have an effect on job placement? A student with back problems should not work where heavy lifting is required. Somebody who is on medication that could make him or her drowsy should not be operating any equipment that requires alertness at all times. Also, if a student has hay fever or allergies, a job on a farm or in a greenhouse would not be suitable.

What are the student's work history and experiences? A student might claim to like fast-paced jobs but in discussing work history may report being fired one or more times for working too slowly. Knowing what types of jobs have and have not been successful helps in placing the student at the job that has the greatest opportunity for success.

What are the student's interviewing skills? It is important for the TS to pay attention to the student's communication skills (e.g., eye contact, verbal ability, voice level), appearance, clarity of job goals, and overall personal presentation. If the TS learns that the participant is interested in retail work but also observes that he or she does not make eye contact or speak clearly, alternatives to retail work should be considered, or training in eye contact and conversation skills may be warranted. It may be important to discuss the importance of cleanliness in getting and keeping a job and to develop a personal hygiene program to address the issue.

Sometimes interviewing a family member is helpful in preliminary job and service development efforts. Family members can be insightful not only about the work habits and strengths of the student but also about deficits that will require additional support and attention. Another benefit of involving family members in service planning is that it establishes a personal connection with the TS. Enlisting the family's support for the program helps generate interest in and promote monitoring of program involvement by both program staff and family. In our experience, this involvement can be helpful should problems arise with the student.

We have also developed an intake interview that focuses on the participant's antisocial behaviors. It is important to realize that only a fraction of the participant's antisocial acts will come to the attention of authorities and be documented in formal records. Accordingly, we administer the Various Indicators of Criminal and Conduct Involvement (VICCI) interview to obtain a profile of the individual's presenting behaviors and needs. The first part of the interview consists of questions to be answered by the participant regarding his or her social history and attitudes. The second part presents a rating scale that the TS completes at the end of the interview, based on the student's responses to the questions and review of other demographic information. A complete copy of the VICCI appears as Appendix B in this book. Although we have been impressed with the forthrightness of most of the persons with whom we have worked, not all participants will admit to their full histories, and not all will respond honestly to all questions. Using the VICCI pulls together the available information and provides a valuable profile of a student's antisocial behaviors. We should note, however, that different local or state laws may preclude asking all questions on the VICCI, or at least asking them in the way they are constructed on the form. Whatever the case, we believe it is essential to gain a clear picture of the individual's history and behaviors before providing services.

When an adult has had the opportunity to evaluate the participant in a work setting, it is very helpful to have that adult fill out a Job-Related Social Skills Checklist (see Figure 3.3). This checklist provides the TS with specific information relating to the student's job skills. The TS also can use the checklist on an ongoing basis to evaluate the progress of an employee and to target specific areas that may require some type of special program.

A second measure, which is time consuming but provides more detailed information on adolescents' job-related social behavior, is the Scale of Job-Related Social Skill Performance (SSSP; Bullis & Davis, 1996; Bullis, Nishioka-Evans, Fredericks, & Davis, 1998). This measure provides skills ratings in six dimensions of job-related social behavior: positive social behaviors, negative social behaviors, self-control, personal issues, body movements, and personal appearance (sample items appear in Figure 3.4). This scale should be completed by someone who has had the opportunity to monitor the student in a job setting for at

Figure 3.3
Job-Related Social Skills Checklist

Student _Quincy_   **TS/interviewer** _Martha_   **Worksite** _Don's Garage_   **Date** _8/22/01_

Work-related behavior	Has skill	Needs training	Item no./comments
1. Checks own work	☐	☑	
2. Corrects mistakes	☐	☑	
3. Works alone without distruptions for specified periods with no contact from supervisor/teacher	☑	☑	#3 — Quincy needs work on being independent in the shop.
4. Works continuously at a job station for specified amount of time	☑	☑	
5. Safety			
a. uses appropriate safety gear	☑	☐	
b. responds appropriately during fire drill	☑	☐	
c. follows safety procedures specific to classroom/shop	☑	☐	
d. wears safe work clothing	☑	☐	
e. cleans work area	☑	☐	
f. identifies and avoids dangerous areas	☑	☐	
g. responds appropriately to emergency situation (sickness, injury, etc.)	☑	☐	
6. Participates in work environment for specified periods of time	☐	☑	#6 — Off-task frequently.
7. Works in group situation without being distracted	☑	☑	#7 — Distractible.
8. Works faster when asked to do so	☑	☐	
9. Completes work by specified time when told to do so	☐	☑	#9 — Off-task frequently.

Figure 3.3
Job-Related Social Skills Checklist (continued)

Student ___Quincy___   Date ___8/22/01___

	Has skill	Needs training	Item no/comments
Work-related behavior (continued)			
10. Time management			
a. comes to class/work for designated number of times per week	☑	☐	
b. arrives at class/work on time	☑	☐	
c. recognizes appropriate time to take break or lunch	☐	☑	
d. recognizes appropriate time to change task	☐		#10d — Has trouble maintaining a schedule.
e. returns promptly from			
(1) break	☐	☑	
(2) restroom	☐	☑	
(3) lunch	☐	☑	
11. Observes classroom/shop rules	☑	☐	
12. Does not leave works tation without permission		☐	
Mobility/transportation			
1. Takes appropriate transportation to and from school/work	☑	☐	#1 — Knows the bus lines well.
2. Moves about class/work environment independently	☑	☐	
Self-help/grooming			
Does independently			
1. Dresses appropriately for school/work	☑	☐	
2. Cleans self before coming to school/work	☑	☐	
3. Cleans self after using restroom	☑	☐	
4. Cleans self after eating	☑	☐	
5. Shaves regularly	☑	☐	
6. Keeps hair combed	☑	☐	
7. Keeps nails clean	☑	☐	

Job-Related Social Skills Checklist (continued)

Student _Quincy_   **Date** _8/22/01_

Item no./comments

#9 and 10 — Has difficulty with personal hygiene (and body odor).

#2 — At times will engage other workers in inappropriate and tangential conversations.

	Has skill	Needs training
Self-help/grooming (continued)		
8. Keeps teeth clean	☑	☐
9. Uses deodorant	☐	☑
10. Bathes regularly	☐	☑
11. Cares for menstrual needs (if applicable)	☐	☐
12. Cares for toileting needs	☑	☐
13. Eats lunch and takes breaks	☑	☐
14. Washes before eating	☑	☐
15. Brings lunch/snack	☑	☐
16. Uses napkin	☑	☐
17. Displays appropriate table manners	☑	☐
Social communication		
1. Does not engage in		
a. self-stimulatory or abusive behavior	☑	☐
b. aggressive/destructive behavior	☑	☐
c. self-indulgent (attention-getting) behavior	☑	☐
2. Engages in relevant, appropriate conversation	☐	☑
3. Responds calmly to emotional outbursts of others	☑	☐
4. Talks about personal problems at appropriate times	☑	☐
5. Refrains from exhibiting inappropriate emotions at school/work	☑	☐
6. Refrains from bringing inappropriate items to school/work	☑	☐
7. Refrains from tampering with or stealing others' property	☑	☐

Figure 3.3
Job-Related Social Skills Checklist (continued)

Student ___Quincy___   Date ___8/22/01___

Social communication (continued)

	Has skill	Needs training	Item no./comments
8. Responds appropriately to changes in supervisors/teachers	☑	☐	#9, 12, and 13—Quincy tries hard to do his job but needs to learn appropriate ways and times to contact co-workers.
9. Interacts with co-workers/students at appropriate times	☐	☑	
10. Responds appropriate to social contacts such as "Hello" or "Good morning"	☑	☐	
11. Initiates greetings appropriately	☑	☐	
12. Ignores inappropriate behaviors/comments of co-workers/students	☐	☑	
13. Refrains from inappropriate sexual activity at school/work	☑	☐	
14. Laughs, jokes, and teases at appropriate times	☑	☑	
15. Responds appropriately to strangers	☐	☑	
16. Approaches supervisor/teacher appropriately when			#16a, 16b, 16d, and 18—Needs training in when to ask supervisor about job tasks and in responding appropriately when receiving corrective feedback.
a. needs more work	☐	☑	
b. makes a mistake he/she cannot correct	☐	☑	
c. tools or materials are defective	☑	☐	
d. does not understand task	☑	☐	
e. is sick	☑	☐	
17. Complies with supervisor's/teacher's requests in specified period of time	☑	☐	
18. Responds appropriately to corrective feedback from supervisor/teacher	☐	☑	
19. Responds appropriately to changes in routine	☑	☐	
20. Follows instructions	☑	☐	

Figure 3.4
Sample Items From the Scale
of Job-Related Social Skills Performance

1. How well does the individual use appropriate head movements to confirm or disagree with a point of conversation or to emphasize particular aspect(s) of a social interaction with the work supervisor?

proficient	somewhat proficient	fair	somewhat inept	inept
5	4	3	2	1

2. How well does the individual give verbal affirmations (e.g., I see, OK, uh-huh), providing feedback that he or she is attending to the co-worker's comments?

proficient	somewhat proficient	fair	somewhat inept	inept
5	4	3	2	1

3. How well does the individual respond if the work supervisor does not allow him or her to take time off from work?

proficient	somewhat proficient	fair	somewhat inept	inept
5	4	3	2	1

4. How well is the individual able to ask co-workers for assistance to complete a work task?

proficient	somewhat proficient	fair	somewhat inept	inept
5	4	3	2	1

5. The individual steals materials or money that belongs to his or her place of employment.

never	infrequently	somewhat infrequently	somewhat frequently	frequently
5	4	3	2	1

6. The individual is physically aggressive towards co-workers.

never	infrequently	somewhat infrequently	somewhat frequently	frequently
5	4	3	2	1

Note. From *Scale of Job-Related Social Behavior for Adolescents and Young Adults With Emotional and Behavioral Disorders* by M. Bullis, V. Nishioka-Evans, H. D. Fredericks, & C. Davis (1998). Available from James Stanfield Company, Inc., PO Box 41058, Santa Barbara, CA 93140. (Toll-free 1–800–421–6534. E-mail stanfield@stanfield.com)

least 1 month. This form is somewhat lengthy, so we recommend using it only at the beginning of the program and at some logical endpoints throughout the project (e.g., end of the school year, exit from the program). Figure 3.5 shows how the information gathered on this form can be used to compare the performance profile of a participating student with norms for vocational education students without disabilities, peers with special education labels, and workers in the targeted job setting.

SELF-DETERMINATION

The Education for All Handicapped Children Act (Public Law 94–142) and more recent special education legislation emphasize the importance of self-determination in the provision of services to persons with disabilities. Self-determination relates to the ability to plan and direct one's

Figure 3.5
Student Performance Profile and Comparison Norms for Different Workers

Name ___Drew___ TS ___Warren___

Job position ___Busing tables___ Date ___10/20/01___

Scale	Student score	Total possible	Worker profile Vocational education comparison	Special education comparison	Co-worker comparison
Positive social behaviors	172	235	193.85	170.54	190
Negative social behaviors	80	100	92.41	91.11	93
Self-control	42	60	50.85	46.75	56
Personal issues	21	35	25.74	23.56	32
Body movements	18	20	17.09	16.50	16
Personal appearance	17	20	17.82	16.57	20
Social skills knowledge	82	120	91.34	79.10	90

own life course in different settings, including settings involving transition (i.e., vocational, postsecondary education, independent living, recreation). Further, this ability may be the most important aspect of human functioning and a key element of success in transition endeavors and adult life (Szymanski, 1994). We should acknowledge that, although the personal choice of the youth with whom we worked regarding their vocational placements was an integral part of both the Sprague High School Program and Job Designs, we did not use a structured curriculum to teach these choice-making skills. Currently, there are several excellent curricula that teach these skills (e.g., Field & Hoffman, 1996; Halpern, Herr, Doren, & Wolf, 2000; Martin, Huber-Marshall, Maxson, & Jerman, 1996) that easily could be incorporated into the program structure described in this book.

We believe it is important to focus on the individual's capabilities, interests, and goals rather than on that person's difficulties and weaknesses. It is always surprising how focusing on a person's strengths results in a more positive and seemingly better relationship, service plan, and results. In line with this orientation, participants should be centrally involved in planning their service programs by (a) identifying their own strengths, interests, and needs; (b) being responsible to the maximum extent possible for securing vocational placements and social services; and (c) making decisions regarding their goals and desires after leaving the program.

PROGRAM PLANS

Youth and young adults with EBD present a number of very real and complicated challenges to the service delivery professional. In order to address these multiple needs, it often is necessary to coordinate services both within the school and with other community service agencies. The Individualized Education Program (IEP) structures these goals and services within the educational setting. The IEP addresses the broad educational needs of students and, at the secondary level, includes vocational objectives. To coordinate services with other agencies focusing on community-based services, we have developed the Integrated Service Plan (ISP). Both of these documents are discussed here.

Each student should have long-range goals and short-term objectives relating to vocational achievements, and related skills should be written into his or her IEP. These goals should reflect skills necessary for the student's transition to the adult world of work and should address both work production skills and job-related social skills. *Work production skills* are those skills necessary for performing the duties of a job. For example, the work skills necessary for a career as a hairstylist include shampooing, cutting, styling, and coloring hair. *Job-related social skills* (also known as associated work skills) are skills necessary for keeping and advancing in the job, such as being on time, asking for help, wearing acceptable dress, getting along with the work supervisor, and interacting appropriately with co-workers.

The goals and objectives on each student's IEP guide the TS in establishing appropriate work placements and implementing vocational training programs that meet the specific needs of the student. Factors to consider when writing these goals include the age of the student, skill level or vocational potential of the student, community resources available to the student as an adult, and preferences of the student and family. Figures 3.6 and 3.7 show the vocational skills portion of the IEP for two students, Tonya and Ben.

Tonya was a 16-year-old student whose mild developmental disabilities required her to receive lifelong vocational and community living support services. Tonya's IEP vocational goals centered on job training that would teach her viable work skills, acceptable work adjustment behaviors, and appropriate social interaction skills valued by these adult vocational agencies. Tonya participated in activities such as completing a work application and interviewing for a job, but competency in these skills were not critical for her success, given the vocational support she would require as an adult. Such training was secondary to teaching her viable work skills.

Ben was a 17-year-old student who did not receive support services after he left school. He hoped to live in an apartment on his own, and circumstances in his life would likely force him to do so when he turned 18. The focus of Ben's IEP vocational goals was preparation for independent competitive work. The goals required Ben to be competent in job search skills, work adjustment behaviors, social skills with his boss and co-workers, and job termination skills. Ben also needed training in work skills that would enable him to obtain employment within his community.

Whereas the IEP focuses on educational services, we found that it usually was necessary to include multiple community agencies in the service provision efforts for most of the individuals with whom we worked. In order to structure these services—and to clarify exactly which service was to be provided, by whom, and when—we developed the Integrated Service Plan. Figure 3.8 presents an example of such a plan for Sally. (Because this is an initial plan, no dates have been given for completion.)

Sally was a 16-year-old girl who had lived in several foster care placements before returning to live with her mother. She had a history of running away and had not attended school regularly. She also had a learning disability and a history of drug abuse, although she had been clean for more than a year. Her goal was to live with her mother and get back into and eventually graduate from high school. She also wanted to gain marketable work skills and move into her own apartment in the next year.

Figure 3.6
IEP Vocational Goals Form (Tonya)

Student _Tonya_   **School** _Pleasant High School_

D.O.B. _6/15/84_   **Review date** _1/18/01_

Present performance level

Tonya has had school-based work experiences in the cafeteria. She has demonstrated the ability to be on time and follow the supervisor's directions. She has had difficulty asking for help at appropriate times, often interrupting the supervisor unncessarily. She has had difficulty getting along with her co-workers, often telling them exaggerated stories to gain acceptance.

Long-term goal

Tonya will demonstrate appropriate work skills and job-related social skills to maintain a community-based work position for at least 3 months.

Objective(s)	Provider	Criteria	Evaluation
Objective 1: Tonya will independently travel to and maintain at least three different work placements lasting at least 3 months.	Vocational program	Three work placements lasting 3 months	Vocational attendance records
Objective 2: Tonya will ask her supervisor for help appropriately (to include acceptable timing and social mechanics).	Life skills class and vocational program	80% competency on task analysis	Total Task Data Form* in role-play and real-life situations
Objective 3: Tonya will demonstrate appropriate conversation with co-workers.	Life skills class and vocational program	80% competency on task analysis	Total Task Data Form
		Zero lying/ storytelling for 4 weeks	Formal behavioral program

*For a description of the Total Task Data Form, see chapter 5.

Figure 3.7
IEP Vocational Goals Form (Ben)

Student _Ben_   **School** _Pleasant High School_

D.O.B. _8/11/83_   **Review date** _5/16/01_

Present performance level

Ben has worked at one fast-food restaurant for 3 weeks. He has had difficulty getting to work on time. Ben can complete a simple work application but has difficulty with job interview skills. He scored 55% on the ability to answer questions appropriately and perform acceptable social mechanics. Ben is deficient in job search, working cooperatively with co-workers, and job termination skills. A vocational assessment indicates that Ben would do well working in vocations that would require him to use his hands, such as plumbing; Ben would like to work in a store.

Long-term goal

Ben will independently obtain and maintain a competitive work placement for 6 months.

Objective(s)	Provider	Criteria	Evaluation
Objective 1: Ben will search, apply, and interview for at least six different jobs in the community.	Life skills class and vocational program	Formal skills-training program	Vocational attendance records
Objective 2: Ben will maintain paid employment for at least 6 months with 0 major infractions.	Vocational program	Paid work for 6 months	Vocational attendance records
Objective 3: Ben will maintain 90% attendance at a work placement for 3 consecutive months.	Vocational program	90% attendance for 3 consecutive weeks	Vocational attendance records
Objective 4: Ben will name three reasons it is appropriate to quit a job and state the steps for terminating a job.	Life skills class and vocational program	80% on written test	Formal skills-training program

Figure 3.8
Integrated Service Plan

Student _Sally_ **D.O.B.** _1/1/80_ **Date of plan** _1/15/96_

Present		Placement date	Stable
Residential	Home with natural mother and sister	Returned 3/95	(yes) no
Vocational	No public school for last year and no vocational training	None	yes (no)
Future		Projected date	Comments
Residential	Independent living	6/99	Apartment
Vocational	Part-time employment and community college	6/99	No

FINANCIAL

Long-term goal	Sally will demonstrate the ability to budget all monthly income to pay monthly expenses for independent apartment living.		
Action	**Agency**	**Timeline**	**Completed**
Sally will be provided instruction in banking and maintaining monthly income to include bills, transportation, supplies, food, recreation, medical, and other expenses.	High school	6/96	
Sally will open a savings account and begin to save money for transition to her own apartment.	Family	6/97	
Sally will be provided instruction in how to use public assistance, low income housing, and food stamps.	High school	6/97	
Sally will open a checking account.	Family	6/97	

VOCATIONAL TRAINING

Long-term goal	Sally will obtain and maintain competitive employment for 6 months.		
Action	**Agency**	**Timeline**	**Completed**
Sally will receive instruction in skills to include work adjustment, job seeking, interactions with supervisors and co-workers, and job exiting skills.	High school	1/96	
Sally will compile a current resume, personal information needed, and reference letters for use in job search.	Vocational program	1/97	
Sally will receive community-based job training in work and social skills necessary in maintaining a job.	Vocational program	1/96	
Sally will participate in a vocational assessment to explore career options.	Community college	1/97	

Figure 3.8
Integrated Service Plan (continued)

Student ___Sally_____   Date of plan ____1/15/96_____

EDUCATION

Long-term goal	Sally will complete her GED and enter the local community college.		
Action	**Agency**	**Timeline**	**Completed**
Sally will attend GED preparation classes.	High school	1/96	
Sally will complete and pass all necessary GED tests.	Community college	1/97	
Sally will explore class options at the community college and apply for enrollment.	Vocational program	1/97	

TRANSPORTATION

Long-term goal	Sally will be able to transport self independently to meet vocational, medical, consumer, and enterntainment needs in the community.		
Action	**Agency**	**Timeline**	**Completed**
Sally will be provided support in maintaining bus transportation.	Vocational program	1/96	
Sally will be povided instruction in purchasing, maintaining, and understanding insurance issues related to owning a car.	High school	1/97	
Sally will be provided driver's education in preparation for her learner's permit.	High school	1/96	
Sally will be provided instruction in driving a car.	Family	1/97	

MEDICAL ISSUES

Long-term goal	Sally will demonstrate the ability to maintain adequate medical and dental care.		
Action	**Agency**	**Timeline**	**Completed**
Sally will be provided instruction in basic health and safety issues.	High school	1/97	
Sally will be provided information regarding free or low-cost medical and dental care services.	High school	1/97	
Sally will receive assistance in using family planning.	TS and family	1/96	

Integrated Service Plan (continued)

Student _Sally_   **Date of plan** _1/15/96_

RESIDENTIAL

Long-term goal	Sally will live independently in an apartment with responsible roommates.			
Action		**Agency**	**Timeline**	**Completed**
Sally will receive instruction in apartment search, money management, getting along with roommates, and shopping skills.		High school	9/98	
Sally will gather and organize personal information necessary for job search and community living.		Vocational program and family	1/96	
Sally will be provided assistance in locating and moving to her own apartment.		Family	1/99	

SOCIAL SUPPORT SYSTEM

Long-term goal	Sally will develop and maintain a socially acceptable social support system outside of paid school and agency personnel.			
Action		**Agency**	**Timeline**	**Completed**
Sally will be provided mentorship support by same-age peers and enrolled in activities acceptable for teenagers.		Vocational program and family	1/96	
Sally will be provided information regarding gangs and gang prevention groups.		Juvenile corrections	1/96	
Sally will attend outpatient support groups for drugs and alcohol.		Juvenile corrections and family	1/96	

SOCIAL SKILLS TRAINING

Long-term goal	Sally will use problem-solving skills to choose socially acceptable ways of coping with social situations encountered in school, work, and the community.			
Action		**Agency**	**Timeline**	**Completed**
Sally will participate in a social skills class that will include instruction in communication, sexuality, parenting, birth control, anger management, relationship building, and problem solving.		High school	1/96	
Sally will learn the rights and responsibilities of being an adult.		Youth and the law class	9/99	

Figure 3.8
Integrated Service Plan (continued)

Student _Sally_   **Date of plan** _1/15/96_

SERVICE INTEGRATION

Contact person	Agency	Reason	Timeline	Completed
Pat	High school	GED preparation and social skills and independent living instruction	Placed	
Tom	Vocational program	Community-based vocational training and transition support	Beginning job exploration	
Joe	Juvenile corrections	Probation and linkage to treatment services	Ongoing	
Sharon	Children's mental health	Referral for drug and alcohol treatment	Has made— will begin 2/1/96	

Page 4 of 4

CHAPTER 4

Job Development and Placement

Vicki Nishioka

An appropriate, competitive work placement is one of the most important factors in creating a successful work training experience. "Appropriate" means a work placement that will minimize conditions that could trigger inappropriate behaviors. Worksites should also provide opportunities to build a successful relationship with the employer and co-workers and enable students to learn marketable work skills. The task of locating paid and unpaid vocational training positions for students is challenging. How does the work of placing a student begin? What steps does one take to place a student? What special considerations need to be made for a student? These are but some of the questions the transition specialist (TS) must consider in matching students to successful vocational training worksites.

CONSIDERATIONS BEFORE PLACEMENT

Before placement, several facts regarding the student should be taken into consideration: (a) antisocial behaviors, (b) skill levels, (c) transportation availability and the individual's ability to use it, (d) medical issues, (e) scheduling concerns, and (f) individual preferences. A great deal of this information can be collected through the intake process, described in chapter 3. If this information has not been collected during intake, then the TS should gather it as the opportunity and need arise. Other considerations include the desirability of multiple job placements, the developmental model of job placements, and aspects of matching the student to the worksite.

Antisocial Behaviors

Assessment information for job matching should include a clear description of the behaviors that may be exhibited by a student in the community or at the worksite. Of critical importance are high-risk behaviors that may threaten the safety of the student or others. For example, inappropriate sexual behaviors, suicide attempts, assaultive or aggressive behaviors, fire setting, and stealing or damaging property are important behaviors to consider in making safe job placements. Information helpful in evaluating a student's potential behavioral risks at the worksite includes the setting in which the behaviors are most likely and least likely to occur, the activities or tasks that are associated with the behavior, the person(s) most likely to trigger or be targeted by the behavior, the times the behavior is most likely to occur, and safeguards that would prevent or limit the occurrence of the behavior.

Jake was a 20-year-old who had a history of aggression, theft, running away, and destruction of property. His behaviors were most likely to occur during sedentary tasks requiring academic skills and least likely to occur during physical activity. The only persons he did not target for aggression were males whom he perceived as physically stronger than himself. Jake's high-risk behaviors required a job placement where natural safeguards would minimize his inappropriate behaviors. The TS placed Jake in a concrete plant with an all-male crew. Jake helped load trucks, thus ensuring an active job. The plant safeguarded the types of items he had stolen in the past, and a one-on-one male TS was assigned to him to prevent his running away.

Of secondary importance are behaviors that might interfere with the student's performance of required job duties but that do not necessarily represent a risk to the community. These behaviors often address work adjustment skills and include appropriate hygiene, attendance, and on-task behavior. Other associated work skills that affect job success relate to the appropriateness of social interactions with supervisors and co-workers.

Dave was a 16-year-old student diagnosed with schizophrenia. He exhibited several at-risk behaviors, including attempted suicide, theft, running away, and aggression toward others. Dave also had problems maintaining consistent attendance due to frequent illnesses, periodic court-ordered incarceration in juvenile detention, and lack of work motivation. The TS placed Dave in a state-operated motor pool. The motor pool was fenced and allowed no access to money. The fence prevented Dave from running away. The supervisor was willing to work with Dave's attendance problem by assigning a co-worker to become his worksite adult mentor. The TS implemented positive rewards for Dave's consistent attendance. With the natural supports of the worksite and the support of the TS, Dave maintained satisfactory attendance for 3 consecutive months.

Skill Levels

To determine job potential, the TS must have knowledge of the student's academic skill levels in math, reading, writing, and reasoning.

Information regarding social competence in work adjustment behaviors, problem solving, interactions with supervisors, and interactions with co-workers is also important in selecting job sites.

In matching students' social skill needs to the job site, the TS should consider the management style of the business. Three management styles have been identified in our work: (a) independent, (b) employer-directed, and (c) co-worker. Each management style requires specific social skills to meet the demands of the worksite. *Independent* worksites require students to work independently to complete routine tasks with minimal interaction with others. *Employer-directed* worksites require students to work independently and interact with and respond appropriately to supervisors. *Co-worker* worksites require students to work independently, interact with supervisors, and work cooperatively with peers at the worksite.

Beth was a 17-year-old student with schizophrenia. Beth displayed bizarre behaviors that included hawking and spitting, comments about the devil, aggression toward others, and theft. Beth also had significant social skills deficits; she did not satisfactorily demonstrate basic social mechanics such as gaining eye contact, smiling, answering others, and making appropriate greetings. When others tried to engage Beth in conversation, Beth would often walk away without answering. Because of these social skill deficits, the TS initially placed Beth at a grocery store, where she sorted bottles and cans. This position did not require Beth to interact socially with anyone besides the TS, and it was a setting that emphasized independent work behavior. Also, in the event of aggression at work, Beth could discreetly be removed to the rear of the store.

Transportation

For many students, a necessary vocational objective is to be able to travel independently to and from work. Therefore, the TS must assess the student's ability to travel to the worksite as well as the availability of various types of transportation. The student's level of skill in pedestrian safety, bicycling, driving a car, or using public transportation is a consideration in placement. Availability of reliable, safe, and feasible transportation will help the student gain independence at the worksite.

When examining transportation options for a student, one must consider the student's capabilities and behaviors as well as the ultimate independence in transportation that will be expected. For instance, a student who has a history of sexually offending and is considered at high risk of doing so again is not a good candidate for a job where independent bus travel will be expected. If the service program is willing to have a TS accompany the individual on the bus to work, then bus travel may be feasible.

Medical Issues

The TS should have information regarding medical issues that might affect the student's work placement. For example, are there impairments in the student's hearing ability? Does the student have a history of seizures? Does the student have physical limitations, such as a bad back, that would affect placement decisions?

Joe was a 14-year-old student with a history of tantrums, defiance toward authority, poor peer relations, and aggression toward others. In addition, Joe had a seizure disorder that was triggered by light, so he was required to wear a baseball cap to help shade his eyes. In consideration of Joe's behavioral and medical issues, he was placed at a pizza parlor in the morning before the place opened so he could be discreetly removed in case of behavioral outbursts. Routine tasks were scheduled to enable Joe to function independently of adult directives. He was given a uniform including a company baseball cap that he was required to wear while at work. This uniform cap naturally addressed Joe's medical problem without causing him undue embarrassment.

Scheduling Concerns

Another area in which the TS must be knowledgeable relates to special scheduling considerations that might affect the job placement. The TS should be aware of required classes that prevent the student from being available for work at certain times. Sports practices and events might cause the student difficulty working in the afternoon. Another scheduling consideration is the presence of behavioral patterns that might interfere with the student's work attendance at certain times of the day. For instance, failure to get up and be motivated in the morning might make it difficult for a student to maintain satisfactory attendance and work performance for early-morning jobs.

Individual Preferences

As much as possible, worksites should be selected to support the student's vocational preferences. Our experiences lead us to believe *strongly* that it is counterproductive to ask students to learn jobs they dislike so they can learn the realities of the world of work.

The vocational program should provide opportunities for the student to self-advocate and exercise choice in his or her vocational training and growth. Moreover, a student's work preferences should be respected to maximize success in the job placement and training process.

Sean was placed on the job as a janitor. Shortly after the job started, Sean told the TS that he would not clean toilets. The TS initially believed that Sean could and should learn to do the bathroom because all employees need to do tasks they dislike. The TS told Sean that he would need to clean the bathrooms successfully before he could move to another worksite. Sean became resistive and demonstrated multiple problems at work. The TS reassessed the situation and allowed Sean to move to another janitorial job that did not require the cleaning of toilets. Sean excelled at the new job.

Multiple Job Placements

Many adolescents with emotional and behavioral disorders (EBD) are unlikely to have had the same number and types of competitive work experiences as have their non-EBD peers. This fact should be balanced with the literature suggesting that most of the general population engages in multiple job placements as one way of deciding what kind of work is rewarding and that should be pursued in the adult years (Dilley, 1965; Gellatt, 1962). It follows, then, that students with EBD should have the opportunity for similar experiences if they are to gain such awareness. Moreover, placement in multiple jobs allows students to learn multiple job skills, competencies that are also crucial in work endeavors.

Developmental Model of Job Placements

Although allowances should be made for multiple job placements, ideally in line with students' interests, these placements should not be made in a random or noncontingent manner. Instead, job placements should be planned carefully, and students should earn the privilege of entering progressively more demanding, and more rewarding, placements through appropriate behaviors and successes. Exactly how such a progression should be structured is a major concern.

According to the Vocational Phase System we have developed (discussed in detail in chapter 5), this progression consists of five phases:

- Phase I: Learning

- Phase II: Responsibility

- Phase III: Transition

- Phase IV: Independence

- Phase V: Employability

There is a definite developmental progression from phase to phase. Some students may spend weeks in one phase, whereas others may be placed in a phase for only a few days before they demonstrate suitable competence to be moved ahead. Following this system means that the program benefits because more control is exercised in the job placements; the student benefits because he or she develops the skills necessary for success in more demanding placements.

Matching the Student to the Worksite

The essence of successful vocational placement is the identification of worksite characteristics that facilitate maximum student success. This requires the TS to integrate knowledge of the student with knowledge of the worksite. The following questions are helpful in matching individuals to potential jobs.

1. Are sufficient safeguards and natural supports in place to minimize the potential risk to the safety of the student, community, and business?

2. Are the job duties appropriate for the student's skill level and interest?

3. Are special considerations required for medical issues the student may have?

4. Are the management style and social demands of the workplace appropriate for the student's social skill level and training needs?

5. Is transportation to the worksite available and reasonable?

Job matching requires attention to detail across multiple areas. The TS should brainstorm with the vocational team to identify potential worksites. Figure 4.1 provides an overview of considerations with regard to matching student behavior with worksites to facilitate community safety.

LOCATING WORKSITES

In each community many resources may be used in finding satisfactory job sites for training students with severe emotional or behavioral disturbances. Some ideas for placements are discussed next.

- Businesses where the TS does business are potential worksites. In these cases, the TS often has the advantage of observing the worksite on different occasions to determine environmental and employer characteristics. This knowledge usually leads to better job matches between the worksite and the student, as well as a smoother job development process. Rapport already established with the potential employer greatly enhances the potential success of the work placement.

- Friends and relatives are good resources for information regarding potential worksites. They usually provide information regarding desirable worksite characteristics and also can recommend the program or the student to potential employers.

- Networking with co-workers or staff from other agencies can lead to information regarding potential worksites.

- Employers currently being used as work placements can be a valuable source of information regarding other potential work placements. Satisfied employers can be used as references during the recruitment process and their names given to potential employers who want firsthand information from participating businesses.

Figure 4.1
Student Behaviors and Worksite Placement Considerations

Theft

- Will the student have access to items to steal, such as other workers' property, cash, or store merchandise?
- Does the business provide for consistent monitoring of workers, or will the student have occasion to work alone?

Aggression or assault

- Who are the people more likely to be targeted, or under what condition is the student more likely to be aggressive? Are these conditions present at the worksite?
- Can the student be discreetly removed to another area or away from the worksite without disrupting the normal course of business?
- Does the student use weapons, and, if so, are there potential weapons present at the worksite?

Inappropriate sexual behaviors

- Will the student have access to potential targets in the workplace?
- Will the student have access to the public? Under what conditions?
- Does the business layout allow the student to be contained in one area (e.g., dishwashing room), minimizing access to others?
- What level of supervision is provided at the worksite for the workers? Will there be times the student would be left alone?

Running away

- Is the physical arrangement of the business a closed setting, or would the student have easy access to the outdoors?
- Is the business location close to areas that would entice the student to run away (e.g., close to a friend's house or freeway)?
- Is the business in an unsafe area due to traffic or other conditions that would place the student at risk if he or she ran?
- Is there easy access to hitchhike or go long distances if the student ran from the business?

Fire setting

- Does the student have access to matches or other undesirable materials?
- Are there areas in the business such as a boiler room or storage area that would be accessible to the student?
- Will the student be left unsupervised at any time?

Suicide

- Are there potential weapons the student could use to attempt suicide?
- Will the student be left unsupervised at any time?
- Will the worksite demands overwhelm or create undue stress for the student?

Figure 4.1
Student Behaviors and Worksite Placement Considerations (continued)

Drug and alcohol abuse

- Will the student have access to materials with abuse potential, such as paint or glue?

- Are there co-workers whose drug or alcohol involvement would have a negative influence on the student?

- Are there machinery or worksite conditions that would be unsafe should the student come to work under the influence of drugs or alcohol?

- Will there be times that the student would be unsupervised, providing opportunities for drug use?

History of abuse

- Will the student be required to work alone with someone who is the same gender as, or otherwise a reminder of, the abuser?

- Will this create problems or undue stress for the student?

Attendance problems

- Will the employer be tolerant of frequent absences as long as the problem improves with training?

- Is the work assigned to the worker critical to the success of the business? Can it be easily reassigned?

Hygiene problems

- Will chronic hygiene problems threaten the production aspects of the business?

- Are the values of the workplace regarding appearance appropriate for the student in relation to the student's values?

Positive recommendations from participating businesses can be the deciding vote in a potential employer's decision to hire a student.

- The local telephone book is always a good source of information, especially if the TS knows the type of job the student desires. For example, if the student desires work in a veterinarian's office, the TS can save many hours by getting a list of potential worksites from the Yellow Pages.

- The local newspaper can also provide information regarding businesses seeking employees.

WORKSITE RECRUITMENT

When the vocational team has selected the job placement most appropriate for a student, the next step is to contact the employer at the targeted worksite. The initial contact can be by phone or meeting. The job recruitment process requires the TS to present himself or herself as a businessperson. He or she is, in essence, selling the vocational program.

Initial Telephone Contact

The purpose of the initial telephone contact is to set up an appointment so the vocational program may be presented to the employer in person. The phone contact should be used *only* to make an appointment, because it is very easy to say no to a job recruitment inquiry over the phone. When calling, the TS should ask to speak to the owner or manager of that business. The call should be short, no longer than 5 minutes, and should briefly outline the agenda for the appointment. It is important for the TS to identify him- or herself and the program and briefly tell the potential employer how the program has been shown to benefit businesses, special students, and the community as a whole. A sample initial phone contact follows.

> *Hello. My name is Dennis Smith. I am a transition specialist for Teaching Research, working with students at Middletown High School. I'd like to talk to you about an exciting vocational program that has been found to benefit employers, students, and the community. We are seeking businesses that would be willing to provide work experiences for these students. Would it be possible for us to meet so that I can present this to you in more detail? (Negotiates a time and date.) Great, thank you, Mr. Ross. I will see you at 10:30 on January 15th at your store. I'm looking forward to meeting you. Good-bye.*

Meeting With the Employer

The purpose of meeting with the employer is to assess the worksite and, if appropriate, elicit a student placement. Prior to the meeting, the TS, most probably in conjunction with the student in question, will need to decide what information should be given to the employer about the individual's skill level and behavioral problems. As a rule, only information that the student agrees to should be shared with an employer—and then only information regarding behaviors that will directly affect the student's ability to perform a specific job.

Prior to the meeting with the employer, the TS prepares to suggest job duties the student could perform at the business and times the student would be available to work. The information to be conveyed at the meeting includes a brief overview of the program, a brief description of the student, and communication of the role of the TS in support of the student and the employer. The following items should be provided to the employer at the time of the meeting: (a) the TS's business card, (b) a letter outlining the goals of the program and benefits to the employer (see Figure 4.2), (c) a list of five employers who have participated in the program and can be called to give references, and (d) information about times the student is available to work.

It is very important that the TS present a professional demeanor through appropriate dress and grooming, clear communication, punctuality, and attentiveness to the employer's concerns. It should be emphasized

Figure 4.2
Sample Letter to Employer

Teaching Research
1234 Main Street
Salem, OR 97302

November 8, 2001

Dear Mr. Ross:

Teaching Research and the public schools are working together to provide a comprehensive vocational education program for high school students who are at risk and having difficulty in school. The purpose of this program is to demonstrate the feasibility of community-based vocational training for these students. Students will be placed in nonpaid or paid employment positions in various businesses in the community. They will be trained to perform vocational tasks successfully and will demonstrate appropriate social behaviors and work skills while on the job. Transition specialists from our program will assist students to perform on the job.

Transition specialists will do the following:

1. Learn various job skills.

2. Teach job skills to students.

3. Work with students on appropriate social behaviors (when necessary).

4. Monitor skills of students involved in the program.

5. Function as contact persons to ensure employer satisfaction.

The goal of this vocational training is to help students gain viable work skills and appropriate work-related social skills. In addition, this project hopes to help students build positive self-concepts, which in turn will facilitate their successful transition to responsible adult life.

Employers will benefit from this program in these ways:

1. Receiving help from a work-experience student trained on the job by a trained transition specialist

2. Having a transition specialist available should a problem arise

3. Having school district insurance coverage for a nonpaid work-experience student

If you have any questions, please call 555-1234. Thank you.

Sincerely,

Dennis Smith
Vocational Coordinator

that the TS is an on-site trainer who will assist students in their jobs and will help them develop positive relationships at work. Finally, if it is a work-experience site, the employer should be informed that school liability insurance will be available to cover both the student and the TS. The following explanation covers the main ideas.

> *Hello, Mr. Ross. I want to thank you for taking the time to meet with me today. As I said, the goal of the vocational training project is to place high school students in work settings so that they can learn job skills that will help them become responsible adult workers. We're hoping that learning job skills will help the students we work with obtain a better understanding of why school is important. We also hope that work will teach students social skills and help their self-esteem. The student I have in mind for this business has reading problems and has had problems in school. Our program will provide a transition specialist who will work with the student at the site, so it won't be any extra work for you or your employees. The transition specialist will be available as long as you or the student believes it is necessary. Also, school insurance is available for students in work-experience placements. Some of the duties the student may be able to learn are putting the salad bar together and vacuuming the floor. I have a letter that describes the program and a list of employers who have worked with us. You are more than welcome to call them. Does this sound like something you would be interested in doing?*

The interview with the employer can take as little time as 10 minutes, with the average time being 20 minutes. Employers are busy, and their time is important to them. If at the end of the interview the employer has not made a decision or would like to call the people on the reference list, then the TS should suggest a time to try to recontact the employer. If the employer agrees to a student placement during the interview, then the TS should set times for the employer to meet the student and for the TS to come to the worksite and learn the duties required of the student.

Selecting Appropriate Employers

The interview can reveal many things about an employer. While waiting for the employer, the TS should observe the surroundings to determine whether the business appears to value safety and organization. Observation of the workers at the business can reveal much about the work habits and overall professionalism of employees, as well as suggest any problems with negativism toward the job or management. Our past experiences have allowed us to establish a list of employer characteristics that facilitate or inhibit successful student employment (see

Figure 4.3). Businesses that display professional standards will provide not only work but also positive role models and social skills training experiences for the student.

Documenting Employer Contacts

Any contact with a business or potential employer should be documented. Even if the site is not considered appropriate, this documentation provides an ongoing record of employers contacted, date of contact, and other pertinent information. Helpful information includes hours available, reasons for nonparticipation, qualities employers deem necessary for satisfactory job performance, and type of management style.

MAINTAINING WORKSITES

The TS should attempt to maintain contact with interested businesses even if no students are currently placed. This contact should be brief and informal. Ongoing contacts of this sort become a vehicle to maintain employer interest in the project. Visits with participating businesses also help maintain connections with job sites that have changed management. These connections enable the TS to learn about changes in management procedures or the work students can perform. In the case of changing management, it is productive to make an appointment for an employer interview with the new manager.

Figure 4.3
Employer Profile

Acceptable employer

- Interested in training job skills
- Willing to accept some behavior problems and work to remedy them
- Accepting of workers with physical/mental disabilities
- Willing to have a job trainer on-site
- Willing to adapt some parts of the worksite to accommodate workers with disabilities
- Monitors all workers, including student trainees
- Flexible in hours/day and scheduling
- Maintains a good rapport with all employees
- Maintains adequate safety on the worksite
- General overall positive response to program needs

Unacceptable employer

- Uninterested in training job skills
- Unwilling to accept some behavior problems
- Unwilling to help workers with physical/mental disabilities
- Unwilling to have a job trainer on-site
- Unwilling to adapt worksite to employees with disabilities
- Does not monitor all workers on-site
- Not flexible in scheduling
- Has obvious personnel problems
- Does not monitor safety on-site
- General overall negative response to program needs

CHAPTER 5

Job Training and Support

Vicki Nishioka

Competitive jobs place many pressures on employees to work rapidly, perform complex tasks, and adapt to changing tasks and demands. Adjusting to these pressures can be difficult for the majority of adolescents and young adults who have had little or no work experience. A significant portion of adolescents with emotional and behavioral disorders (EBD) who are hired in competitive jobs leave these positions under less than positive circumstances (various studies estimate that 50 to 70 percent of these adolescents with EBD will be fired from at least one job placement). Although unsuccessful work experiences are a fact of working with this population, many job failures can be prevented with adequate preparation, training, and monitoring of the adolescents in question.

The focus of this chapter is on procedures for ensuring that students perform job tasks successfully. The importance of understanding employer expectations and demands, combined with task training appropriate to the needs of individual students, is critical to maintaining worksites and providing students with real-life work experience, from which they will benefit after leaving school. This chapter addresses the major phases of job training: (a) orientation to the job, (b) task instruction and data collection, and (c) ongoing support. Issues in providing support to the student and the employer in the workplace are also discussed.

JOB ORIENTATION

Preplacement Contact With the Employer

Vocational/transition program staff should make few if any assumptions about what employers already know about the needs of individuals with EBD or about the program in which they have agreed to participate. It is crucial for the transition specialist (TS) to meet with every employer before the student is hired to reiterate the program assurances and guidelines (see chapter 4). It is our experience that employers may recall part, but not all, of conversations they have had with our staff. It is therefore the responsibility of the TS to establish clear communication with the employer regarding the expectations of all parties involved: the employer, the student, co-workers, and participating program staff.

The TS should not assume that employers who agree to hire a student with EBD truly understand the student's training needs when they agree to the student's on-the-job training and supervision. Often, students present themselves as capable and personable during the job interview. Behaviors that can result in job failure (usually job-related social skills deficits relating to interactions with work supervisors and co-workers) may present themselves after the student has been on the job for a brief period of time (e.g., 2 weeks to 1 month). It is important to recognize that business owners and managers are usually busy people who are interested in producing results that will increase their profit margin while providing quality products or services. This is not to say that employers are uninterested in providing students with learning opportunities but rather that student needs are not their number-one priority, especially if those needs detract from the business priorities. Therefore, the TS should emphasize to the employer the necessity of notifying the TS as soon as the employer notices any aberrant behavior, as well as reinforce the assurance that the program will provide training and intervention if the employer needs assistance. The end result of these prework preparations should be for the employer to understand possible problems with the student and the role of the TS. There also should be a clear understanding of how problems in the workplace will be handled should they arise.

Orientation to the Workplace

Generally, the TS accompanies the student to the job in the early stages of job placement and training. The TS can take this opportunity to evaluate potential concerns in the specific placement setting by observing the physical setting, co-worker interactions, and employer responses to both the student and co-workers. The following case example illustrates the process of job orientation.

James was a 16-year-old student who lived in a residential treatment center. James was hired at a small accounting firm as an office assistant and file clerk. The following procedures occurred prior to James's arrival at the worksite for the first day of work. First, the TS arranged to meet with the employer for a set amount of time to clarify work rules (e.g., what to do if the student does not come to work as scheduled) and job training and monitoring procedures.

The TS and the student next met to accomplish the following goals:

1. Prepare an agenda for meeting with the employer. *James wanted to know about lunch and break times, how and when he would be paid, and official or unofficial work policies.*

2. Decide on appropriate dress and appearance for the job. *The student and TS developed a checklist for the student to use before leaving for the job. The list included clothing items (in this case, clean slacks and a button-up shirt) and personal hygiene (i.e.., shower, shave, and brush teeth).*

3. Clarify the student's school and meeting schedule. *James's weekly schedule included cottage meetings, school activities, counseling appointments, and a drug and alcohol treatment group. The TS assisted James in updating his calendar to reflect any changes result-ing either in his schedule or associated with the employer's labor needs.*

4. Make arrangements for transportation to and from work. *The trans-portation plan was coordinated with the cottage supervisor and staff. James was able to ride the city bus to work, and cottage staff pro-vided transportation home.*

5. Arrange training regarding appropriate social interactions. *This training was scheduled to begin in the program's vocational support group* (discussed in chapter 9). *It also took place on a one-to-one basis in which the TS worked with the student through role playing and modeling prior to the student's orientation visit to the worksite.*

The TS and the student arrived for the first day of work 5 minutes early. Throughout the meeting with the employer and orientation to the work-site, the TS guarded against speaking for James, allowing him to be as independent as possible from the first day of placement. James initially was shy and very quiet with the employer; however, he took the lead, with cues from the TS to ensure that information and questions were communicated. James referred to his list of questions so that his con-cerns were addressed. The employer provided specific information regarding break and lunch times and clarified the policy regarding the employee's responsibility to call before a designated time if unable to come to work.

An important area of discussion relates to the handling of prob-lems with student attendance, work quality, and co-workers. It is critically important that secondary-level vocational programs for this population have written program policies. A Work Policy Form for James is presented in Figure 5.1. The policy is a written agreement

Figure 5.1
Work Policy Form

Worksite ___Accounting, Inc.___

We agree to the following points:

1. Employee will give the transition specialist and the employer 2 days notice if there will be a change in his work schedule or school schedule. This notice will make it easier to change transportation arrangements, and the employer can plan ahead.

2. Employee will call both the transition specialist and the employer before 8:00 A.M. if he is ill and cannot go to work.

3. Employee will give the transition specialist and the employer at least 5 days notice when requesting 1 day off.

4. Employee will give 2 weeks notice to the transition specialist and the employer when requesting more than 1 day off.

5. Employee will give the transition specialist and the employer at least 2 weeks written and verbal notice of resignation from the job.

6. If an emergency occurs that causes the employee to be late for work, he will call the transition specialist and the employer as soon as possible.

7. The breaking of any state or federal law by the employee will result in the same legal action as any other employee would face.

I, ___James Jones___, have read and understand the above policies. I agree to follow the policies as set forth.

_____James Jones_____   3/14/01
(Signature of employee)   (Date)

I, ___Dennis Smith___, have clarified the above policies as set forth.

_____Dennis Smith_____   3/14/01
(Signature of transition specialist)   (Date)

signed by the student and the TS that clarifies expectations and holds the student accountable to the employer and the program. When shared with the employer, the form provides written clarification of what the program staff expects of the student. These forms vary according to the needs of each student and are thus individualized.

The TS can often pinpoint possible social and work skills training needs by listening, observing, and touring the worksite on the first day of work. For example, it appeared that James would be working independently most of the time. There were only two other employees, and they performed completely different tasks. Opportunities for James to improve social and interpersonal skills would occur frequently, however, because his desk was in the front office, and he would be the first person with whom clients would interact. James would need some social skills training to ensure that his greetings were appropriate. (Social skills training procedures are described in chapter 8.)

TOTAL TASK INSTRUCTION AND DATA COLLECTION

This section describes the steps in task instruction by outlining a specific method of task training, the *total task method*. This method, used originally for students with mild cognitive disabilities or with average and above cognitive abilities, was used to assure that students had learned the job tasks required of them. The method involves the use of three forms: the Total Task Data Form, the Program Cover Sheet, and the Task Checklist. A fourth form, the Work Data Form, is helpful in signaling when a problem is occurring at work or home that could be detrimental to job success.

The total task method is based on a task analysis: breaking a job down into the steps necessary to complete the task. The specific job, then, is learned in a step-by-step fashion. The student's ability to learn the task is reflected in the number of trials he or she needs to complete the job. During the teaching process, all steps are completed every time so that the work objective is met. The TS supervises the student and provides appropriate cues, reinforcers, and corrections.

The capabilities of each student, as well as the complexities of the work tasks, determine the need for and nature of the task analysis. In our experience, students who benefit most from this teaching approach are those with learning disabilities or below-average cognitive abilities; however, students who are easily distracted may also benefit.

Task Analysis

The TS can develop a task analysis either by performing the task or by observing someone else performing the task. When possible, the TS should perform the task in order to gain a firsthand knowledge of the demands and nuances of the job. It is wise to write out the task analysis as each of the components of the task are completed. Each step in the task analysis must conform to certain guidelines (Sailor & Guess, 1983). Specifically, steps must meet the following criteria:

1. Consist only of student behavior (except where interactive behavior of others is part of the action)

2. Consist of discrete, quantifiable action

3. Be of difficulty equal to other steps whenever possible

4. Be written as a simple sentence

5. Be essential to the completion of the job

Two examples of task-analyzed jobs are presented to illustrate the differences in the degree of difficulty of the steps when one student's cognitive abilities are average and the other student has mild cognitive disabilities. Figure 5.2 is a sample Total Task Data Form for James, introduced in the previous section. As stated earlier, James's worksite was a small accounting firm. The program objective for his task analysis was designated as "filing federal tax coordinator (FTC) packets." A task analysis was helpful for this job because filing the information accurately was of the utmost importance to the employer. Note that high-level reading skills and attention to details were required to complete the task. James's physical and cognitive abilities matched the degree of complexity in the steps of the task analysis.

The second example (Figure 5.3) is a task analysis developed for Susan, 18 years old and labeled as having EBD. She also had a learning disability and functioned several levels below the norm for her age in reading and math, but her expressive and receptive language skills and physical abilities were average. Susan worked in a pizza parlor and was responsible for busing tables and light dishwashing. The task objective for Susan was "busing tables." Note that the breakdown of the job in the task analysis provides discrete, incremental steps to ensure that Susan performs the details of the task. The training requirements for Susan's successful learning of this task differed from the requirements for James. Susan's task analysis had 19 steps. If James were learning this job, a task analysis for this job would not be required at all, although he might need a general checklist of job responsibilities for the first few weeks to remember numerous tasks. The distinct steps to ensure that Susan did quality busing of tables also differed from what would be necessary for an individual with severe developmental disabilities. For example, whereas Susan could complete cleaning and pushing in chairs (Step 12) as one action, for an individual with severe physical and cognitive disabilities it is possible that this step alone could be considered the program objective from which to develop a task analysis. The key point to remember in preparing a task analysis of a particular job is that the complexity of the steps in a task analysis must be tailored to the physical and cognitive abilities of the student who is being trained to complete the task.

Figure 5.2

Total Task Data Form (James)

Student _____James_____ **TS** _____Dennis_____ **Program** _Filing FTC packets_

Terminal objective _100% independence for 3 consecutive days_ **Date** _1/10/02_

Task																	
1. Put FTC packets in order by date with the oldest on the top.	O	O	X	X	X	X											
2. Bring first 10 FTC books from library.	O	X	X	X	X	X											
3. Read filing directions on the cover sheet of FTC packet.	O	O	X	X	X	X											
4. Remove and throw out pages as indicated.	O	X	X	X	X	X											
5. Insert new pages into the space where pages were removed.	O	O	O	X	X	X											
6. Cross off the page numbers on the cover sheet as completed.	X	X	O	X	X	X	PROGRAM COMPLETE. PROBE FOR 1 MONTH.										
7. Repeat steps 3–6 for the first 10 volumes.	O	O	X	X	X	X											
8. Return first 10 volumes to the library.	O	O	X	X	X	X											
9. Remove next 10 volumes from the libarary.	O	O	X	X	X	X											
10. Repeat steps 2–10 until packet is completely filled.	O	O	O	X	X	X											
11. Start on next packet.	X	X	X	X	X	X											
Total no. of Xs / Total no. of steps	$\frac{2}{11}$	$\frac{4}{11}$	$\frac{8}{11}$	$\frac{11}{11}$	$\frac{11}{11}$	$\frac{11}{11}$											
% independence	9	36	73	100	100	100											
Dates/baseline _1/10, 1/11_	$\frac{1}{10}$	$\frac{1}{11}$	$\frac{1}{14}$	$\frac{1}{15}$	$\frac{1}{16}$	$\frac{1}{17}$											

Figure 5.3
Total Task Data Form (Susan)

Student _Susan_ **TS** _Pat_ **Program** _Busing tables_

Terminal objective _100% accuracy for 5 consecutive days_ **Date** _4/9/01_

Task																
1. Get a clean rag.	O	X	O	X	X	X	O	X	X	X	X	X	X	X		
2. Get an empty tray.	X	X	X	X	X	X	X	X	X	X	X	X	X	X		
3. Locate a dirty table.	X	X	X	X	X	X	X	X	X	X	X	X	X	X		
4. Place plates, garbage, and glasses on tray.	X	X	X	X	X	X	X	X	X	X	X	X	X	X		
5. Put pizza pan under tray.	X	X	O	O	O	X	X	X	X	X	X	X	X	X		
6. Set tray/pan on a chair or table.	X	X	X	X	X	X	X	X	X	X	X	X	X	X		
7. Wipe off (table-wiping motion should go with the wood grain).	X	X	O	X	X	X	X	X	X	X	X	X	X	X		
8. Wipe off napkin holder.	O	O	X	X	X	X	X	X	X	X	X	X	X	X		
9. Check to see if napkin holder is full. If full, place horizontal; if low/empty, place vertical.	O	O	X	X	X	X	X	X	X	X	X	X	X	X		
10. Replace napkin holder.	X	X	X	X	X	X	X	X	X	X	X	X	X	X		
11. Wipe/replace salt and pepper shakers.	O	O	X	X	X	X	X	X	X	X	X	X	X	X		
12. Clean and push in chairs.	O	O	X	X	X	X	X	X	X	X	X	X	X	X		
13. Take tray with used dishes and pizza pan to dishwashing area.	X	X	X	X	X	X	X	X	X	X	X	X	X	X		
14. Put glasses on the counter on the left side of the dishwasher.	X	X	X	X	X	X	X	X	X	X	X	X	X	X		
15. Put cans/bottles under the counter on the left side of the dishwasher.	O	O	X	O	X	O	O	O	O	X	X	X	X	X		
16. Put silverware in sink.	O	X	X	X	X	X	X	X	X	X	X	X	X	X		
17. Throw out garbage/leftover food.	X	X	X	X	X	X	X	X	X	X	X	X	X	X		
18. Stack dishes and trays.	X	X	X	X	X	X	X	X	X	X	X	X	X	X		
19. Put dishes/trays in dishwashing area (located through window).	X	X	X	X	X	X	X	X	X	X	X	X	X	X		
Total no. of Xs / Total no. of steps	12/19	14/19	16/19	16/19	18/19	17/19	18/19	18/19	18/19	19/19	19/19	19/19	19/19	19/19		
% independence	63	74	84	84	95	89	95	95	95	100	100	100	100	100		
Dates/baseline _4/9, 4/10_	4/9	4/10	4/11	4/12	4/13	4/16	4/17	4/18	4/19	4/20	4/23	4/24	4/25	4/26		

PROGRAM COMPLETE. PROBE FOR 1 MONTH.

Instructional Strategies

In the total task method, all steps in the task analysis are taught sequentially during instructional trials. This method does not require that one step be mastered before the next step is undertaken. The student learns each step within the context of completing the entire task. For example, the steps in the task analysis for busing tables must all be completed each time tables are bused. If Susan did not complete a step independently, the TS was responsible for helping her so she could complete the task to the satisfaction of the employer. Following is a description of the instructional process, data collection procedures, and analysis of data to determine necessary changes in Susan's program for busing tables.

As Figure 5.3 shows, the form on which the task analysis is written is also used to record the instructional data used as evidence that a task has been mastered and to make decisions about program changes that may be necessary. Before instruction begins, a baseline is established to determine the student's ability to complete the task. First, the TS shows the student how to perform the task by modeling and providing a verbal description as the steps are modeled. For students with mild cognitive disabilities, such as Susan, this modeling may need to be done only twice before the student attempts to perform the task independently.

Second, the student must perform the task. As this occurs, the TS takes baseline data on the student's performance of each component task. Baseline data should be taken for 2 days on at least one occasion per day. The data collection procedure involves writing an X when the student completes the step independently or an 0 for an incorrect response.

The baseline data, recorded on the Total Task Data Form once each day over a 2-day period, are used to calculate a percentage of correct responses for each day. For example, on April 9 Susan correctly performed 12 out of 19 steps (63 percent). On April 10 she performed 14 out of 19 steps (74 percent). These results dictate the way in which a student will be taught. As a rule, if the baseline percentage is below 50 percent, the TS continues to model the steps before the student starts that task each day. Modeling continues until the number of correct responses exceeds 50 percent. In Susan's case, baseline data were above 50 percent on both baseline days, with roughly a 10 percent increase on the second day of baseline. Therefore, Susan began the work task and received assistance from the TS only when she did not complete a step.

Instructional Decisions

Once the task has been analyzed and a baseline established, the TS must make decisions regarding ways to teach the job task. This information is recorded on the Task Program Cover Sheet. The sample shown in Figure 5.4 for Susan includes information detailed enough that program staff other than the TS who develops the program would have no problem following the instructional guidelines. Thus, the sheet

Figure 5.4
Task Program Cover Sheet

Student _Susan_   **TS** _Pat_   **Program** _Busing tables_

Terminal objective _100% accuracy for 5 consecutive days_   **Date** _4/9/01_

Materials Clean cloth Clean tray	**Nonverbal cues (setup)** Tables that have used items on them
Instructional cues Susan will read the written employee work schedule to determine assigned jobs for that day. **Reinforcement procedure** Social praise from transition specialist and co-worker Four positive statements, one correction	**Criterion** 100% accuracy for 5 consecutive days Probe weekly for 1 month Fade probe to every 2 weeks for 1 month Fade probe to monthly for 3 months
Correction If Susan starts working on the wrong task or work area, ask her to check her work schedule. Praise Susan when she starts work correctly. If Susan makes a mistake or does a job poorly, ask her to check her work. If Susan fails to correct her mistake, tell her or model what she should do to complete the task correctly. Praise Susan when she corrects the mistake.	**Teaching notes** Susan interrupts and asks questions when she is supposed to be listening to feedback. Point this out. Continue speaking when she stops. Susan responds best when receiving a lot of attention.

is a means of maintaining instructional consistency in case of staff turnover.

The "materials" section of the form identifies the materials necessary for the student to perform the work in a satisfactory manner. In this case, Susan needs a clean cloth and tray to do a good job. The cues (or setup) for instruction consist of simply stating that the tables need busing. The nonverbal cue is Susan's seeing tables that have used items on them. Sometimes the nonverbal cue may be a diagram of the physical space or objects, as might be appropriate in production tasks.

The initial decisions regarding cues, reinforcement, and correction are based on student behavioral characteristics and setting. Specifically, instructional interactions with the student depend on both the business environment and the student's responses when cued or corrected. The key guideline is for instruction to be as natural and unintrusive as possible—in other words, to maximize the learning experience without drawing attention to the student. For example, when confronted in an aggressive tone, Susan tended to act hurt and sometimes stated that she was ill or actually became ill. The choice of tone of voice in presenting instructional cues and correction to Susan was based on these known responses. A nonthreatening approach provided Susan with the ability to maintain her demeanor and feel good about herself in spite of needing assistance.

We try to provide the least amount of assistance necessary to complete a step in a task analysis. A continuum of cues (i.e., physical assistance, modeling, direct cues, indirect cues, and environmental cues) is available. One should use the least intrusive cue because the ultimate goal is for students to complete routine tasks independently, with solely environmental cues. In our experience, the preferred level of assistance for the majority of students with whom we have worked is the indirect cue. The indirect cue, which can be either verbal or nonverbal, provides the student with the opportunity to use cognitive processes to figure out the next step. When the student does so, the steps in a task become established in the student's memory, a situation that supports the student's maintenance of information over time and adds to his or her ability to generalize the task to other settings. For example, on the fourth day of busing tables, Susan needed assistance to complete Step 15, "Put cans/bottles under the counter on the left side of the dishwasher." The TS used an indirect verbal cue: "Susan, where do the cans and bottles go?" With that cue, Susan processed what she remembered from the previous day and recalled where to put the cans and bottles.

Once the TS has given an indirect cue, it is important that he or she give the student enough time to figure out what to do before providing a direct cue. Should the student fail to complete the step, the TS should initiate the corrective procedure. For example, Susan responded positively to a firm but caring corrective approach combined with social reinforcement and compliments regarding factors unrelated to work performance (e.g., her appearance). In a public setting, if Susan became upset and pouted or cried, the behavior would draw attention to her, and should similar responses occur on a frequent basis, Susan might be at risk of losing her job. Therefore, any correction was done in a direct but calm and caring way. The TS followed each correction with four reinforcing statements. Emphasizing positive aspects of the interaction increased the chances that Susan would perform the task successfully.

Susan needed only minimal assistance from the TS, even during the first week of busing tables. In fact, by the end of the second week, she completed the task independently. The criterion, or "terminal objective," set by the TS for successful program completion was 100 percent accuracy for 5 consecutive days. Data analysis has shown that when a student performs a task at 100 percent accuracy for 3 to 5 days, the task is usually mastered. After criteria are met, the TS collects data, called "probe data," on either a random or a scheduled basis. The "criterion" section of the Task Program Cover Sheet (Figure 5.4) includes the probe data schedule. The probe data for Susan's busing tables program was collected on a weekly basis for the first month after program completion and was faded over time. Probe data are important because students may need assistance to maintain performance on the job task over time.

The "teaching notes" section of the program cover sheet provides a place for the TS to write pertinent information about the student that will be useful to other staff. For example, the notes shown in Figure 5.4 regarding Susan point to two behavioral areas of concern: (a) Susan sometimes interrupted the TS by asking questions and making statements that were not work related when she should be listening to feedback and (b) Susan responded best when receiving adequate positive attention. This section can be very useful as a means to highlight student needs and strengths that might otherwise not be immediately apparent.

Task Checklist

The Task Checklist is used by the TS to keep an ongoing record of the tasks for which a student is responsible while employed in a specific job. The form includes a listing of tasks, brief description of each, date each task is begun, and the date the task is mastered. Over the years, we have learned that most students with EBD whose cognitive abilities are average and above can succeed at work with little task training from the TS. Although some students with cognitive difficulties may learn by using the Task Checklist alone, they usually learn job tasks more easily when the total task method is used. The following case example describes Marie, a student with cognitive abilities in the average range.

Marie was a bright and capable 17-year-old high school senior. A sexual abuse survivor with a history of drug and alcohol abuse, she had lived in a series of foster homes and residential treatment facilities. She was interested in attending college and majoring in business. As an employee at a computer software and consulting business, Marie was responsible for a variety of important tasks. The task training was done by the employer or co-workers because Marie could easily follow directions.

The Task Checklist, shown as Figure 5.5, provided the TS with information regarding what tasks Marie had learned, what new tasks she was being taught, and the level of challenge the job presented. This information could easily be transferred to Marie's resume and to future job applications.

The TS used the checklist to monitor the student's work activities through systematic communication with the instructor (in Marie's case, a co-worker), the supervisor, and the student. During periodic visits to the worksite, the TS conducted informal observations of the student performing work tasks.

ONGOING SUPPORT

A consistent finding in the programs we have operated, obtained through surveys of the employers with whom we have worked, relates to their appreciation of the level of support they are provided once a student is placed with them. The working relationship between the employer and the TS, including the clarity of expectations and agreements regarding job monitoring described earlier in this chapter, is critical to job success. We have developed three mechanisms to structure this process: regular staff meetings, the Vocational Phase System, and ongoing monitoring.

Regular Staff Meetings

A simple yet effective monitoring procedure involves regular meetings of all of the program staff. We established weekly staff meetings concerning each student and adhered religiously to this schedule. With all of the unforeseen events that can occur with and to this population—coupled with an everyday workload—it is easy to miss meetings or schedule them with less and less frequency (e.g., every 2 weeks to every month). We found that staff enjoyed these opportunities to share their students' progress and problems and that the meetings actually served as a "support group" for our staff.

In the meetings, each TS presents a profile of the progress and problems each of his or her students has experienced since the last meeting. Problems are discussed, and staff offer possible solutions. The TS, having the greatest firsthand knowledge of the student, considers each option before deciding on a general path of intervention. We have been fortunate to have had several staff members highly skilled in developing behavioral programs (see chapter 6) to operationalize these interventions. Less frequently, staff from related agencies or programs attended these meetings to review a student they also were serving. In these instances, it is important to address such students first and to ensure that the concerns staff raise in the visit have been addressed.

Figure 5.5
Task Checklist

Student _Marie_   **TS** _Kendra_

Worksite _Computer Systems_   **Date** _1/2/01_

Task	Description	Date begun	Date mastered
Pre-bills	Print record of work done and products bought for each client; three-hole punch and place in folder.	1/2	1/8
Bills	Same as above; make corrections as indicated by supervisor.	1/4	1/8
Invoices	Match invoice with purchase order, put PO no. in checkbook, file in unbilled POs.	1/15	1/19
Deposits	When a payment is received: 1. Write payment in checkbook ledger. 2. Complete a deposit slip. 3. Credit the sending company's account.	2/2	2/7

Vocational Phase System

The Vocational Phase System, outlined in Figure 5.6, offers students a way to monitor progress in their vocational placements. The phase system uses positive incentives—such as increased independence, longer work hours, and participation in work breaks—to reward students for responsible work behavior. The system outlines clear and gradual expectations for students that increase only as they demonstrate the necessary work skills to be successful. This incentive system provides students with the security of knowing that they are not immediately expected to be "perfect workers" and that the TS is available to provide support as needed to ensure their vocational success.

Phase I: Learning

In the learning phase, students work side by side with the TS at all times. Students work 3 to 5 hours a week and are transported to and from work by the TS. This transportation time provides a one-to-one training opportunity in which the TS can assist students to prepare mentally for work. For example, the TS may ask a student, "What is the first thing you're going to do at work today?" or "What are you going to say to your boss when she gives you your schedule?" These questions help students make the transition from the role of student to the role of worker. These sessions also provide training opportunities in social interactions and work adjustment behaviors that are important for student success at the worksite. The return trip allows the TS to give students support and specific feedback about the day's events and their progress toward job-related social skills training goals. The final important feature of Phase I is that the TS manages all behavioral consequences for the student. In this way, the TS can use behavioral contracts and management techniques he or she knows are effective with the student. In addition, problems can be managed without unnecessarily inconveniencing the employer.

Phase II: Responsibility

In the responsibility phase, the TS remains at the worksite but does not work side by side with the student at all times. This phase allows the TS to begin "testing" the student by leaving the immediate work area but not the worksite and by checking work performance on a random schedule. During this phase, the student may work 5 hours each week and may begin to travel independently to work by bus or by other modes of transportation. As in Phase I, the TS still assumes primary responsibility for managing the behavioral consequences for the student.

Phase III: Transition

In the transition phase, the TS no longer remains on-site with the student. Instead, the TS checks in with the student and employer on a random basis. The student is responsible for his or her own transportation

Figure 5.6
Vocational Phase System

Phase I: Learning

1. The student is supervised and trained on all tasks and duties by the TS.
2. The student learns various job duties required at the worksite.
3. The student learns and follows all rules and regulations of the worksite.
4. The student begins to identify and work on skills and behaviors exhibited at the worksite.
5. The TS collects and records all data from skill and behavior programs.
6. The TS, in conjunction with the student, begins to explore transportation options, such as city buses, bicycling, walking.
7. The student begins bus training, if appropriate.
8. The student maintains a minimum of 3 working hours per week.
9. The TS delivers all consequences and makes all contacts with the student.

Phase II: Responsibility

1. The trainer makes intermittent quality checks while remaining on the worksite.
2. The student begins to maintain various job duties independently.
3. The student begins to follow all rules and regulations of the worksite independently.
4. The student begins to set own goals with the TS and watches own behaviors.
5. The TS collects and records all data from skill and behavior programs.
6. The student begins traveling to and from work, using public transportation if available, with guidance and supervision by the TS.
7. The student uses vocational time wisely and maintains satisfactory work rate and quality.
8. The student maintains at least 5 working hours per week.
9. The student begins to receive and respond to occasional feedback from employer.
10. The TS delivers all consequences and maintains the majority of contacts with the worker.

Phase III: Transition

1. The TS is not at the worksite but makes intermittent quality checks.
2. The student is independent in all job duties and tasks.
3. The student follows all rules and regulations of the worksite independently.
4. The student works toward vocational goals and maintains own behaviors.
5. The student's work skills and behavior data are monitored.
6. The student travels independently to and from work.
7. The student maintains work quality equal to that of regular employees.
8. The student maintains at least 10 working hours per week.
9. The student responds to the employer in all job-related matters.
10. The employer delivers the majority of consequences.

Vocational Phase System (continued)

Phase IV: Independence

1. The TS makes intermittent quality checks by phone.
2. The student is independent in all job duties and tasks.
3. The student independently follows all rules and regulations of the worksite.
4. The student continues to work toward vocational goals and monitors own behaviors.
5. The student has no formal behavior programs.
6. The student travels independently to and from work.
7. The student maintains work quality equal to that of regular employees.
8. The student maintains at least 15–20 working hours per week.
9. The student responds to employer in virtually all job-related matters.
10. The employer delivers nearly all consequences.
11. The student is eligible for placement in paid employment with TS support.

Phase V: Employability

1. The TS assists with administrative issues.
2. The employer trains and manages.
3. The student reaches vocational goals.
4. The student travels independently to and from work.
5. The student maintains at least 20 working hours per week for 6 months.
6. The student is able to gain paid employment independently.

and works 10 to 15 hours per week. If there is a problem at work, the student is given consequences cooperatively by the employer and the TS. In the event of a behavioral problem, the TS and the employer negotiate the disciplinary measures to be taken with the student. Sam's example shows how this works.

Sam had trouble with a customer one day. The customer started teasing and calling Sam names. Instead of ignoring the customer, Sam started teasing back until an argument and fistfight erupted. The TS and employer discussed the problem and decided the employer would reprimand Sam and reduce his work hours for a week. The TS and employer then met with Sam to review the work infraction and the corrective action that was being implemented. In addition, the TS met with Sam both before and after the meeting with the employer to ensure that Sam understood the infraction, accepted his responsibility in creating the problem, and could identify other options for handling the situation. As a result of this intervention, Sam understood the seriousness of the problem and learned other coping skills for dealing with customer problems.

Phase IV: Independence

At this phase, the TS makes intermittent checks by phone on an average of once each week. The student travels independently to work and is working 15 to 20 hours each week. Work problems that arise are handled by both the TS and the employer; however, the employer assumes major responsibility in the decision making and in issuing of consequences. At the completion of this phase, the student is ready for competitive employment. If at the completion of this phase the student is not hired at the current job, the TS moves the student to a different worksite to ensure that quality vocational training continues.

Phase V: Employability

The student at this phase applies and is hired for competitive work and maintains the work placement for at least 6 months. The TS offers minimal support to the student, primarily in the area of completing tax forms, compiling a resume, or filling out insurance papers.

Generally, all students at a new worksite should begin by being placed at Phase I regardless of their previous work history. Phase I provides an opportunity for the TS to assess student skills in meeting the work and social skills objectives of the new worksite. For students without previous work experiences, it is recommended that the TS advance students systematically phase to phase as outlined. It is not uncommon for students to take several weeks to several months to progress from Phase I to Phase III at their first worksite. In fact, to establish adequate rapport with the student and employer, we recommend that the TS remain at the first worksite well past the time a student demonstrates confidence in performing the work and meeting social skills expectations. At subsequent worksites, students may progress more quickly through the phase system, and, in many instances, phase levels may be skipped. Many students being placed at their second vocational worksite are promoted to Phase III and IV within days of their placement. The decision to promote students should be a team decision based on behavioral and skills information provided by the TS.

Even if the student is stable and successful in his or her job placement, we make it a practice to provide ongoing support and checks. A consistent finding in our projects has been the cyclical nature of the job skills, satisfaction, and attendance of adolescents and young adults with EBD. It is all too common for an individual to be performing well on the job, express satisfaction, and appear happy but then to express diametrically opposing views seemingly overnight and for no apparent reason. In these situations, the TS must be able to talk to the individual, identify the problem, assist in developing a strategy to resolve the issue, and—in some cases—contact the employer regarding the placement. In certain instances, the TS can either save the placement for the student or save the placement for another participant.

Ongoing Monitoring

For even the most capable student, work infractions and nonwork stressors occur that may jeopardize work success unless intervention takes place in a timely manner. The Work Data Form provides a way to document and profile issues and problems in a concrete manner (see Figure 5.7). These data can be gathered by phone contact with the employer and by direct observation at the worksite. Each category has a written definition to ensure consistency in interpretation. Additional information is written in case notes in the Student Worksite Notebook (see chapter 7).

Figure 5.7 shows the relationship between Susan's work infractions and stressors and illustrates the role of her TS in identifying the underlying issues and providing effective intervention.

Susan worked hard busing tables at the pizza parlor and appeared to enjoy being with people. Susan's Work Data Form included three checks in the work infraction section under the category "inappropriate dress" during the week of July 9. These marks signaled the TS to investigate the reason for the change in appearance. The TS observed Susan at work. She looked unkempt, and her clothes were wrinkled and smelled bad. When interviewed, the employer reported no changes in job tasks and expectations or in staffing patterns. The employer had noticed that Susan was spending more work time talking with her co-workers and supervisor and frequently asking whether she was doing a good job.

The TS then spoke with Susan during nonwork time. The causes for the change in Susan's appearance and work behavior seemed to be family related. The family was getting ready to move, and Susan's father, who was away from home much of the time, had decided that they could no longer afford a housekeeper. Susan was alone when she got up in the morning and when she came home at the end of the day. She indicated being stressed about the forthcoming move and feeling lonely. The TS addressed the immediate need by meeting Susan at her home to make sure she was clean and neat for work and by developing a checklist for Susan to use before she left the house each day. The TS's positive attention also helped Susan to feel better about herself. To address the issue of Susan's response to the changes in the home, the TS met with Susan's father. He agreed to refer Susan to counseling. In addition, he agreed that Susan was socially isolated from her peers and gave the TS permission to explore possibilities for developing Susan's social network.

Susan's deterioration in grooming habits came to be seen as a symptom of her feeling alone and needing additional support and positive attention. As a result of the intervention, the work problem was addressed immediately, and Susan was able to keep her job.

Figure 5.7
Work Data Form

Student: _Susan_

Worksite: _Pizza Restaurant_ Date initiated: _7/2/01_ TS: _Pat_ Date terminated: _8/31/01_

Week of	Vocational phase	Phone/visit	Late	No show/ no call	Theft	Work quality	Aggressive	Noncompliant	Inappropriate dress	Staff change	TS change	Task change	Boss problem	Co-worker problem	Boredom	Personal/ nonwork	Volunteer extra time	Positive interaction/ boss	Positive interaction/ co-worker	Initiative	Time management	Follow worksite policies
								Work infraction				Client stressors							Positive performance			
7/2																				/		
7/9	I	V							///								/			/		
7/16	I	V														/						
7/23	I	V																		/		
7/30	II	V																		/		
8/6	II	P															/					
8/13	II	P																		/		
8/20	II	P																		/		
8/27	II	P																		/		
8/31	II	P														/				/		

Work Data Form (continued)

Student _Susan_

Worksite _Pizza Restaurant_

Week of	Comments	Follow-up	Date complete
7/9	Student's clothes unclean, wrinkled.	TS spoke with employer.	7/10
		TS discussed with Susan.	7/10
		TS developed checklist for Susan and arranged to meet her at her home before work.	7/16
8/6	Susan enjoys filling salt and pepper shakers—volunteered to do the job.	Employer and TS gave verbal praise.	8/6

CHAPTER 6

Behavioral Interventions

Vicki Nishioka

Community-based vocational programs that serve students with emotional and behavioral disorders (EBD) should be prepared to cope with an array of disruptive behaviors at the worksite. These behaviors may include minor work infractions that might threaten a student's employment, such as tardiness, inept social behaviors, or working too slowly. In other instances, the behaviors could be crisis situations—involving such behaviors as theft, assault, or property damage—that might damage the vocational program's reputation and result in the employer's unwillingness to work with the program. Our experience indicates that even serious situations can become positive learning experiences for the student if effectively managed by the transition specialist (TS). The goals of the TS are to (a) support the student in responsibly resolving the problem, (b) minimize any damage to the employer's business, and (c) collaborate professionally with the employer so that the firm will be willing to continue to work with the vocational program.

A comprehensive behavioral intervention program that provides maximum safety for the community and for the training of job-related social skills should address three areas: prevention planning, to minimize opportunities for the student to exhibit inappropriate behavior; job placements at worksites that provide students with positive training experiences; and emergency procedures that ensure effective responses from the TS in the event of a serious behavior problem.

This chapter first briefly describes strategies for preventing severe acting-out behaviors through adequate student assessment, case management of support services, and careful job matching of worksite characteristics to the needs of the student. Next considered are strategies for creating a positive vocational training site through the use of the Vocational Phase System, the 4-to-1 ratio of positive statements made to students, and consistent behavior management. Finally, emergency procedures to assist the TS in effectively managing severe acting-out, runaway/no-shows, and theft are described.

It may be comforting to note that most students placed in community-based vocational training sites generally do not exhibit the high-risk acting-out behaviors at the job that have been reported in their behavioral histories or that they are currently exhibiting in home, community, and school settings. However, it is important that the TS have adequate assessment information to develop worksites with natural supports that will minimize the risk of potential behavioral problems. These natural supports can involve the physical layout of the worksite, the level of supervision provided to workers, the management style of the employer, the location of the worksite, and the type of work tasks expected. The following case example illustrates the function of some of these natural supports.

William, a 20-year-old with schizophrenia, had a history of theft, property damage, and aggression toward anyone he perceived as weaker than himself. He was placed at a landscaping business, bagging bark dust. The business employed primarily strong male workers, and the work assigned did not require use of tools that would be potential weapons. The worksite also limited access to items that William might steal. Finally, the TS provided William with continuous supervision for training and behavior management purposes. In this instance, the worksite natural supports that prevented or minimized William's acting-out behavior were the type of personnel employed and the type of work.

Another component important to prevention of behavioral problems at work is an integrated support system that addresses the medical, treatment, housing, financial, and other support needs of the student (for a sample Integrated Service Plan, see Figure 3.8, p. 51). For some youth, this case management support might mean development of a mentor relationship to assist in coping with day-to-day problems such as conflicts with family or roommate, money management, arguments with a girlfriend, or filling out an application for an apartment. In the case of William, psychiatric services to manage his schizophrenia, treatment for his physical aggression, probation and court mandates to motivate his cooperation in treatment, and residential program supervision were factors that contributed to his vocational success. (As is true for almost everyone, students who have stability in their home or residential situations often experience greater vocational success.)

WORKSITE INTERVENTIONS

The goal of the TS is to use positive training strategies that will facilitate students' success in their vocational placements. Factors considered important in creating positive structure at the worksite are the implementation of a vocational phase system, maintenance of positive training interactions, and the use of informal behavioral interventions to manage inappropriate work behaviors. Detailed discussion of the Vocational Phase System is given in chapter 5. Positive training interactions and informal behavioral interventions are discussed next. The subsequent section details procedures in conducting formal behavioral interventions.

Positive Training Interactions

The maintenance of a ratio of four positive interactions to each negative interaction or correction directed toward student workers is of critical importance in creating positive vocational training experiences. We believe that students who receive 4-to-1 positive interactions, or 80 percent positive feedback, are more likely to perceive the worksite as beneficial and supportive of their training needs. Positive feedback is defined as smiles, pats on the back, verbal praise, increased privileges, and anything else that tells students they are being appropriate at work. Negative feedback is defined as frowns, dirty looks, reprimands, loss of privileges, or any other criticism that tells students they have made a mistake. Figure 6.1 presents examples of positive and negative interactions.

This is not to say that negative feedback should not occur at the worksite. On the contrary, students need to be informed of mistakes they make so that a clear understanding of work expectations is achieved. However, for each correction, four positive interactions should be given. Students have reported that ratios of less than 4-to-1 positive feedback result in feelings of frustration, nervousness, inadequacy, and anger, all of which negatively affect their work performance. In addition, a 1-to-1 ratio of positive to negative feedback causes students to view the job as punishing and creates dissatisfaction with the worksite. Providing 80 percent positive feedback is important in creating a positive work training site and in preventing inappropriate behaviors at work.

Informal Behavioral Interventions

We have used the informal behavior management system next described in many environments—classroom, residential, and vocational—for over a decade and have found that it provides staff with a guide to handling inappropriate behaviors not deemed suitable for a formal behavioral program. Such behaviors include those that occur infrequently or are of low intensity. This informal response system has frequently been found to be sufficient to change behaviors without the implementation of a formal behavioral program. However, if inappropriate work behaviors threaten the student's potential vocational success or do not appear to be managed effectively by the informal behavior management system, then a baseline and functional analysis of the behavior should be conducted to determine whether a formal behavioral intervention program or another course of action is required to help the student achieve success at work.

Figure 6.1
Positive and Negative Interactions

Positive interactions	Negative interactions
• Smiles	• Frowns
• Pats on back	• Dirty looks
• Positive work evaluation	• Verbal reprimands
• Special privileges	• Loss of work privileges
• Special attention from boss	• Poor work evaluation
• Special attention from co-workers	• Teaching corrections for mistakes
• Verbal praise	• Loss of work hours
• Break time	• Nonpreferred work assignments
• Increased hours	• Loss of break
• Preferred work assignments	• Suspension from work
• Raise in salary	

The system separates problem behaviors into four different categories: (a) failure to follow directions, (b) self-indulgent behavior, (c) aggression, and (d) self-stimulation. These behaviors and recommended TS responses are described in the following paragraphs. (Figure 6.2 presents a summary of the informal behavior management system.)

Failure to Follow Directions

This behavior includes failure to comply with reasonable employer requests or work demands. One example of this behavior is the student who is asked to do a task, says no, and blatantly refuses to follow the employer's directions. Another example is the student who is asked to do a job but does the job incorrectly or sloppily when he or she has previously demonstrated proficiency at the assigned task. A third example is the student who dawdles and completes the task too slowly to be acceptable to the employer. The final example of failure to follow directions is breaking a known rule, such as when a student who knows that smoking is not permitted inside the work building disregards the rule and smokes a cigarette in the bathroom. Refusal to do a task, doing a poor job, doing a job too slowly, and breaking a known rule are all defined as failure to follow directions.

The recommended intervention for this behavior is to make a reinforcing activity or privilege dependent on the performance of the required work task or behavior. For instance, telling the student he or she can take a break only after a specified number of work tasks are done creates a situation in which the student must complete the work requirements before a work privilege can take place. The TS is encouraged to choose reinforcing activities that occur naturally at the worksite

Figure 6.2
Informal Behavior Management System

Category of behavior	Examples	Treatment	
		When behavior occurs	**When behavior does not occur**
Failure to follow directions	Slow to comply (slow to task) Refusing to follow a directive Poor or incomplete job Breaking a known rule	Assist to comply or arrange natural consequence	Reinforce compliance
Self-indulgent behavior	Tantrums Screaming Whining Pouting Negative statements Complaints Irrelevant comments and questions Crying	Withdraw attention	Reinforce appropriate behavior
Aggressive behavior	Spitting Biting Pinching Punching Kicking Stealing Lying Breaking or throwing objects	Time away from group	Reinforce prosocial behavior
Self-stimulation or self-abuse	Rocking Putting objects in mouth Grinding teeth Hitting self Biting self Head banging	Interrupt behavior	Reinforce appropriate behavior

and that the student genuinely enjoys as contingent on completing desired tasks. When a rule is deliberately broken, the student may lose a planned privilege. Another consequence, such as apologizing to the boss, may be equally appropriate.

Self-Indulgent Behavior

This category includes negative attention-getting behaviors the student generally uses to protest a decision previously made, to get a decision changed, to escape a situation, or to gain attention.

Debbie worked in a restaurant. She wanted to make friends with her co-workers but didn't have adequate social skills. Instead, Debbie made up outlandish stories about her many boyfriends and terrible living situation to get her co-workers' attention and sympathy. Debbie's storytelling behavior was an inappropriate means to gain her co-workers' attention.

The TS should withdraw attention or *ignore* self-indulgent behavior so that students are not rewarded with the attention they are seeking. It is important to note that students who exhibit severely self-indulgent behaviors are often accustomed to negative feedback such as frowns, scolding, or lectures. In fact, these reprimands may become the attention that maintains and strengthens these self-indulgent behaviors over the years. The rate of these behaviors may initially increase because of the change in the TS's ignoring response.

Aggressive Behavior

The third category includes aggression against other people in any number of ways: (a) hitting, biting, scratching, hair pulling; (b) aggression against other people's property, such as breaking windows or stealing; and (c) aggression against social boundaries, such as swearing, lying, and cheating. In other words, aggression includes any verbally or physically hostile act toward another person or another person's property. Mild aggression includes gentle pushing or verbal aggression, such as swearing or lying to manipulate. The response to these mild behaviors is to withdraw attention so that the student does not gain the desired attention or privilege as a result of the inappropriate behavior. Aggressive behaviors that should not be ignored are those in which a student injures another, destroys property, or steals. These behaviors call for the TS's immediate intervention in the form of removing the student from the work setting. Emergency procedures for these more serious aggressive behaviors are described at the end of this chapter.

Self-Stimulation or Self-Abuse

Self-stimulation behaviors include nervous habits such as nail biting, hair twirling, and knuckle cracking. These behaviors generally are not exhibited to get attention and require intervention only if they interfere with the student's success at work. The recommended response for this category is to interrupt the behavior and redirect the student toward work or toward a socially appropriate behavior. Self-abuse behaviors may include the student's hitting himself or herself, cutting or burning the skin, or more extreme mutilating actions. These behaviors may demand more intensive and structured interventions or even removal from the workplace.

Formal behavioral interventions consist of strategies designed to teach specific work skills and to remediate specific problem behaviors. These programs involve clear behavioral objectives to describe the goal of the program; a data system to track the program's effectiveness; a specific procedure for reinforcing the desired work skill or behavior; and a correction procedure designed to decrease inappropriate behavior and encourage use of the desired work skill.

Prior to implementing a formal behavioral intervention program, the TS should become familiar with the policies and procedures of his or her district regarding such interventions. In particular, policies concerning parental consent, parental involvement, and procedural safeguards should be followed.

The following paragraphs describe the steps included in developing a formal behavioral intervention program:

1. Pinpointing and defining the problem behavior

2. Baselining the problem behavior

3. Conducting a functional behavioral assessment

4. Establishing a program objective

5. Designing and implementing the behavioral intervention program

6. Evaluating and modifying the behavioral intervention program

7. Maintaining behavioral change over time

Pinpointing and Defining the Problem Behavior

Behavior to be remediated should be accurately defined in observable and measurable terms so that the student, the TS, and other involved persons clearly understand what behavior is targeted. If possible, all dimensions of the behavior should be included in the description. For example, a tantrum behavior is best described by identifying all the behaviors actually exhibited during the tantrum. The following case example illustrates.

Kevin worked at a nursing home as a dishwasher. When Kevin became upset, he often yelled, called people names, squirted water, and threw objects. For Kevin's behavioral intervention program, his tantrum behavior was defined as yelling, name-calling, and throwing objects.

Baselining the Problem Behavior

The first step in initiating a behavioral program is to collect baseline data. Baseline data are the "pretest" of formal intervention programs, describing the frequency and severity of the pinpointed behavior prior to implementation of the formal behavioral intervention program.

Baseline data are collected without changing current behavior management strategies or informing the student. This information allows the vocational team to determine whether an inappropriate behavior is severe enough to warrant a formal behavioral intervention program and, if so, helps the team establish realistic program goals and behavioral objectives for the student.

In selecting the strategy for collecting baseline data, the TS should choose simple procedures that will promote program accuracy and program fidelity. Behaviors are measured in terms of their frequency, duration, and percentage.

Frequency

Frequency is a measure of how often a behavior occurs. It is the simplest way to measure a behavior that has clearly defined start and stop points. Typical problem behaviors that can be measured in terms of frequency are arguing, complaining, hitting, and making negative comments. To record frequency data, simply tally each occurrence of the behavior in the given observation period. Figure 6.3 shows a Behavior Data Form used to record a frequency baseline for Tom. This form records the student's name, the TS's name, the date baseline data collection is initiated and terminated, a description of the behavior to be remediated, and the student's baseline data for each day. The form permits recording of multiple weeks of data.

Tom made negative comments at work. Examples include "I hate this job," "Why are you bossing me around?" and "I hate cleaning shelves." To record the frequency of Tom's negative comments, the TS simply tallied the number of times the behavior occurred for each day worked. The total number of negative comments made for the week was then summarized and recorded. According to the baseline data, Tom made a total of 90 negative comments during the first 5 days of baseline data collection. Given this ongoing behavior, data gathering continued for a second week, in which Tom's negative comments were reduced to 72.

Duration

Duration is a measure of the length of time over which a behavior occurs. To obtain accurate measures of behaviors that last varying lengths of time—such as tardiness, tantruming, or running away—it is helpful to measure the duration of each event so that both the number of times the behavior occurred and how long each behavioral incident lasts are available to evaluate behavioral change. Figure 6.4 shows sample baseline data for duration collected on Joe.

Joe had difficulty arriving to work on time, often being 10 to 20 minutes late for his shift and asking co-workers to "cover" for him. Joe was late four times during the first 5-day work week, totaling 55 minutes. The second week he was late four times, for a total of 45 minutes.

Figure 6.3
Behavior Data Form (Frequency)

Student _Tom_ **Worksite** _Mid-Town Dry Cleaning_ **TS** _Karen_

Date initiated _11/05/01_ **Date terminated** _11/16/01_

Behavior	Date								Total
	11/5	11/6	11/7	11/8	11/9				
Negative comments (e.g., "I hate this job," "I want to quit")	////// //// //// //// //// //	//// //// //// //// ////	//// //// //// ///	//// //// ////	//// ////				90 per week
	11/12	11/13	11/14	11/15	11/16				
(same)	//// //// //// ///	//// //// //// ////	//// //// ///	//// //// ///	//// ///				72 per week

99

Figure 6.4
Behavior Data Form (Duration)

Student __Joe__   Worksite __Arbors Nursery__   TS __Russ__

Date initiated __5/7/01__   Date terminated __5/18/01__

Behavior	Date					Total
Late to work	5/7 10 minutes	5/8 15 minutes	5/9 0 minutes	5/10 20 minutes	5/11 10 minutes	4 days late 55 total minutes
(same)	5/14 10 minutes	5/15 10 minutes	5/16 0 minutes	5/17 15 minutes	5/18 10 minutes	4 days late 45 total minutes

Percentage

This data collection technique measures the percentage of times the student follows the employer's or TS's directions in relation to the total number of requests made. Percentage is used to measure compliance with routine and spontaneous requests. *Routine requests* concern work adjustment behaviors and responsibilities that are required by the worksite as a matter of course; the employer does not give verbal requests or reminders. The employer might review the requirements for these routine tasks at the beginning of the work placement and then expect the student to fulfill these duties without further reminder. Examples of routine tasks are following written rules, completing a time card correctly, being punctual, dressing appropriately, and staying on task. *Spontaneous requests* are requests made or directions given by the employer during the course of a working day. These requests usually reflect tasks that need to be completed to ensure that the work shift operates efficiently—for example, asking the student to answer the phone, clean up water spilled on the floor, or clear off a table that patrons just left. These tasks differ from routine tasks in that the employer does not expect the student to complete these tasks without verbal requests or directions from his or her supervisor. Figure 6.5 shows a form for recording spontaneous requests. The layout of this form allows recording of several behaviors or events across a week's time.

Tina worked in a grocery store, stocking shelves. She had difficulty responding to authority figures and would often ignore her employer's requests, stating she wanted to do the job her own way. During the baseline week Tina followed 25 of 50 directions, or 50 percent of the directions given by the employer.

Ideally, baseline data should be collected for a period of at least a week, preferably more. If the behavior improves during the baseline period, the TS continues the baseline to gather more information prior to determining whether a formal behavioral intervention program is necessary. If the behavior is insignificant and does not seem to interfere with the student's work performance, then formal behavioral intervention strategies are not warranted, and the TS should terminate baseline data collection. However, if the baseline data indicate behavioral problems that are a barrier to student success at the worksite, then the TS should continue gathering information regarding the behavior through the functional behavioral assessment process, described next.

Conducting a Functional Behavioral Assessment

The focus of all behavior management for students should be teaching appropriate work skills. Accomplishing this goal requires a careful assessment of the circumstances surrounding a problem behavior.

Figure 6.5
Behavior Data Form (Compliance With Spontaneous Request)

Student __Tina__   Worksite __Kwik-Mart__   TS __Gail__

Date initiated __10/1/01__   Date terminated __10/5/01__

Behavior	10/1	10/2	10/3	10/4	10/5			Total
1. Follows employer directions	/ / / /	⊬⊤⊤	⊬⊤⊤ /	⊬⊤⊤	⊬⊤⊤			25 compliances 50 total
2. Total number of employer directions	⊬⊤⊤ ⊬⊤⊤	⊬⊤⊤ / / /	⊬⊤⊤ ⊬⊤⊤ / /	⊬⊤⊤ ⊬⊤⊤	⊬⊤⊤ ⊬⊤⊤			50% compliance

Factors to consider in this assessment include the person with whom the behavior occurs, times the behavior is most likely to occur, triggers that could cause the behavior, and motivations of the student. In other words, why is the behavior occurring? This process, known as *functional behavioral assessment,* may best be completed at a vocational meeting in which staff brainstorm and share information toward a better understanding of the nature and causes of the behavior problem. This information will then become the basis for developing a hypothesis as to why the behavior occurs so strategies to prevent the behavior and suggestions for design of a behavioral intervention program can be determined. In addition, appropriate work skills training can be initiated to help the student achieve his or her goals without using the problem behavior.

Functional behavioral assessment questions that may help the vocational team hypothesize the reasons the inappropriate behavior occurs and determine the most effective intervention are as follows:

- What is the severity of the behavior in terms of frequency, duration, or intensity? Has there been a recent increase or decrease?

- What are the antecedent events (i.e., events that occur immediately before the occurrence of the behavior)?

- What environmental factors are related to the behavior (e.g., settings, time of day, people involved)?

- What possible reinforcers or conditions are maintaining the behavior?

- What are possible punishers or conditions that may prevent or reduce the occurrence of the behavior?

- What interventions have worked in the past? What is the history of the problem?

- Is the student trying to communicate something but does not know how (e.g., trying to ask for help or for praise)? From the student's perspective, what is being gained from the behavior?

- Is the student using the behavior to escape or avoid unpleasant events? Does the student feel that he or she does not have enough opportunity to exercise choice or independence?

- Are too many requests or demands being made of the student?

- Is the student having difficulty in another environment that may affect work (e.g., problems at home, in school, or with friends)?

- Does the student have problems that affect work performance and that require treatment, such as medical ailments, substance abuse, or emotional problems requiring professional therapy?

Once the vocational team has completed the functional behavioral assessment for the target behavior, they may use this information to determine an effective intervention. Possible interventions include a schedule change, staff training or change, medical treatment, a skills-training program, worksite change, referral for treatment (e.g., counseling), or implementation of a formal behavior management program.

The following case example illustrates the importance of a functional behavioral assessment in determining an effective response to problem behavior. The Functional Behavioral Assessment Form organizes the information to be compiled by the vocational team. This information includes a description of the target behavior, medical conditions that may be influencing the occurrence of the target behavior, hypothesis as to what the student is gaining or avoiding with the behavior, environmental conditions or triggers for the behavior, possible reinforcers maintaining the behavior, possible punishers that may remediate the behavior, history of the behavior, and skills that might be taught to replace the behavior. This form also allows the vocational staff to record and rank the interventions recommended by the staff during the functional behavioral analysis. Figure 6.6 is a Functional Behavioral Assessment Form for Tony.

Tony worked at a small deli doing basic janitorial tasks. He had never worked before and had very poor job-related social skills. Tony had a long history of problem behaviors, including fire setting, running away, theft, and lying. He had a very low tolerance for stress and often pretended he was sick to avoid unpleasant tasks. The first day of work went great for Tony. The second day he told the TS he was sick and asked to leave work early. For the remainder of the week, Tony did not attend work 2 days and was late 1 day, complaining of being sick. However, in the classroom he seemed healthy and willingly participated in all activities. The TS reviewed the situation with the vocational staff, who completed a functional behavioral assessment of Tony's behavior. They determined that Tony had no medical problems causing the behavior, nor did he have other treatment issues interfering with work. Because the worksite was so new and Tony had a long history of feigning illness to avoid unpleasant situations, the vocational staff decided that the most effective intervention would be a behavior contract in which Tony earned increases in support and tangible rewards for attendance and on-time arrival. The plan proved effective, and Tony completed training at the worksite successfully.

In some instances, a functional behavioral assessment is conducted to protect the citizens of a community or to prevent the youth from committing a felony. The most prevalent felonies are theft and assault. With a youth who has a history of theft, the functional behavioral assessment should involve examining the youth's history to learn the types of thefts and the circumstances surrounding them. The student prone to stealing money should not initially be placed in a vocational environment where the opportunity to pilfer is present. However, not all thefts involve money. For example, one young man with whom we worked had an attraction to tools. He was known to

Figure 6.6
Functional Behavioral Assessment Form

Student _Tony_   **TS** _Sara_

Worksite _Pop's Deli_   **Date** _12/4/01_

Target behavior

Lying about being sick and refusing to go to work, arriving late, and leaving early

---

1. Do prescribed medication or medical conditions influence the occurrence of the target behavior? If so, explain.
   Tony is overweight and has history of a heart problem. Currently appears healthy in the classroom.

2. Is the behavior used to get something and/or to avoid or escape something? Explain.
   Tony has a history of low tolerance to stress and often pretends to be sick to avoid unpleasant tasks.

3. What are common triggers for the behavior?

Events/situations	Behavior most likely to occur	Behavior least likely to occur
Time of day	*Vocational work time 10 A.M.–12 noon*	*Lunchtime, afternoon*
Settings	*Worksite, math class, reading class*	*PE, lunchroom, community activities, art room*
Persons	*TS, new staff, classroom aide*	*Peers, classroom teacher*
Activities	*Vocational or work time*	*Leisure activity, free time, PE*
Other		

Page 1 of 2

Figure 6.6
Functional Behavioral Assessment Form (continued)

Student _____Tony_____   Date _____12/4/01_____

4. What are warning signs or precursor behaviors that the individual may exhibit prior to the target behavior?
   Tony arrives at school tired.

5. What reinforcers may be maintaining the behavior?
   Tony may be reinforced by getting extra attention for being sick and having fewer work expectations during that time period. Tony often puts his head on his desk and sleeps.

6. What punishers or conditions may help remediate the behavior?
   On days Tony is "sick," he should not participate in school fun activities and should not be allowed to go on community activities.

7. What has worked in the past to treat this behavior?
   Withdrawal of attention for complaining of being sick, behavior contracts for responsible attendance.

8. What skills could be taught to replace this behavior?
   Tony needs to learn problem-solving skills that will assist him in selecting more appropriate social skills to verbalize needs, assertiveness skills, negotiation skills.

9. What is the hypothesis for why this behavior is occurring?
   Attendance problems are an attempt to avoid work demands.

10. What intervention(s) does the staff recommend? Number the choices 1–4, with 1 being the intervention to initiate first, 2 second, and so forth.
    _____ Behavior does not warrant intervention
    _____ Schedule change
    __2__ Staff change/training
    _____ Medical treatment
    __4__ Skills training program
    _____ Referral for intervention (e.g., counseling, drug/alcohol treatment)
    __3__ Environmental change
    __1__ Behavior program change or other modification

Page 2 of 2

shoplift tools from hardware stores and take them from neighbors' garages. This young man was not assigned to vocational placements where tools were present.

After two or three successful placements in which the opportunity to offend is not present, the TS should try placements where this opportunity does exist. The youth should be informed that this placement is a test to determine whether he or she can be trusted with this new responsibility. The employer should be informed of the risk and know that the TS and the vocational program will be responsible for reimbursement if irrecoverable loss occurs.

With the adolescent who has a history of assaultive behaviors, a functional behavioral assessment should be conducted to determine the circumstances likely to trigger an assault. Initially, the placement may have to be in a job where the individual is working alone or with one or two very carefully selected peers who have characteristics unlikely to antagonize the youth. Ideally, the student should receive anger management training during these early vocational placements so that later placements can test the youth's ability to control outbursts and maintain cordial relationships with fellow workers.

Ian had a long history of school difficulties. His first job placement lasted less than 2 days because of a severe temper outburst accompanied by a forcible push against his supervisor's shoulder. Although the TS had been informed that Ian had a bad temper that could easily escalate into hitting, pushing, or shoving, the TS had little history regarding Ian's victims or the circumstances around these events. The school staff were quite nonspecific. After the vocational incident, the TS went back to the school and attempted over a period of several days to talk to various staff members to discover why Ian would become angry. The pattern emerged that Ian could not accept correction or forceful direction from a female. Almost every incident of school-based assault was directed against female staff. In fact, only one known incident occurred in which Ian became angry with a male staff member, and that incident resulted in yelling and no physical assault. The vocational incident was also directed against a female supervisor.

Ian was placed in a job with a male supervisor. Advised of the nature of Ian's assaults, the anger management therapist Ian was seeing indicated that he would try to learn why Ian was so resentful of female correction and direction. After 9 months of vocational training with male supervisors, both the anger management therapist and the TS felt it was time for Ian to practice his newly learned anger management skills, and so he was assigned a job with a female supervisor. Over the next 2 months Ian had two minor verbal outbursts but no assaults. Ian continued to be supervised by a woman.

Establishing a Program Objective

A program objective, or goal, should be developed for problem behaviors that are to be remediated by formal behavioral interventions. This objective should state the level of performance for the behavior that the student must exhibit before the behavioral intervention program is considered complete. Specifically, it should tell for whom the behavior intervention is designed, what behavior is targeted for remediation, the criterion for acceptable behavior, and how long the criterion of acceptable behavior must be maintained to ensure that the behavior change will persist over time. Sample program objective statements are as follows:

- Joe will increase work attendance to 80 percent each week for 4 consecutive weeks.

- Shirley will decrease incidence of arguing with employer to one time per week for 4 consecutive weeks.

In establishing a program objective, the vocational team must strive to set realistic expectations in view of the student, type of behavior, and work setting. For example, it is reasonable to expect that aggressive behaviors such as hitting, theft, and property damage will be eliminated to ensure safety of the community. It might be unfair and unrealistic, however, to expect behaviors such as arguing, complaining, tardiness, or interrupting to be completely eliminated unless they present a severe social barrier to the student. For these behaviors, the vocational team must set program objectives that include criterion levels of acceptable behavior that are reasonable for the student's skill level and that will help present the student as a responsible employee. Figure 6.7, a Behavioral Intervention Program Cover Sheet for Tammy, lists this type of program objective.

Tammy was a 16-year-old student who worked in a restaurant as a kitchen helper. When she was given corrective feedback, Tammy would respond by telling the employer that someone else had made the error. This response was obviously untrue and unacceptable. In addition, Tammy would often tell untrue stories about herself and her family to co-workers at break. The vocational staff conducted a functional assessment regarding Tammy's lying. The staff concluded that Tammy's lies to the employer were intended to avoid punishment and that she required instruction in how to accept corrective feedback. These evasive lies were deemed a barrier to her work, thus requiring formal intervention. On the other hand, Tammy's lying about herself and family was looked on as a means of making herself look good and of participating in conversations with co-workers at break. For this behavior, Tammy was provided instruction in conversation skills, with lying behavior being redirected to more appropriate conversation topics. No formal intervention was implemented for the "storytelling" behavior.

Figure 6.7
Behavioral Intervention Program Cover Sheet

Student _Tammy_   **TS** _Ann_

Date initiated: _10/1/01_   **Date terminated** _11/2/01_

Program: Home ☐ **School** ☑ **Vocational** *(specify worksite)* ___Country Kitchen___

Program objective
Tammy will exhibit zero incidents of lying to avoid trouble for 3 consecutive weeks.

Collection procedure
Frequency, or tally each lie that occurs.

Dates	Baseline data	Comments and treatment
10/1/01 to 10/5/01	15 per week	Tammy's lies were ignored. (Treatment 1)

Program summary

Week of	Weekly total	Treatment no.	Date	Weekly total	Treatment no.
10/8	5	1			
10/15	0	1			
10/22	0	1			
10/29	0	1			

Posttreatment follow-up

12/3	0	1			
12/10	0	1			
12/17	0	1			

If program terminated, state reason ___Criterion achieved.___

Designing and Implementing the Behavioral Intervention

In designing a formal behavioral intervention program, the vocational team uses the information obtained from the functional behavioral assessment. The first step is to identify the target behavior to be remediated—stating it in clear, observable terms—and the desired social skill to replace the inappropriate behavior. In the case of Tammy's lying, her behavioral program specified the target behavior as lying to avoid trouble. The social skill to increase was accepting negative feedback in an appropriate way. In addition, if she did not lie to avoid punishment during the work period, she earned an extra 10 minutes at break.

The next step is for the vocational team to determine and describe clearly the response of the TS and employer if the behavior to be decreased occurs. The TS met with Tammy to discuss the problem, and they role played appropriate ways to deal with two types of employer criticism—valid and invalid. At work, the TS gently corrected Tammy if she lied to get out of trouble and assisted her in responding to the employer correctly. In addition, Tammy did not earn her extra break if she lied to get out of trouble.

In setting up a schedule of reinforcement for a formal behavioral intervention program, it is necessary to determine how often reinforcers are needed to help the student maintain the appropriate behavior at work. Some students are able to meet behavioral goals with a weekly reward, whereas others require both daily and weekly rewards. The vocational team will need to examine the type of behavior, the frequency of occurrence, intensity of the behavior, and the type of reward attractive to the individual. In Tammy's case, the vocational team decided that Tammy needed a daily reward.

Figures 6.8 and 6.9 show behavior data and treatment forms for Tammy. Note that in the treatment form the reinforcement and correction procedures are clearly and concisely written, detailing the behavior, reinforcer, and schedule of delivery.

Evaluating and Modifying the Behavioral Intervention

Once the behavioral program has been implemented, daily behavioral data should be collected. The vocational team should then analyze these data weekly to determine whether the program is effectively managing the behavior or program modifications are needed. Weekly data summaries are recorded on the cover sheet to assist in weekly review of the program (see Figure 6.7).

As a general rule, if data collection for a behavioral program shows improvement from the previous week, the treatment should remain the same. If the data do not show improvement for 2 consecutive weeks, then the program should be modified. Exceptions to this rule may occur if unusual circumstances have caused changes or stress for the student at work. For example, a substitute TS, student illness, problems at home, or changes in the work setting could cause temporary behavioral changes.

Figure 6.8
Behavior Data Form (Treatment 1)

Student __Tammy__ Worksite __Country Kitchen__ TS __Ann__

Date initiated __10/1/01__ Date terminated __11/2/01__

Behavior	Date					Total
BASELINE Lying to get out of trouble	10/1 ⊬⊤	10/2 ///	10/3 ///	10/4 /	10/5 ///	15 per week
TREATMENT 1 Lying to get out of trouble	10/8 //	10/9 /	10/10 0	10/11 /	10/12 /	5 per week
(same)	10/15 0	10/16 0	10/17 0	10/18 0	10/19 0	0 per week
(same)	10/22 0	10/23 0	10/24 0	10/25 0	10/26 0	0 per week
(same)	10/29 0	10/30 0	10/31 0	11/1 0	11/2 0	0 per week

Figure 6.9
Behavioral Intervention Treatment Form

Student	Tammy	TS	Ann
Worksite	Country Kitchen	Date	10/1/01

Behavior to increase

Accepting negative or critical feedback in an appropriate fashion

Behavior to decrease

Lying to get out of trouble

Treatment no. and date	When behavior to increase occurs, do this	When behavior to decrease occurs, do this
Treatment 1 10/8/01	Socially praise Tammy for listening to employer criticism and responding appropriately. If Tammy exhibits zero lies for the work period, she may earn an extra 10 minutes at break.	Prior to starting work, TS reminds Tammy of appropriate ways to respond to employer criticism. If Tammy lies to get out of trouble or blames others, TS helps Tammy apologize to the employer and accept criticism in the appropriate manner. If Tammy lies to avoid trouble at work, she does not earn an extra 10 minutes at break.

If the data indicate no improvement in the behavior and there are no extenuating circumstances to explain the lack of behavioral change, then a modification of the behavioral program is probably indicated. As a general rule, only one program change should be made at a time. If a program change is recommended by the vocational team, the team should first examine the strength and schedule of the reinforcers for the original behavioral program. The first modification that should be made is to increase the power of reinforcers. Generally, a change in reinforcers sufficiently enhances the behavioral intervention and results in increased program effectiveness. If reinforcer changes do not increase the desired behaviors, however, then the TS should explore other options—for example, changing the schedule, switching staff, changing the correction procedure, adjusting the environmental setting, or modifying the behavioral program's objective.

Maintaining Behavioral Change Over Time

After the objective for a behavioral intervention program has been achieved and reinforcers not naturally provided by the work setting have been faded, the student "graduates" from the program. The TS then periodically observes the student at the worksite to determine whether the behavioral change has been maintained. If the TS suspects that the behavior is becoming a problem again, then he or she should collect baseline data again for 1 week. If the baseline data indicate that the behavior has been maintained at the level specified by the program objective, no further action is necessary. If the data indicate that the behavior change has not been maintained, the formal behavioral intervention procedures are reimplemented.

BEHAVIOR CONTRACTS

Formal behavioral intervention procedures have been used successfully to teach a variety of job-related social skills to students while at the worksite and to remediate behaviors that pose a barrier to the student's success. Another intervention that may be used to manage inappropriate behavior at the worksite involves a behavior contract. A behavior contract system is effective with students who need to assume more responsibility for their behavior or who demonstrate problem behaviors on an infrequent basis. The contract system allows the TS to deal with more than one behavior at a time and is an excellent tool for building self-management skills. Figure 6.10 presents a sample contract for Ted.

Ted was a 17-year-old student who could demonstrate appropriate social behaviors at work. However, every 4 to 6 weeks he would exhibit a problem behavior at work, such as no-call/no-show, argument with a coworker, or poor work quality. A behavior contract was written with Ted to specify exactly what was expected each week, and a reward was selected for Ted's meeting these expectations.

Figure 6.10
Behavior Contract

I, _____Ted Smith_____ , understand that I am expected to maintain acceptable work habits

and courteous social skills at _____Burger Palace_____ . I understand that if I perform

the work expectations at a satisfactory level I will be entitled to the work incentives described.

Work expectations

1. I will attend work as scheduled unless I am sick or have a preapproved day off.

2. If I am sick, I will call the employer as early as possible but no later than 1 hour before my shift is scheduled.

3. I will work cooperatively with my co-workers.

4. I will maintain satisfactory work quality.

Work incentives

1. I will be able to have a free pop at break each day.

2. I will be able to get a pizza coupon on Friday.

I, _____Ted Smith_____ , agree with this contract and will cooperate with the expectations

listed.

Ted Smith	_11/29/01_
Student	Date
John Smith	_11/29/01_
Parent/guardian	Date
Jane Doe	_11/29/01_
Transition specialist	Date
Bob Johnson	_11/29/01_
Employer	Date

The information in a behavior contract should include the student's name, date the contract is initiated, schedule on which the contract will be reviewed, and behavioral expectations for the student. The contract should also specify the rewards the student will earn for meeting the contract expectations and say how often these rewards will be delivered.

VOCATIONAL CRISIS INTERVENTION

Vocational training for students with EBD often creates stressful situations. Some of the severe behaviors exhibited by students at our community-based worksites have included theft, assault of the TS, accusations of sexual abuse toward employers, major breakage or property damage, creating a fire hazard, threatening suicide at work, and no-show as a result of runaway or juvenile detention. It should be noted that these emergencies became viable training situations for the students through appropriate responses by the TS. It should also be noted that all worksites at which these problems occurred either continued to work with the students, took other students, or were otherwise willing to continue participation in our vocational training program.

Handling crisis situations such as these requires that the vocational program have established policies and procedures so that the TS may respond as quickly as possible. The employer relies on the TS to be the advocate for the student and to be the "expert consultant" if a problem arises. The TS must be ready to give professional, confident guidance to employers in dealing with difficult behaviors and to assure employers that their best interests are the most important concern of the vocational program. Figures 6.11, 6.12, and 6.13 outline generic crisis intervention procedures for severe acting-out, runaway/no-show, and theft, respectively.

One of the most important components of successful crisis intervention is an open, honest rapport with the employer. As noted previously, employers need to view the TS as an honest and knowledgeable professional. They must feel that the TS is a viable resource for them, regardless of the problem, and that their business's best interests are of concern to the TS.

The second component on which good crisis intervention relies is quality communication with employers. It is essential that the TS have at least weekly contacts with employers to build rapport and to keep abreast of problems that may arise. Often, good communication can *prevent* crisis situations from erupting. If they do occur, the TS will be aware of any work factors that may have influenced the occurrence of the behavior, such as new co-workers, student dissatisfaction with the work, manager schedule changes, or recent social or performance problems. Of the major problems that have been documented at work, many can be attributed to students' seeking termination from their jobs as a result of a change in the work environment.

The remaining pages of this chapter describe the steps that should be followed for effective management of an extreme behavioral problem

Figure 6.11
Vocational Crisis Intervention: Severe Acting Out

Behavior	Staff action	Brief description
Student has history of assault, tantruming, property damage, or disruptive behavior.	Prevent	1. Carefully select worksite that has natural supports to prevent behavior: • Positive, supportive employer and co-workers. • Physical surroundings enable discreet intervention if behavior occurs. • Access to machinery, tools, etc., does not promote unsafe conditions if behavior occurs. 2. Provide continuous TS supervision as needed. 3. Implement behavioral program if needed.
Student exhibits minor disruptive behavior.	Intervene	4. Discreetly instruct student to calm down. If severe, remove from area. 5. If student calms, return to work and carefully monitor student during remainder of vocational training period.
Student exhibits severe disruptive behavior, refuses to calm down, or both.	Remove	6. Remove student from worksite. Tell the employer you will call later to explain decision.
Employer calls to inform you of situation, or you have removed student from worksite.	Gather information	7. Question employer regarding incident; obtain as much detail as possible about antecedent events, recent work stressors, actual incident, etc. 8. Question student regarding incident to corroborate facts, explore causes for behavior and student goals regarding work.
	Alert staff	9. Contact vocational supervisor: Communicate all information gathered. Coordinate a plan of action to include the following steps: • Determine whether team will advocate for student to remain at worksite. • Determine consequences for student. • Determine recommendations/plan to be suggested to employer. • Determine need for juvenile court/police intervention. • Determine additional support vocational program should provide. 10. Contact employer and review student actions, precipitating events, and your recommendations regarding placements and consequences. *Negotiate* and *confirm* plan with employer to include: • Description of incident • Hypothesis as to why behavior occurred • Consequences for student • Employer's role • Student responsibilities • Follow-up to be conducted by TS 11. Set up meeting time with student if needed as soon as possible.

Vocational Crisis Intervention: Severe Acting Out (continued)

Behavior	Staff action	Brief description
Student is to be given consequences by employer.	Prepare student	12. Discuss problem and consequences with student. Discuss alternatives student could have used to deal with problem.
		13. If student is to meet with employer, role play how student should respond to employer. (Do not tell student what employer will say; instead advise student of all options the employer has.)
	Meet with employer	14. Be punctual to meeting with employer. Assist employer and student as needed. Ensure all steps of plan of correction are completed.
	Follow up	15. Debrief with student regarding employer's meeting.
		16. Follow up by phone or personal visit to ensure employer is satisfied with the plan of correction. Restate prevention measures project will implement if student is to stay at worksite. Thank employer for the support and training the worksite has provided for the student.

at the worksite (i.e., how to get the facts and investigate the behavioral incident, factors to consider in defining the intervention, strategies to follow in communicating with the employer and student, and, finally, follow-up steps that should be considered).

Know the Student

To assist in emergency situations, the TS must know the student's history, behavior problems, current treatment issues, and medical and/or psychiatric issues. The TS must also be aware of any court involvement, court orders for juvenile detention or mandatory disciplinary actions, and actions from other agencies providing support services. Finally, the TS must have sufficient knowledge and rapport with the student to discern the facts regarding a major infraction and to help the student use problem-solving skills so an effective solution can be selected.

Get the Facts

On becoming aware of a problem, the TS must get the facts surrounding the incident. If it is the employer who calls to notify the TS, then as much information as possible regarding the incident must be obtained from the employer. Details such as what the infraction was, amount of damage if any, persons involved, time of the incident, possible causes of the behavior, and any intervention that has occurred should be obtained. It is also helpful to determine from the employer whether there is doubt regarding the student's participation in the inappropriate behavior or whether evidence definitely confirms guilt. The TS *should not* at this point try to negotiate an intervention plan with the employer. Instead, the TS should thank the employer for the information, assure the employer that the incident will be investigated, and schedule a time to

Figure 6.12
Vocational Crisis Intervention: Runaway/No–Show

Behavior	Staff action	Brief description
Student has history of attendance or runaway problems.	Prevent	1. Carefully select worksite that has natural supports to prevent behavior: • Worksite is well supervised by staff. • Employer, co-workers are positive and supportive. • Physical surroundings are enclosed, preventing easy departure.
	Change monitoring or support on the job	2. Implement behavioral program if needed. 3. Provide continuous TS supervision as needed. 4. Alert employer if TS suspects attendance will be a problem, and set up a backup substitute to replace student.
Student runaway or no-show is reported by employer.	Gather information	5. Express concern and apologize to employer for any inconveniences, and obtain information on incident. Offer to help with completion of job. Tell employer you will call later to explain student absence. 6. Question parents, school personnel, etc., to determine student whereabouts, probable return time, reason for no-show or runaway, and student goals regarding worksite. Obtain as much detail as possible.
	Alert staff	7. Contact immediate supervisor and communicate all information gathered. Coordinate a plan of action to include following decisions/steps: • Determine whether student should remain at worksite. • Determine consequences for student. • Determine additional support to be provided by vocational program. • Determine recommendations/plan to be suggested to employer. • Determine need for juvenile court/police intervention. 8. Contact employer and review student actions, probable causes for actions, and program recommendations regarding continued placement and consequences. *Negotiate* and *confirm* plan with employer and program to include: • Description of incident • Hypothesis as to why behavior occurred • Consequences for student • Student responsibilities • Employer's role • Follow-up to be conducted by TS 9. Set up meeting with student if needed as soon as possible.
Employer is to give student consequences.	Prepare student	10. Discuss problem and consequences with student. Discuss alternatives student could have used to deal with the problem. 11. If student is to meet with employer, role play how student should respond to employer's message. (Do not tell student what employer will say; instead advise student of all options the employer has.)

Vocational Crisis Intervention: Runaway/No-Show (continued)

Behavior	Staff action	Brief description
	Meet with employer	12. Be punctual to meeting with employer. Assist employer and student as needed. Ensure all agreed steps of plan of correction are completed.
	Follow up	13. Debrief with student regarding employer's meeting.
		14. Follow up by phone or personal visit to ensure employer is satisfied with the plan of correction. Restate prevention measures or plan of trainer support if student will stay at worksite. Thank employer for the support and training the worksite has provided for the student.

meet to discuss the results of the investigation. The TS should express concern and sympathy for the employer's inconvenience.

After learning of the problem, the TS needs to investigate the incident to determine the significance and truth of the allegations. This investigation could include interviews with teachers, other students, and parents to corroborate the facts the employer or other source has provided. The final step in the investigation is to interview the student regarding the incident. During the student interview, the TS should try to gather facts, assist the student in problem solving, and facilitate the student's selection of an appropriate solution—one that will resolve the problem and keep the student out of trouble in the future. If at all possible, the student should accept responsibility for the incident before having contact with the employer.

Determine the Intervention

Once the facts are known, it is up to the vocational team to determine and propose an intervention or consequences. If at all possible, the team should not recommend firing students if they have exhibited the behavior as a means to avoid or escape the job. In these instances, students should be given other consequences for the infraction and then given support and training in job termination skills.

The questions to consider when determining consequences for students are as follows:

- Was the infraction a violation of a current court order for the student? If so, the court officer should be notified and consulted regarding consequences.

- Does the infraction warrant police involvement? If so, should the employer be asked to file formal charges?

- Did the infraction cause the employer to lose money? If so, restitution should be made to the employer, preferably by the student. If this is not possible, then the program should offer to reimburse the employer.

- Was the infraction serious enough to warrant termination? If so, firing the student may be a viable option if the employer suggests it.

Figure 6.13
Vocational Crisis Intervention: Theft

Behavior	Staff action	Brief description
Student has history of theft.	Prevent	1. Carefully select worksite that has natural support to prevent behavior: • Worksite is well supervised by staff. • Belongings or objects to steal are not accessible. 2. Provide continuous TS supervision as needed. 3. Implement behavioral program if needed.
TS apprehends student stealing.	Intervene	4. Instruct student to return item. 5. Carefully monitor student during remainder of vocational training period. 6. Ensure student has consequences for behavior.
Student becomes defiant or refuses to return item.	Remove	7. Remove student from worksite. Tell the employer you will call later to explain decision.
Employer or other source alerts you to theft by student.	Gather information	8. Question student regarding incident to determine whether student stole items, reason for stealing, times of theft, what student did with items, and student solutions to problem. Question parent/guardian, school staff, or other persons to determine whether stolen items have been seen or noted. Ensure that student is supervised continuously until consequences are set.
	Alert staff	9. Contact vocational supervisor or director. Communicate all information gathered. Coordinate a plan of action to include the following decisions/steps: • Determine whether student should remain at worksite. • Determine consequences for student. • Determine recommendations/plan to be suggested to employer. • Determine need for juvenile court/police involvement. 10. Contact employer and review student actions and your recommendations regarding continued placement and consequences. *Negotiate* and *confirm* plan with employer to include: • Description of incident • Hypothesis as to why behavior occurred • Employer role • Student responsibilities • Consequence for student • Follow-up needed by program 11. Set up meeting time with student if needed as soon as possible.
Student to be reprimanded by employer as part of consequences.	Prepare student	12. Discuss problem and consequences with student. Discuss alternatives student could have used to deal with problem. 13. If student is to meet with employer, role play how student should respond to employer's message. (Do not tell student what employer will say; instead advise student of all options the employer has.)

Vocational Crisis Intervention: Theft (continued)

Behavior	Staff action	Brief description
	Meet with employer	14. Be punctual to meeting with employer. Assist employer and student as needed. Ensure all agreed steps of plan of correction are completed.
	Follow up	15. Follow up by phone or personal visit to ensure employer is satisfied with the plan of correction. Restate prevention measures project will implement if student is to stay at the worksite. Thank employer for support and offer praise for the work done with the student.

- Did the student commit the behavior as a result of a change at work? Stress at home? Was the student trying to escape work? Ask for help? Protest an unfair situation?

- Does the student's success at this worksite require that more vocational support be made available? If so, what kind of support?

- Does the student have a sincere attachment to the job? What does the student want to have happen? Remain at the job? Exit the job?

The TS should clearly outline consequences that will be effective with the student. However, the TS *should not tell the student* these consequences until the employer has been contacted and the consequences confirmed.

Talk to the Employer

The TS must talk to the employer once the facts have been established and a proposed intervention plan outlined. If possible, this encounter should be face to face. At this meeting, the TS should present the facts briefly and explain the student's possible motivations. For example, a TS explained Ken's theft problem to the employer in the following manner: "Ken seemed to like his job for a while, but his attitude changed recently. He told me he wanted to quit but didn't want to let the program down, so he stole something because he knew he would be fired."

The TS should then outline the *proposed* consequences for the employer, detailing what the TS would like to have happen to the student, the student's role in the consequences, the TS's role in the consequences, and what support the TS can offer the employer. Remember that the TS should *recommend* an intervention plan to the employer, not *tell* the employer what to do! Typically, employers will agree to consequences that are well planned and will often provide effective suggestions.

Talk to the Student

Once the consequences have been finalized, the student should be told what is to happen. If the plan is for the employer to talk directly to the student, then the TS should prepare the student for this encounter through role playing. It is important that the student apologize to the employer and accept the consequences in a polite manner. If the TS feels this is not within the student's capabilities, then the TS should recommend that the program deliver the consequences to the student. If the TS tells the student about the consequences of his or her behavior, then one responsibility assigned to the student should be a written or verbal apology to the boss. (Even if the program delivers the consequences, the student is still responsible for providing a written or verbal apology.)

The TS should then ensure that all the consequences are delivered as planned and that the student clearly understands the infraction, reason for the consequences, and more effective ways to deal with the problem.

Follow Up

The final step in vocational crisis intervention is to follow up with the employer. Follow-up involves updating the employer about the student, expressing thanks for the help, and assuring the employer that the behavioral incident has been a learning experience for the student.

CHAPTER 7

Tracking Student Progress

Vicki Nishioka

Record keeping is a critical component of a vocational transition program for students who exhibit high-risk behaviors. The information gained from careful tracking and monitoring of students is the basis for developing effective interventions. Records adopted should be updated on a regular basis by the student's transition specialist (TS) to document the student's progress toward individualized training goals. Of course, the system should require minimal daily maintenance from the TS and the worksite employer.

STUDENT WORKSITE NOTEBOOK

Over the years, we have developed a record-keeping system that is comprehensive yet relatively simple to use and maintain. This system involves the creation of a Student Worksite Notebook. For each student, this notebook is a place to collect relevant previous records, documentation of vocational and other training and education, and details of employment history. Materials include any and all of the forms discussed in this and other chapters and gathered in Appendix A.

The TS uses this notebook to record the student's daily progress and refers to the information in it to make decisions regarding program modifications. As discussed in chapter 3, each student with EBD should have long-term and short-term objectives relating to vocational achievements and skills. These objectives should reflect skills necessary for the student's transition to the adult world of work and should address both work production skills and job-related social skills. Briefly, *work production skills* are the skills necessary for performing the duties of a job. For example, the work production skills necessary for a career as a hair stylist include shampooing, cutting, coloring, and styling hair. *Job-related social skills* are skills necessary for keeping a position and advancing in the workplace, such as being on time, asking for help, wearing acceptable dress, getting along with work supervisors, and interacting appropriately with co-workers.

Indicators of job success include increases in work hours, increases in independence at the worksite, decreases in the level of TS support required, and decreases in intensity and frequency of behavioral infractions. To gauge these improvements, we use several forms, next discussed, to monitor the following areas:

- Attendance and total student work hours per week

- Amount of TS support provided per week

- Rate of progress through the Vocational Phase System (as discussed in chapter 5)

- Infractions at work

- Work production skills training progress

- Job-related social skills training progress

- Employer contact and evaluation information

Worksite Record Form

The purpose of the Worksite Record Form is to document basic demographic information about the worksite, the student's attendance and total work hours, and the amount of time the TS spends supporting the student. As shown in Figure 7.1, the first page of the form includes space for recording general information regarding the worksite—specifically, the names of the student and TS; name, address, and phone number of the business; the names of the supervisor and alternate supervisor; and transportation arrangements. The sample form shows that Jack is working for Court Restaurant and that he will be traveling to work by city bus. His supervisor is Rick, and his alternate supervisor is Darla.

Space on this first page is also given for detailing the program objective and social/behavioral objective that have been established for the student in the specific worksite. The student's attainment of these goals guides decisions regarding the student's continued placement, graduation, or termination from the worksite. In Figure 7.1, Jack's work objective at the restaurant is to complete 100 percent of entry-level kitchen preparation duties independently—in other words, to learn all the work production skills necessary to perform the kitchen preparation job. His social/behavioral objective is to exhibit 100 percent appropriate social behavior and zero incidents of drug involvement for 4 consecutive weeks. To achieve these objectives, the TS will provide training in required tasks and in assertively asking for help to cope with difficult situations at work and will support Jack in using these skills. When Jack completes the program and social/behavioral objectives, a decision will be made as to whether to continue the placement with new behavioral goals, have Jack graduate and move to another worksite, or advocate that Jack be hired at this worksite.

The second page of the Worksite Record Form documents student attendance, the amount of time the TS spends at the worksite in supervision, and the amount of time the student works at his or her

Figure 7.1
Worksite Record Form

Student _Jack_

TS _Sandra_

Supervisor _Rick_

Alternate supervisor _Darla_

Transportation _City bus_

Placement date _9/12/01_

Worksite _Court Restaurant_

Address _123 Waverly St._

Anytown, USA 12345

Phone _555-1234_

Program objective

Jack will demonstrate 100% of entry-level kitchen preparation duties independently.

Social/behavioral objective

Jack will exhibit 100% appropriate social behavior and zero incidents of drug involvement for 4 consecutive weeks.

Comments

Jack will check in with his TS daily regarding his work and social experiences on the job.

On a weekly basis the TS will check with Jack's supervisor regarding his work and social experiences for the week.

Figure 7.1
Worksite Record Form (continued)

Student __Jack__   Worksite __Court Restaurant__

Week of	Mon	Tu	Wed	Th	Fri	Total time	Comments
9/10	No work	No work	110/110	120/120	130/130	360/360	Jack is working quickly and efficiently with others.
9/17	120/120	90/120	120/120	120/120	90/120	540/600	Doing well and attitude is good.
9/24	10/120	0/120	15/120	0/120	0/120	25/600	Working independently and seems to enjoy job.
10/1	10/120	10/120	10/120	10/120	10/120	50/600	Working well with minimum support.
10/8	0/180	60/180	JDH	JDH	JDH	60/360	Bought drugs from co-worker and went to JDH.
10/15	0/180	0/180	OFF	OFF	5/180	5/540	Co-worker approached Jack again to buy drugs.
10/22	5/180	0/180	5/180	10/120	10/120	30/780	Change in hrs to 11–2.
10/29	30/180	5/240	OFF	5/180	OFF	40/600	New owner took over restaurant.
11/5	20/180	20/180	OFF	OFF	20/180	60/540	Jack seems to like new hours.
11/12	20/180	0/180	0/180	OFF	OFF	20/540	Argument with co-worker and supervisor.
11/19	10/180	0/180	10/180	Holiday	Holiday	20/540	Thanksgiving–off.
11/26	5/180	5/180	0/180	OFF	0/180	10/720	Doing well overall.
12/3	No work	OFF	0/240	10/240	0/240	10/720	Missed work 12/3 due to school problems.
12/10	0/180	No work	0/240	10/240	OFF	10/660	Went to court for review 12/11. Backtalk to Darla.
12/17	OFF	OFF	OFF	OFF	OFF	0/0	Cut finger 12/15 (off work for 1 week).
12/24	Vacation	Holiday	Vacation	Vacation	Vacation	0/0	On vacation.
12/31	OFF	Holiday	10/240	60/240	10/180	80/660	Laid off 1/5.

placement. Each row shows 5 days of work attendance, with each box corresponding to a day at work. Figure 7.1 shows that attendance for Jack was taken beginning with the week of September 10 and continued through the week of December 31.

The numbers in the box for each day reflect the amount of time the TS and the student are present at the worksite. The amount of time the TS spends supporting the worksite placement for that day is entered first, and the amount of time the student works at the site for the day is entered next. On Monday, September 24, for example, Jack's TS spent 10 minutes at the worksite checking in with Jack. Jack worked 120 minutes, or 2 hours. The column for "total time" gives a total for the week for the TS and the student, with the number given first indicating the TS's total time and the number given second reflecting the total time for the student.

The "comments" column on this second page allows the TS to note major events that occurred for the student during a particular work week—for example, progress at the worksite, behavioral infractions, and changes in work hours or work supervisors. For example, during the week of September 10, Jack worked "quickly and efficiently with others." In contrast, during the week of October 8, he was sent to the juvenile detention home for buying drugs from a co-worker.

Vocational Phase Form

The Vocational Phase Form documents the dates the student progresses within the Vocational Phase System. (For an in-depth discussion of this system, see chapter 5.) Figure 7.2 shows an example of the Vocational Phase Form completed for Jack during his placement at the restaurant. As the figure shows, Jack achieved Phase IV (independence) on November 26.

Space is also provided on this form to record all behavioral infractions at the worksite and the procedures the TS uses to correct the problem behaviors. As shown, among Jack's infractions were his attempts to buy drugs from a co-worker, arguing with a co-worker and supervisor, and reluctance to follow instructions given by his alternate supervisor. Recording this type of information assists the TS in understanding reasons for work infractions and in determining appropriate corrective action. In Jack's case, the TS began to notice a correlation between the work infractions involving Jack's attempts to buy drugs and the schedule of a particular co-worker. The co-worker's offers of drugs were difficult for Jack to resist. A conversation with Jack confirmed the connection, resulting in Jack's and the co-worker's schedules being changed so their shifts would not overlap.

Vocational Log

The Vocational Log is helpful in keeping a running record of daily events, especially when a substitute takes the place of the regular TS. This communication system is helpful in providing consistent support to both the student and the worksite employer, as well as for ensuring

Figure 7.2
Vocational Phase Form

Student _____ Jack _____

Intake date _____ 8/21/01 _____   Worksite _____ Court Restaurant _____   TS _____ Sandra _____

Placement date _____ 9/12/01 _____   Expected termination date _____ 1/4/02 _____

Reason for termination _____ Employee layoff _____

Phase I 9/10/01 Learning	Phase II 9/24/01 Responsibility	Phase III 11/5/01 Transition	Phase IV 11/26/01 Independence	Phase V Employability

Date	Infraction	Consequence
10/9	Bought drugs from co-worker (David).	Jack sent to JDH for 3 days (10/10–10/12). TS discussed with supervisor—next infraction with drugs will result in termination.
10/15	David approached Jack again with offer to sell drugs. Jack left work 1 hour early (unable to cope with situation).	TS spoke with supervisor. Supervisor will reschedule Jack and David so their shifts do not overlap.
11/12	Problem arguing with co-worker (Lucy), then talking back to supervisor when he intervened.	TS and supervisor agreed that Jack will lose bus privileges for the rest of the week.
11/13	Walked to work—late 1/2 hour.	Supervisor reprimanded.
12/3	Missed work because of behavior problems at school.	Co-worker took Jack's shift on 12/3. TS scheduled a meeting of vocational staff to discuss school issues.
12/13	Noncompliance with alternate supervisor (Darla). Will take direction only from supervisor.	Supervisor reprimanded and explained Darla's position. Jack agreed to try harder to cooperate with Darla.

that follow-up action for problems or concerns is taken in a timely manner. Figure 7.3 shows sample entries from a Vocational Log kept by a substitute ("DB") during days Jack's regular TS was absent.

Skills-Training Program Data Form/Skills-Training Program Log

Information for recording teaching strategies and student progress in formal skills training programs is organized on two forms: the Skills-Training Program Data Form and the Skills-Training Program Log.

The first page of the Skills-Training Program Data Form documents the teaching plan for a formal skills-training program, including the program objective, reinforcement schedule, correction procedure, and teaching notes. Figure 7.4 shows the skills program used to teach Jack to perform the entry-level skills for the kitchen help position. In this example, the TS demonstrated the task to Jack and then worked alongside Jack to ensure that he maintained acceptable rate and quality of work. The TS withdrew support gradually as Jack gained skills.

The second page of this form presents Jack's progress in learning the desired work skills. The left-hand column lists the work duties the student is to learn or, if needed, a task analysis of a specific work task. (As described in chapter 5, a task analysis is a systematic breakdown of the steps required to complete a work task.) Having a task analysis permits the TS to monitor student progress closely and to decide when to teach a task in smaller steps if the student is having difficulty learning. The right-hand columns consist of a series of data boxes in which the TS can record student progress data on a daily basis. If the student demonstrates the selected skill at the desired level of independence and competency, the TS marks an *X* in the corresponding data box. If the student requires assistance or does not demonstrate the skill at an appropriate level of competency, the TS records an *O* in the data box. If a student demonstrates little or no success learning desired work skills in two teaching trials, then the TS should offer more teaching support. Figure 7.4 shows that Jack demonstrated little difficulty in learning the desired work tasks. However, the data indicate that he did have problems setting up the tables. The TS determined that Jack could not remember the exact placement of the silverware. The TS took a picture of a correct table setting, and Jack used it until he had the table arrangement memorized.

The second form for documenting student progress on formal skills-training programs is the Skills-Training Program Log. This form allows the TS to record anecdotal information about the student's progress. These notes can highlight strengths that may assist the student in developing long-range career goals, or they may highlight training problems and provide specific information about why the student is having difficulty. Figure 7.5 shows sample entries on this form for Jack.

The Skills-Training Program Data Form may also be used as an aid in teaching job-related social skills. Figure 7.6 shows an example of a skills-training program to help another student, Sarah, learn to ask for help from her supervisor and co-workers. Again, the first page of this form gives program objective, reinforcement schedule, correction

Figure 7.3
Vocational Log

Student _Jack_   **TS** _Sandra_

Worksite _Court Restaurant_   **Placement date** _9/12/01_

Date	TS initials	Program	Comments
9/17	DB	Restaurant	Rick said they could use another person for busing tables, etc. (At 8 A.M. said Jack and other person could switch off.)
9/18	DB	(same)	Darla likes Jack's work and wants to know when he can come by himself.

procedure, and teaching notes. The teaching notes in the example outline an instructional strategy requiring the TS to choose an appropriate situation in which Sarah will ask for help. Before Sarah approaches her boss, she and the TS will role play the situation to assist Sarah in planning what she will say and how she will say it. After Sarah asks her boss for help, the TS will give her immediate feedback about her performance.

The task analysis for this social skill (i.e., asking for help) is shown on the second page of the form. This task analysis lists the social mechanics (e.g., eye contact, body posture, facial expression) and suggests dialogue to initiate the skill ("Excuse me").

Employer/Co-Worker Contact Form

The Employer/Co-Worker Contact Form (see Figure 7.7) documents the date, name of contact, time spent, type of interaction, and anecdotal information for both phone and face-to-face contacts the TS has with the employer or other worksite staff. We recommend that employers be contacted at least weekly but that most contacts last only 5 to 10 minutes. Our experience indicates that, if employers are not contacted weekly or if the contacts are lengthy, communication breaks down, sometimes to a degree that causes employers to terminate program participation.

As shown, columns are provided for recording date, name of contact, and time (duration of contact). The remaining columns, for type of interaction and for comments, allow the TS to record the content of the interaction with the employer or co-worker. "Type of interaction" refers to whether the content concerns work-related behavior problems (discipline), the student's mastery of work responsibilities (training), the employer's delivery of support for the student (praise), or coordination of scheduling or completion of other tasks (administration). This information should be recorded very briefly.

Figure 7.4
Skills-Training Program Data Form (Work Skills)

Student _____Jack_____   **Date program started** __9/12/01_____

TS __Sandra_____   **Date program completed** ___9/21/01_____

Worksite ____Court Restaurant_____

Program objective

Jack will demonstrate 100% of entry-level kitchen preparation duties independently.

Reinforcement schedule

Social praise for each correct response

Correction procedure

If Jack makes an error, give him a teaching hint that will encourage him to self-correct the error. If Jack corrects the error, give him social praise. If he does not correct the error, help him do the task.

Teaching notes

Demonstrate the task for Jack, then work cooperatively with him to ensure work quality is satisfactory. Gradually fade support when Jack does task at acceptable level for 5 consecutive days.

Page 1 of 2

Figure 7.4
Skills-Training Program Data Form (continued)

Student _____ Jack _____   Worksite _____ Court Restaurant _____

Job description/task analysis	Date															
	9/12	9/13	9/14	9/17	9/18	9/19	9/20	9/21						PROGRAM COMPLETE		
1. Wash dishes.	O	X	X	X	X	X	X	X								
2. Prepare vegetables.	O	X	X	X	X	X	X	X								
3. Butter bread.	O	X	X	X	X	X	X	X								
4. Bus tables.	O	X	X	X	X	X	X	X								
5. Prepare butter and jellies.	O	X	X	X	X	X	X	X								
6. Prepare hamburgers.	O	O	X	X	X	X	X	X								
7. Prepare meats.	O	O	X	X	X	X	X	X								
8. Set up tables.	O	O	O	X	X	X	X	X								
Total no. of Xs / Total no. of steps	0/8	5/8	7/8	8/8	8/8	8/8	8/8	8/8								
% independent	0	63	88	100	100	100	100	100								
TS initials	SR	SR	SR	DB	DB	SR	SR	SR								

Figure 7.5
Skills-Training Program Log

Student ___Jack___   **TS** ___Sandra___

Worksite ___Court Restaurant___   **Placement date** ___9/12/01___

Date	Comments	TS initials
9/12	Jack worked quickly and was eager to learn. Needed assistance in doing all tasks. I worked with him, which seemed to help with his frustration level.	SR
9/13	Jack learned quickly and performed most tasks independently. Needed reminders in preparing meats and setting up tables re minor issues (e.g., right dishes, utensils).	SR
9/14	Worked independently on all tasks. Needed some cues regarding social behavior only.	SR

Student Progress Report

The Student Progress Report (Figure 7.8) provides the student and TS with information regarding the employer's perception of the student's performance and competency. This information is useful in determining progress toward work production skills and job-related social skills. The schedule for conducting evaluations for students who are receiving on-the-job training from the TS might include evaluations completed at the end of the first 2 weeks of training and at the termination of a 3-month period of work experience. If the student receives on-the-job training from the employer, then the evaluation may be conducted on a weekly basis to provide the TS with consistent feedback regarding the student's work performance. This information then guides the TS in providing specific help to the student in identified areas of weakness.

In either case, we *strongly recommend* that the TS complete the evaluation during a brief face-to-face interview with the employer rather than leave the form for the employer to complete on his or her own. This strategy strengthens the program's relationship with the employer and provides an opportunity to obtain detailed information regarding the employer's perception of the student's work performance.

GUIDELINES FOR TRANSITION SPECIALISTS

When gathering and sharing the information in these various forms with students, parents, employers, and other members of the vocational staff, as a TS you will need to exercise professional judgment. When giving the student feedback, cover the student's performance,

Figure 7.6
Skills-Training Program Data Form (Social Skills)

Student ___Sarah___ **Date program started** _7/9/01_

TS _Warren_ **Date program completed** _7/19/01_

Worksite _Office of Building Codes_

Program objective

Sarah will ask for help in a socially acceptable manner across three different social situations in the work setting.

Reinforcement schedule

Praise Sarah for correctly asking for help.

Correction procedure

Observe Sarah as she asks for help. After Sarah is done, praise her for steps she did correctly and explain steps she could have done better. Role play the situation with Sarah to help her practice the correct way to ask for help.

Teaching notes

Choose a situation for Sarah to ask for help from her boss or a co-worker, to include asking for physical help to perform a task, asking for information, or asking for clarification of directions. Discuss and role play how she may do this correctly.

Page 1 of 2

Skills-Training Program Data Form (continued)

Student   *Sarah*   Worksite   *Office of Building Codes*

PROGRAM COMPLETE

Job description/task analysis	7/9	7/10	7/11	7/12	7/13	7/16	7/17	7/18	7/19
1. Chooses an acceptable time.	O	X	X	X	X	X	X	X	X
2. Makes eye contact.	O	O	X	X	X	X	X	X	X
3. Smiles at person.	O	X	X	X	X	X	X	X	X
4. Stands at arm's length away.	O	X	X	X	X	X	X	X	X
5. Uses polite voice.	O	O	O	X	X	X	X	X	X
6. Greets person.	O	O	O	O	X	X	X	X	X
7. Says, "Excuse me," if needed.	O	X	X	X	X	X	X	X	X
8. States request.	O	O	X	X	X	X	X	X	X
9. Listens to answer.	O	X	X	X	X	X	X	X	X
10. Asks questions to clarify answer.	O	O	O	X	X	X	X	X	X
11. Thanks the person for help.	O	O	O	O	X	X	X	X	
Total no. of Xs / Total no. of steps	0/11	5/11	7/11	9/11	11/11	11/11	11/11	11/11	11/11
% independent	0	45	64	82	100	100	100	100	100
TS initials	WS	WS	WS	WS	WS	WS	WS	WS	WS

Figure 7.7
Employer/Co-Worker Contact Form

Student ___Jack___

Worksite ___Court Restaurant___

Placement date ___9/12/01___

Supervisor ___Rick___   TS ___Sandra___

Alternate supervisor ___Darla___

Date	Name of contact	Time	Type of interaction					Comments
			Discipline	Training	Praise	Admin.		
9/12	Rich	5 min		X		X		Briefly explained tasks to be done.
9/13	Darla	5 min				X		Discussed free lunch policy. Jack may eat before or after shift.
9/17	Rick	8 min		X				Said they may need another person for busing tables, etc.
9/18	Darla	5 min			X	X		Likes Jack's work. Would like him to come alone next time.
9/26	Darla	10 min			X			Jack is working independently and is an excellent employee!
10/2	Rick	8 min				X		Advised about being careful with new uniforms.
10/5	Darla	5 min			X			Working well with minimum support.

Figure 7.8
Student Progress Report

Student ___Jack___ TS ___Sandra___

Worksite ___Court Restaurant___ Evaluation period ___9/12/01–1/5/02___

	(lowest)				(highest)
1. Gets to work regularly and on time.	1	2	3	4	⑤
2. Reports if unable to work.	1	2	3	4	⑤
3. Completes tasks to best ability.	1	2	3	④	5
4. Uses work time efficiently.	1	2	③	4	5
5. Works at reasonable speed.	1	2	③	4	5
6. Uses equipment properly and safely.	1	2	3	4	⑤
7. Works independently.	1	2	3	④	5
8. Dresses appropriately.	1	2	③	4	5
9. Has good grooming habits.	1	2	③	4	5
10. Complies with standards and rules of job.	1	2	3	4	⑤
11. Gets along well with others.	1	2	3	4	⑤
12. Is willing to take criticism.	1	2	③	4	5
13. Exhibits appropriate behaviors.	1	2	③	4	5
14. Exhibits appropriate attitudes.	1	2	③	4	5
15. Works at same rate/quality as regular worker.	1	2	③	4	5

Would you hire this student? At minimum or submininimum wage? Why or why not?

Yes—at minimum wage. Jack does an acceptable job for this type of work.

What problem areas do you identify?

Jack needs to work on talking and working at the same time. Evaluations marked at a lower score are due to Jack's needing to learn to work while he's talking.

Additional comments

Jack has difficulties focusing at work but when he tries he does well. Employer would like to hire him to "help him out."

Date ___1/7/02___ Evaluated by ___Darla___

Please contact ___Sandra___ at ___555-1234___ if you have any questions or concerns.
If you need more space, please continue on the reverse.

your concerns about problems or suggestions for improvement, and the employer's concerns. Be sure to discuss any unusual events, and address any concerns the student may have.

If you need to discuss a student's problems with an employer, keep in mind the fact that information other than that pertaining to work-related issues will need to be kept confidential, and avoid talking about other students, parents, or vocational staff unless that information applies directly to the student's work performance.

Finally, always remember to be as professional and as unobtrusive as possible at the worksite. It is important to maintain a cooperative and friendly approach. Employers, co-workers, and students all expect and appreciate a professional attitude.

CHAPTER 8

Job-Related Social Skills Training

Vicki Nishioka and Michael Bullis

One of the most critical components of a vocational training program for adolescents with emotional and behavioral disorders (EBD) is training in the social interaction skills and responsible work behaviors necessary to obtain and maintain competitive employment—competencies we have come to call *job-related social skills*. Research indicates that this group of individuals has a high rate of unemployment and, when employed, tend to secure menial and low-paying jobs. A substantial number of studies indicate that adolescents with EBD tend to have trouble in the workplace or lose their jobs primarily because of deficient job-related social behaviors and not because of deficits in work production tasks (e.g., Bullis, Nishioka-Evans, Fredericks, & Davis, 1993, 1998; Cook, Solomon, & Mock, 1988). Competency in work-related social behaviors is of critical importance to the successful employment of this population and their successful transition to the adult world of work. Accordingly, we and many others believe that job-related social skills training must be a central part of transition programs for this population.

Unfortunately, job-related social skills training programs often are piecemeal, do not focus on relevant skills (i.e., those skills the individual needs to succeed in specific jobs), and are taught in a manner that is weak and does not promote generalization of the skills across settings. In this chapter we discuss ways to address these problems and to provide effective job-related social skills training.

PHILOSOPHY

Teaching social skills is a complex and difficult task, but it is enormously important to students' success while they are enrolled in the transition program and during later work and community adjustment. The instructional approach presented in this chapter is grounded in our experience of providing social skills training to over 100 adolescents with extreme forms of emotional and behavioral problems. Over this time, we have experimented with different instructional approaches and content emphases. From this background, we derived two underlying assumptions that guide our social skills training approach. First, we strongly believe that a major reason that adolescents with EBD do poorly in the secondary grades and exhibit seemingly self-defeating behaviors is that they are rebelling against an educational system that is not meeting their needs and is too academic in its orientation. The adolescents with whom we have worked are homogeneous in their dismal academic performance. Their educational files resonate with academic difficulties across schools, classes, and grades. Their early educational experiences have been so negative and punishing that the less structured environment of the secondary school provides a setting that accommodates, at least to some degree, subpar academic performance and that offers an escape when students turn 16 and drop out. Although others may disagree with our position, we believe it is critical at this point in these individuals' lives and school careers to emphasize training in vocational and independent living skills. The simple reality is that the great majority of these students do not go on to postsecondary education or receive services from other agencies after leaving school. The instruction they receive in the secondary grades is likely to be the last concentrated service they receive, so those services must focus on critical skills and be as powerful as possible. Adolescents with EBD *must* be trained in the specific social, vocational, and life skills they need to make the transition to responsible adult life.

Second, this type of training should reflect employers' values and perspectives—a view foreign to most educators. Educators generally do not receive training in these areas in their academic programs, nor are employers generally involved in a central and meaningful manner in many transition programs. Thus, this type of instruction can be disconnected from the skills students need to succeed in the competitive work placements they receive through transition programs, as well as in placements they may secure after leaving school-based programs.

To address this type of skills training most effectively, we first discuss the benefits of concurrent training across school and vocational settings and then offer suggestions regarding teacher qualifications that are helpful in establishing successful job-specific social skills training.

Training in the Classroom and Worksite

Teaching job-related social skills *requires systematic teaching strategies in both classroom and community-based work settings to attain maximum benefits*. All too often, classroom social skills training programs require students to learn job-related behaviors, to be practiced in work settings in the community, only through class-based discussion, modeling, and practice. This "work readiness" philosophy advocates that students attain an acceptable level of appropriate behavior in school and in the social skills training class before they can be placed in community-based jobs. This strategy can result in students' never participating in community-based vocational training and never being placed in competitive jobs. Figure 8.1 shows how the classroom and vocational setting may interact effectively. The following case example points up some of the issues involved in this interaction.

Figure 8.1
Classroom and Vocational Setting Interactions

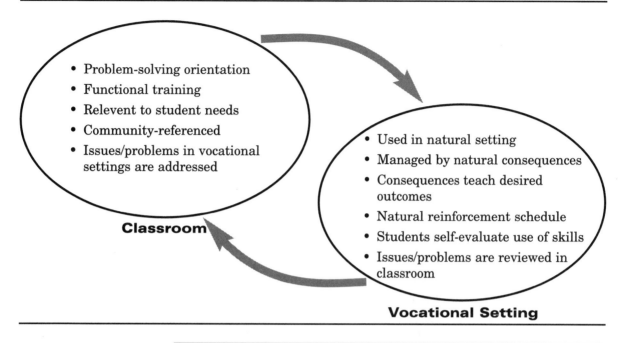

- Problem-solving orientation
- Functional training
- Relevent to student needs
- Community-referenced
- Issues/problems in vocational settings are addressed

Classroom

- Used in natural setting
- Managed by natural consequences
- Consequences teach desired outcomes
- Natural reinforcement schedule
- Students self-evaluate use of skills
- Issues/problems are reviewed in classroom

Vocational Setting

Leroy was 17 years old and enrolled in an alternative education program. He had been in the program for over a year and had not earned the opportunity to participate in community-based vocational training despite the educational team's awareness that placement in vocational training was critical for Leroy's successful transition to adult life. Further, Leroy wanted to work in the community and was debating whether or not to drop out of the alternative program, and out of school altogether, because of his dissatisfaction with the program. However, given Leroy's failure to earn that placement through his school-based behavior, educators were reluctant to place him in work training and feared that he would not fully appreciate the work opportunity and could develop poor work values. Another concern was that the inappropriate behaviors he exhibited in school could also be exhibited at the worksite, creating an unsatisfactory training experience and a dissatisfied employer. To reverse this situation, the educational team decided to change their incentive system to offer work experience to students regardless of their school-based behavior. Leroy was then placed in a community-based job and worked successfully in several increasingly difficult and demanding placements. He expressed satisfaction with the placements and the program, and he eventually graduated and was placed in a full-time, competitive job.

If the previous incentive system had been maintained, with Leroy's being required to exhibit acceptable school behavior prior to participation in vocational training, it is unlikely that he would have learned to work. Educators often believe that a student's inappropriate behaviors from school will transfer to the worksite, creating problems for the training specialist (TS), the employer, and the transitional program. Our experience indicates that exactly the opposite occurs: The placement of students in a competitive and community-based worksite generally enhances their school and vocational experiences and satisfaction.

Employer Perspective

Effective teaching of job-related social skills requires that the classroom teacher and the TS think like competitive employers and understand fully the work principles that guide the mission and conduct of the workplace. They must convey these principles and values to their students for optimum success in vocational training.

The first and foremost principle is to get the job done! Students simply will not be maintained in a competitive placement if they cannot adequately perform the job or if they demonstrate social problems in the workplace.

The second principle is to remember that employers are busy. If students are (a) unable to learn the job with minimal help from the employer, (b) lack the skill to ask others for help, and (c) require excessive amounts of employer supervision, the students' jobs will be in jeopardy. Some caring employers will hire students for altruistic reasons—in fact, surveys of the employers with whom we have worked emphasize this point—but no competitive employer is in business to be a counselor or to help employees solve all their work or home problems. Our experiences with hundreds of adolescents with EBD and numerous employers strongly indicate that employers value workers who will take initiative in appropriately resolving problems on their own and who can discriminate problems they should bring to the employer.

The third principle is that employers do not want to be responsible for resolving conflicts among co-workers; thus, employees must possess the skills necessary to work cooperatively and effectively with others. In turn, educators must understand that the first solution to a work problem should not automatically be "to talk to the boss." Employers should be informed of problems that may disrupt or damage their businesses, but other issues should be handled first by the student.

Finally, competitive employers demand workers who conduct themselves in a businesslike manner, who will keep their business safe, and who will report problems that may affect the success and safety of the business.

JOB-RELATED SOCIAL SKILLS

Job-related social skills are those skills and behaviors necessary for workers to (a) secure entry into the employment setting, (b) work cooperatively and successfully with others in the workplace, and (c) exit the employment setting in an acceptable manner. Broadly, these behaviors are exhibited in reference to the work supervisor, co-workers, and—in some cases—customers. These job-related social skills require students to demonstrate the ability not only to perform the required job duties but also to build positive work relationships with both supervisors and co-workers. Figure 8.2 presents a summary of these core skills, discussed in more detail in the following paragraphs. Figure 8.3 lists *social skills mechanics,* consisting of the array of verbal and nonverbal behaviors that constitute and support effective social interactions (Spence, 1981). Examples of these behaviors include facial expression, body posture, gestures, eye contact, and physical touch during social interactions.

Jeanne was a 15-year-old student employed at a deli. Jeanne worked very hard delivering orders. However, she slouched constantly, making her appear lazy and bored. Her poor posture caused problems with her boss, looked "bad" to the public, and ultimately reduced her potential as a respected worker at this placement.

Job-Seeking Skills

Skills necessary to gain entry into competitive employment are included in this category. They include the ability to obtain information regarding employment opportunities, secure an employment application, complete the application, demonstrate appropriate hygiene and dress for job search, exhibit competent performance at a job interview, and follow up appropriately to a job application or interview. This cluster of skills also includes the ability to complete necessary paperwork once employment is obtained, including income tax forms, W-4 forms, and insurance forms. Completion of preservice training activities is necessary for some competitive jobs—for example, successful completion of a course of study or licensure before the placement can begin.

Work Adjustment Behaviors

This category describes the skills necessary to adjust to the routine demands of most competitive jobs: being on time, appropriate hygiene and dress, taking breaks when appropriate, following work rules, displaying safe work habits, staying on task, and using time cards. Also included in this cluster of skills is the ability to act in a manner appropriate for the worksite—that is, not to act in a bizarre, aggressive, or strange way that would alienate others.

Fred was a 16-year-old student who worked at a computer job and performed work production skills very well. However, he made bizarre noises while waiting for the computer to finish the requested program, causing his co-workers to become uncomfortable around him. This behavior created a barrier that reduced his ability to build a social network at work.

Figure 8.2
Job-Related Social Skills Components

Job-seeking skills
- Reads help wanted ads.
- Uses phone book for job search.
- Uses local vocational agencies.
- Uses job announcement boards.
- Has work permit if needed.
- Has Social Security number.
- Has birth certificate if needed.
- Obtains job application.
- Completes simple application.
- Completes complex application.
- Has appropriate appearance at interview.
- Answers interview questions appropriately.
- Asks appropriate questions at interview.
- Follows up application/interview.
- Uses telephone professionally to inquire about jobs.
- Completes tax forms.
- Completes basic insurance forms.
- Conducts self appropriately during inservice.
- Discusses any disabilities with boss that may affect job (e.g., reading).

Work adjustment behaviors
- Wears clothing appropriate for work setting.
- Maintains satisfactory personal hygiene.
- Observes basic rules of setting.
- Follows established routine/schedule.
- Works independently on specified tasks.
- Works cooperatively in group settings.
- Remains on task during work period.
- Works at appropriate rate/speed.
- Finished work is of satisfactory quality.
- Checks own work.
- Punctual in arriving to work.
- Punctual in returning from lunch/break.
- Uses time clock/card.
- Follows safety procedures of setting.
- Uses safety gear.
- Responds to emergency situations.
- Transports self to work.
- Locates bathroom, break room at work setting.
- Obtains paycheck in timely manner.
- Does not steal at work.
- Does not damage property.
- Does not display aggression at work.
- Does not display bizarre behavior at work.
- Does not display childish behavior at work.
- Does not display self-abusive behavior at work.
- Does not lie.
- Applies problem-solving skills to work setting.

Interactions with work supervisor
- Applies problem-solving skills in work setting.
- Greets employer appropriately.
- Asks simple small-talk questions.
- Initiates conversation with boss at appropriate times.
- Answers simple small-talk questions.
- Uses appropriate body language.
- Asks for help when needed.
- Listens to supervisor directions.
- Acknowledges supervisor directions.
- Asks appropriate work questions if needed.
- Answers work-related questions.
- Acknowledges supervisor help if needed.
- Initiates co-worker questions/statements if appropriate.
- Keeps supervisor/co-worker informed of work progress.
- Thanks supervisor for praise given.
- Jokes and teases with supervisor appropriately.
- Responds to jokes and teasing of supervisor.
- Asks for time off appropriately.
- Discusses work problems appropriately.
- Chooses appropriate topics to discuss with supervisor.
- Requests schedule change if needed.
- Refuses/confronts supervisor when appropriate.

Interactions with co-workers
- Greets co-worker.
- Asks simple small-talk questions.
- Chooses appropriate time to talk to co-worker.
- Answers simple small-talk questions.
- Has appropriate body language, eye contact, posture, etc.
- Asks co-worker for help when needed.
- Answers work-related questions.
- Acknowledges help given.
- Thanks co-worker for praise.
- Gives co-worker praise.
- Initiates co-worker questions (e.g., "Would you vacuum? I'll go set the table").
- Keeps co-worker informed of progress.
- Jokes and teases with co-workers appropriately.
- Responds to jokes and teasing of co-workers.
- Discusses work problems appropriately.
- Chooses appropriate topics to discuss with co-workers.
- Asks co-workers for duties appropriately.
- Refuses/confronts co-workers when appropriate.

Exiting a job
- Appropriately decides to leave job.
- Seeks another job.
- Schedules dates of notice appropriately.
- Gives verbal notice to supervisor.
- Gives written notice to supervisor.
- Maintains work quality during notice period.
- Adjusts to relationship changes with supervisor and co-workers.

Figure 8.3
Social Skills Mechanics

- Gestures
- Fidgeting
- Gross body movements
- Smiling
- Appropriate head movements
- Eye contact
- Dysfluencies

- Attention feedback responses
- Amount spoken
- Interruptions
- Questions asked
- Initiations
- Latency of response

Interactions With the Work Supervisor

This category addresses skills that will enable student workers to interact appropriately with their supervisors in a variety of work-related social situations. These social situations include (a) following directions, (b) asking for help, (c) accepting criticism, (d) asking for time off, (e) talking about job-related problems, and (f) engaging in social conversation. All too often, the skill errors a student makes are minor in nature but happen so frequently that the student fails to make a favorable impression with the supervisor.

Randy was a 17-year-old student who worked at a restaurant. The management style at the site required Randy to be continually directed to tasks by the employer—that is, when Randy finished a task, he then went to the employer and asked for more work. Each time the employer gave instructions, Randy walked away without making eye contact or saying anything when the employer had completed his instructions. In contrast, all the other employees made eye contact with the employer and would acknowledge the direction by saying, "I'll get right on it" or "No problem—I will do it right now." Randy was regarded as different and "slow" by his co-workers and supervisor. The TS was informed of the situation, so she conducted regular observations to assess the problem. After gaining perspective on what was wrong, the TS instructed Randy to look at his boss and answer him while being given instructions. After some practice, this intervention resolved the problem. In this problem, Randy understood the work production skills of doing his job and remaining on task but was deficient in knowledge and use of social interaction skills with the supervisor.

Interactions With Co-Workers

Skills for interacting with co-workers enable students to build appropriate work relationships with other workers in both work and nonwork situations. In particular, these skills emphasize cooperative work behaviors needed to complete work projects with others. This area is often overlooked; educators tend instead to focus their instructional efforts on general work adjustment skills and social skills for interacting with the work supervisor. Such an emphasis may result in the students' becoming overly dependent on the boss for support and inept at socializing with co-workers—the most important natural supports available to students in the workplace. Co-workers can provide support in coping with day-to-day stress and dealing with problems involving the supervisor, and they also provide social outlets that make the job more satisfying and appealing. Poor relationships with co-workers are a primary cause of job dissatisfaction and students' decision to leave their jobs.

Sam, age 16, became attached to his boss and often made it a point to talk to him each workday. However, when talking to his co-workers, Sam would lie about his personal life to gain acceptance. For example, he told his co-workers that he owned several cars and that he had been arrested for robbing a bank. Sam's lying alienated him from his co-workers to the point that they referred to him jokingly as "the convict." One issue was the boss's concern regarding Sam's poor relationship with his co-workers. Sam felt like an outsider at work because of his co-workers' attitudes, and these feelings caused the worksite to be unpleasant and unrewarding for him. Eventually, Sam left the job.

Exiting a Job

Skills for exiting a job are necessary for students to assess whether they have adequate reason to leave their current job (by weighing the pros and cons of the position against what could be gained and lost in a new job) and, if they decide they should leave, to leave the job in an appropriate manner. Some students have good reason to quit a job, and we generally encourage students to change jobs to gain different work experiences and to experience quitting in an appropriate way. For other students quitting becomes an easy way out of a difficult situation. This escape response may result in a pattern of poor work history, as well as an inability to deal with daily stressors at home and at the workplace. Thus, teaching students to deal with upsets at work and to make sound decisions when leaving a job will benefit them greatly in the adult world.

Often students will feel comfortable in a work situation until there is an overt change, or even a slight variation, in the job, such as (a) new supervisor, (b) new co-worker(s), (c) changes in scheduling and work hours, (d) boredom with routine, (e) new job tasks, (f) problems with the supervisor or co-workers, or (g) an embarrassing situation at work. Other factors that may cause students to consider quitting their jobs are problems with family, problems with boyfriends or girlfriends, scheduling conflicts, and poor time management. These circumstances can cause students to become dissatisfied with their jobs and, rather than adjusting to the change, may cause them to display inappropriate behaviors so that they will be fired from their work placement. This type of self-sabotage is frequent among the persons with whom we have worked. Often the "choice" to be fired results from students' inability to cope with stressful events at work and their inadequate knowledge of the mechanics of quitting the job. Compounding this problem is their assumption that quitting the job will not be acceptable to their family or the TS.

Paul was a 17-year-old student who worked in a garden shop. The employer was very pleased with Paul's work and had recently increased his hours. Paul's only friend at work was a co-worker who was having performance difficulties. When this co-worker was fired, Paul no longer wanted to work at the site. Paul did not discuss this problem with the TS or the employer. Instead, he called in sick on the day following the co-worker's termination and then failed to call in or go to work the next 2 days. When asked why he didn't call, he stated that he wanted to quit the job but didn't know how.

If quitting the job is a viable option, students must be able to give appropriate verbal and written notice. They also must deal with changes in relationships with co-workers and supervisors, whether it means ending the relationships, maintaining them on an acquaintance level, or making plans to continue the friendship(s) after the job is ended.

TEACHING JOB-RELATED SOCIAL SKILLS IN THE CLASSROOM

Job-related social skills training should occur in a supportive classroom environment and then be applied and practiced in the natural work setting with the support of the TS. Information shared in the classroom should be job specific and include instruction in all areas of job-related social skills. In addition, this training should emphasize group discussion, group social interaction activities, and role playing of specific skills and situations instead of reading and writing exercises, which can be difficult for many students. Strategies for structuring and organizing a job-related social skills class are described next, along with suggestions for curriculum areas and teaching activities.

Class Organization

The job-related social skills class should address the following content areas: (a) job-seeking skills, (b) work adjustment skills, (c) interactions with supervisors, (d) interactions with co-workers, and (e) job-exiting skills. The class should include six to eight students, who can be in varying job placements and of varying skill levels, and it should meet once a day for a minimum of 1 hour. A positive and effective class requires clear and reasonable rules and a positive instructor who is well acquainted with the employers' values and viewpoints.

The rules for the class should be simple and emphasize the value of interacting with other students in a respectful manner:

- Use a polite tone of voice.

- Listen attentively to others.

- Take turns talking.

- Show respect to others.

The classroom should be furnished so each student has seating and a table or desk. The setting should be private, to foster honest social exchanges, and there should be enough space to allow group activities and role-playing assignments to be conducted in a comfortable manner. The classroom should have a chalkboard or another whole-class format that the instructor may use to present information visually to students.

It is usually helpful to begin the lesson with a 5- to 10-minute warm-up activity, either through review of the previous lesson or a short, enjoyable activity. A 15- to 20-minute group discussion should then follow to present the instructional material for the lesson. We suggest that a second 15- to 20-minute activity or role-playing session, requiring that students practice the skills learned, follow the group discussion. Finally, a short (5-minute) review of the lesson should be conducted to emphasize key points.

Teaching Strategies

Successful teaching strategies are those that motivate and reward students for active participation in their learning process and growth, and that avoid lectures and workbooks. The teacher should utilize group discussion, group activities, and role-playing strategies in teaching students job-specific skills. It is also important for curriculum materials and lesson plans to reflect the challenges students will encounter in the "real" world and for students to recognize the relevance of what they are learning to their success as adults in their own community. One classroom teacher with whom we worked researched statistical information on the job market across various occupational areas throughout the United States. His students found the information irrelevant to their needs and misbehaved badly. Once the teacher began to address local job possibilities, the students grew interested, and the misbehavior ceased.

Making the lesson "real" for the students is of critical importance in maintaining their interest. The goal for each lesson should be to provide information to students that they may use that day in their life outside of the classroom. Activities for a job-related social skills class should be meaningful and demonstrate to students how skills learned in the class will help them accomplish their goals. When possible, these activities should directly increase their potential for success. For example, an activity for a class on applying for a job could be for students to write their resumes, look in the want ads for jobs, call potential employers, go pick up actual applications, and describe problems or interactions they have experienced in the workplace similar to the content of the class's instruction.

The following paragraphs describe strategies for conducting group discussion using problem solving, group discussion, and role playing to teach skills.

Problem-Solving Approach

Social problem solving is defined as

> *a behavioral process, whether overt or cognitive in nature, which (a) makes available a variety of potentially effective response alternatives for dealing with the problematic situation and (b) increases the probability of selecting the most effective response from among these various alternatives. (D'Zurilla & Goldfried, 1971, p. 108)*

This process can be summarized in a five-step model (D'Zurilla, 1986). First, the student must be able to recognize accurately the presence and characteristics of a presenting social interaction or problem (*problem recognition*). Second, to formulate possible responses to the situation, the individual must be able to assume the role of the "other" actor in the interaction (*role taking*). Third, it is necessary to generate a number of possible solutions or responses to the interaction (*generation of alternatives*). Fourth, from the array of possible responses, the individual must choose the best possible response to the social situation (*decision making*) and implement or exhibit that behavior. Finally, once the response is displayed, the individual must be able to evaluate whether the response was effective or not (*analysis of consequences*).

To teach job-related social skills successfully, the teacher should employ a problem-solving strategy that will enable students to evaluate a given social problem at work and choose an acceptable, effective response to resolve the problem. Coupled with this thinking process should be structured role plays in which students are required to enact the scenario, then critique one another's performance. (See Kelly, 1982, for excellent guidelines on this process.) Examples of problem social situations include failure to follow directions, not asking for help when needed, not accepting criticism, taking time off without permission, talking inappropriately about work-related problems, and losing the job. To deal with these problems, students must know how to apply the problem-solving approach to each situation and then display the correct social response within that context. Simply teaching students to comply with their supervisor or co-workers each time there is a problem is inadequate because such an approach does not reflect reality. In our experience (personal as well as professional), supervisors have never been right *all* of the time.

A problem-solving approach is efficacious for both instruction and practical application of job-related social skills because each social situation represents a variety of different scenarios as the problem, goals, circumstances, and persons involved in the basic interaction change. Depending on the specific circumstances, a scenario based on a work problem could easily require any of several different correct responses, or combination of responses, to resolve. For example, suppose Tom's boss asks him to finish vacuuming the restaurant's dining area. Tom tells his boss, "I'll get right on it" and pleases his boss by completing the job. However, if Tom's boss asks him to vacuum the dining area while Tom is in the middle of mopping the kitchen area, it would be more appropriate for Tom to say, "I'm almost done mopping. I'd like to finish this so the floor dries before we open the restaurant, then I'll do the vacuuming. Will that be OK?" In yet another variant, Tom's boss asks Tom to vacuum, but Tom knows the vacuum is broken. Telling his boss, "I'll get right on it" will not be helpful for Tom because he can't perform the job until the vacuum is fixed. Instead, he tells his boss the vacuum is broken and asks for advice on how to get it fixed.

These scenarios are all ways to respond to a work supervisor's directions. However, the appropriate response to each social situation is different because of variations in the work setting. For this reason, teaching appropriate social interactions requires that students be instructed in applying problem-solving skills to a variety of problem situations that can occur on the job and to perform appropriate social responses in an acceptable manner.

The teaching process is outlined in the sample lesson plan (Figure 8.4). Each class begins with a discussion of the importance of each type of social behavior to be learned (e.g., requesting assistance from supervisors, working cooperatively with co-workers). The teacher asks students to volunteer brief examples of similar types of problems or interactions they have experienced in a work placement, stressing the importance of these interactions and their direct relevance to the students' work placements. The teacher then shows a video presenting a content-specific social interaction. The students are required to critique the interaction (*problem recognition*) and to specify the specific roles and positions of the persons in the interaction (*role taking*). Once the problem is defined, the group generates possible behavioral solutions (*generation of alternatives*), and a "correct" response, or group of correct responses, is identified (*decision making*). After this part of the process, students discuss and identify why one type of response is effective and another is not (*analysis of consequences*). To highlight important aspects of effective behaviors, the teacher pays attention to both the content of the response and the mechanics of the social skills used by the actors (e.g., eye contact, fidgeting, smiling, etc.) in both the effective and ineffective responses. Specific steps in the problem-solving process are as follows:

1. Identify the problem.

2. Stop and get the facts.

3. Brainstorm choices.

4. Make a decision.

5. Evaluate the decision.

Students are then asked to give examples of similar problems they have encountered, and the teacher selects a problem generic to the

Figure 8.4
Sample Lesson Plan

Goal

Students will use a problem-solving approach to asking for help with work situations in which they need to ask for help and will demonstrate satisfactory mechanics in performing this job-related social skill.

Warm-up activity (5–10 minutes)

- Ask students to think of situations in which they have asked for help at school, at work, and at home.
- Write down students' answers on the chalkboard in the appropriate category (i.e., home, work, school).

Instructional activity (15–20 minutes)

Group discussion

- Ask students what you must remember when asking for help. Encourage them to think of social skills mechanics. Write their answers on the board—make sure the list is sequential.
- Ask students whom you would ask to help you at work. They should state co-workers and the boss. Help them to think of things they would ask co-workers and things they would ask the boss.

Application activity (15–20 minutes)

- Put role-play scenarios in a hat. Ask two students to role play the scenario. Write the problem on the board and ask the class to complete the problem-solving steps.
- Ask the students to complete the role play.
- Assist class in giving supportive feedback to the students.
- Continue until all students have completed at least one role play.

Review (5 minutes)

- Have class review social skills mechanics of asking for help.
- Give students worksheet to complete problem-solving process.

group. The group engages in the problem-solving process to identify an effective response or solution to the problem chosen. The group then discusses that response and practices by using role-playing techniques. (Figure 8.5 describes a number of problem situations and details facts, choices, and decisions relating to them.)

Group Discussion

Group discussion is an excellent strategy for teaching not only the instructional material but also for teaching group interaction, problem-solving, listening, and communication skills. This teaching strategy differs from the typical lecture approach in that the instructor must gather the desired information from students, using a question/answer format. For example, an instructor who wants students to learn how to dress for an interview might show students a picture of someone dressed in a very businesslike way, someone dressed sloppily, and

Figure 8.5
Role-Play Scenarios

Problem	Facts	Choices	Decision
1. Fred can't remember how to turn on the copy machine.	• Fred needs to copy a report right away. • The boss is busy. • Fred has never used this machine before.	• Ask the boss for help. • Ask a co-worker for help. • Try to figure out how to turn on the machine by himself. • Wait until someone needs the machine and turns it on.	Find a co-worker who is not busy and ask for help politely.
2. Tina is helping a customer who has asked a question she doesn't know how to answer.	• The question is about store policy. • The customer is angry. • Tina's co-worker is new at the job.	• Make up an answer to get rid of the customer. • Tell the customer he has no right to be angry with her. • Yell at the customer. • Ask a co-worker for help. • Ask the boss for help.	Tina should ask the boss or co-worker for help.
3. Pete wants to know what restaurant is good for lunch.	• Pete's lunch hour is an hour away. • Pete has only 5 dollars to eat lunch. • Pete has to finish two assignments before lunch. • The boss and co-workers are busy.	• Ask the boss for suggestions. • Ask a co-worker for suggestions. • Finish the assignments and then ask for suggestions. • Go without lunch. • Wait until a co-worker is not busy and then ask for suggestions.	Wait until a co-worker is not busy and then ask for suggestions.
4. Lisa wants to learn how to use a feature on the computer so she can be promoted.	• Lisa doesn't need to know about the feature to do her job. • Lisa is respected at work. • Lisa has finished all her work.	• Ask the boss for help. • Ask a co-worker for help. • Take a computer class. • Ask for the promotion. • Try and figure out the feature before asking for help.	Try and figure out the feature before asking for help.
5. Ted has a family emergency and needs to leave work early.	• Ted has good attendance at work. • Ted's family needs his help.	• Ask the boss for help. • Ask a co-worker for help. • Leave without asking. • Stay and work.	Ask the boss for help (i.e., to leave work early).

someone dressed casually. The instructor would then open the group discussion with a very general question, such as "If you were interviewing people for a job, which one would you hire?" The instructor would then guide the group discussion by asking carefully formulated questions. Ideas for guiding a group discussion include (a) gradually adding questions that require more detailed answers, such as "Why would you hire this person?" or "What is wrong with this person's appearance?"; (b) asking questions that require use of the skill or information in different situations, such as "Would you be dressed for an interview today?" or "What would you wear to an interview?"; (c) using questions that require negative answers from the student to clarify ideas, such as "Would the person dressed casually get hired at an interview for a job as a business executive?"; (d) using negative examples to guide students in formulating personal opinions and understanding the gray areas of issues, such as "Would the person dressed casually get hired at an interview for Morrow Accounting Firm, where everyone wears suits? What about at a factory where all the executives dress casually?"; and (e) using hypothetical cases to give students practice in applying skills learned, such as "What would you wear to interview for a job at Sam's garage to pump gas?"

We have found the chalkboard a useful tool to organize lessons and discussion points, as well as to maintain student interest, because it presents material visually in conjunction with verbal explanations. When using the chalkboard, be sure to simplify the concepts that are being taught and to write ideas in concise and simple terms, at a reading level the students can understand. In teaching a series of related skills, write the skills the student needs to learn in simplified terms that can easily be read, as in the following.

Being Assertive

- Look the person in the eye.

- Stand at the right distance.

- Talk in a clear, calm voice.

- Use "I" statements.

- Tell the person what you want.

A list such as this can then be used as a guide for students in answering questions during role-playing activities, with the students' correct responses to questions being written down for display and comment. This technique gives the student reinforcement for correct answers and organizes information visually to structure group discussion activities.

Role Playing

Role plays are a very important teaching strategy in helping students practice basic communication skills (Kelly, 1982). Having students practice responses to specific social interactions through role playing is effective in reinforcing the generalization and application of skills to real-life situations. The teacher should offer role plays as a central part of the social skills class and should structure them carefully to ensure that this practice occurs in a supportive and positive setting.

Suggestions for using role plays in social skills training classes are as follows:

- Use role-playing practice in response to specific work interactions *after* the students have gained a rudimentary understanding of the social interaction in question and of what response is expected to resolve the situation.

- Choose role plays of situations students have or are likely to encounter in the work setting. In fact, asking students what social interaction problems or situations they have encountered in their own jobs is a good way of making sure the skills learned and practiced are related directly to pragmatic application.

- Provide students with a list of simple steps that clearly outline what is expected to resolve the situation in question. Following this, help them to develop a suitable way to operationalize the steps. This response will then be role played.

- Ask the students in the class who are not involved in the role play to give those who are involved praise or recommendations for their role playing based on criteria such as eye contact, voice volume, posture, and the like. Take a leadership role in the beginning to ensure positive and supportive suggestions.

- Whenever possible, have students role play with different people. Some students may need to role play with the teacher initially to overcome shyness and self-consciousness.

- Have students carefully set the stage to simulate the setting. For example, a table and chairs are needed for job interview skills.

SOCIAL SKILLS TRAINING IN THE WORKSITE

The goal of vocational training is to prepare students to cope with the social skills problems and work demands that may arise in their paid employment experiences. In addition to classroom instruction in these areas, specific training at the students' work placement is necessary to ensure generalization of skills to the natural work setting. There is an important connection between what is learned in the classroom and the worksite. The process of selecting worksites to teach specific job-related social skills and strategies for training at the worksite is discussed next.

Types of Worksites

Teaching job-related social skills in the worksite requires that the TS identify the management or interaction style of the supervisor and co-workers in the worksite in which students are placed. We have identified three types of management style: independent, supervisor directed, and co-worker directed. Each management style demands specific social behaviors to meet the social demands of the worksite successfully. In addition, the social skills needed to meet the expectations for each of these worksites differ in level of difficulty, so it is critical to take into account the social interaction styles and requirements of these sites.

The *independent worksite* is one in which the worker has minimal or no contact with the employer and co-workers in the performance of job duties. Social interaction with others generally occurs at the beginning or end of the work period and consists of brief small talk, exchanges about how specific jobs or tasks should be performed, or scheduling conversations. Students are expected to work independently during the work period. Jobs generally categorized as independent include reshelving books at the library, factory or assembly-line work, dishwashing, and restocking shelves in a retail store. This type of worksite is well suited to teaching skills such as on-task behavior, following a schedule, using a time clock, and checking one's own work. These types of worksites are good choices for placing new students who have minimal work experience or work skills. These sites are not effective for teaching more than minimal social interaction skills with supervisors or co-workers.

In a *supervisor-directed worksite,* students are expected to respond to directives and assignments by the employer or work supervisor. Work duties are scheduled continually throughout the work period as students complete assigned tasks. Students are expected to work independently at assigned tasks, but the employer or work supervisor checks the students' work quality throughout the work period. Worksites that generally fall within this category are small businesses in which the employer works with a small number of employees. This type of worksite teaches work adjustment behaviors (e.g., on-task behavior, punctuality), but it also provides an excellent opportunity for teaching appropriate interactions with the supervisor.

In a *co-worker–directed* worksite students are required to work cooperatively with their co-workers. The work supervisor may delegate supervision to an experienced and trusted co-worker, who is either formally designated as a leader or who has assumed such a position in an informal way over time. A common example of this site is a pizza parlor. Typical co-working interactions on a pizza parlor worksite are "Joe, I'll get the phone if you'll shred some more cheese" or "I finished the dough, so I'll start the salad bar now." Co-worker–directed worksites have a high level of social interaction and may or may not have a supervisor present. The distinguishing feature is that workers need to interact to coordinate duties and complete tasks. This type of worksite requires a wide array of complex social behaviors not needed at independent or employer-directed worksites.

Training Strategies

To teach effective and relevant job-related social skills, the TS must understand the job performance requirements of the worksite and its unique social skill demands, as well as the strengths and weaknesses of the student who is placed in that setting. To begin the on-the-job training process, the TS should establish at least one job-related social skills training goal for each student at each worksite. Each goal should be identified in conjunction with the student, specify what particular behavior is to be addressed, clearly describe an acceptable performance level, and place the goal within an appropriate time frame. Once the TS has discussed these issues in depth with the student to ensure that he or she understands what is expected, and a written contract is drawn up and signed, the TS should decide on the most effective and appropriate teaching strategy to achieve the goal. Strategies could be as simple as reminding the student prior to work of the skill goal and then role playing the behavior to ensure that the student understands what is expected.

Jeremy was an 18-year-old student who had difficulty listening to criticism. Whenever his boss would start to correct him, he would interrupt and tell the boss, "I know, I know, I know." The job-related social skills goal identified for Jeremy was to "decrease incidences of interrupting boss during corrective feedback to 0 incidences for 4 consecutive weeks." Because Jeremy was a very skilled student and had previous classroom training in accepting criticism, the TS privately explained to him what the problem was. The specialist then used a problem-solving approach to help Jeremy understand why giving "I know, I know, I know" answers was not helpful and worked with him to decide on a different social response. The TS role played the response with Jeremy to ensure that he would not only accept criticism using appropriate dialogue but also exhibit acceptable social mechanics (e.g., good eye contact, standing an appropriate distance from employer, using a polite tone of voice). The TS then shadowed Jeremy at work, giving discreet support for the desired social skill. Finally, the TS gave Jeremy feedback privately after work regarding his performance.

Another effective way to help students apply social skills knowledge to the worksite is to plan a strategy with the employer to remediate the problem. Employers should not be expected to make anything but minor accommodations to support students.

Kate was a 16-year-old student with a history of severe aggression, property damage, and drug abuse. At work she would often "space out" and not answer the employer or respond verbally to instructions. She would usually walk off and do the job requested. The goal for Kate was to "decrease her incidence of not answering the employer to zero incidents per week for 4 consecutive weeks." Once the goal was set, the TS talked to the employer and asked her to please require Kate to respond to directions. The TS suggested that the employer tell Kate, "Please answer because I don't know if you heard me unless you say OK." The TS then spoke to Kate about the problem and role played with her so that she understood what was expected. The TS gave Kate feedback while at the worksite and after the work shift ended. In addition, the TS gave support to the employer for her help in training Kate.

A third strategy to teach social skills interactions is for the TS to collaborate with the classroom teacher to develop a formal behavioral intervention.

John was 18 years old, diagnosed with bipolar disorder. Before John was medically stable, he talked incessantly about bizarre topics and often did not listen to people's responses. After John's medication issues were resolved, John still continued to babble and often did not listen to people's responses. The TS hypothesized that John used this behavior to avoid social situations in which he felt inadequate. The social skill goal developed for John was to "participate in a social conversation with co-workers at work for a period of 3 minutes, using 90 percent appropriate social mechanics, for 5 consecutive days." Due to the severity of John's social deficits, the TS placed John on a formal teaching program in which the social skills mechanics of a small-talk conversation were task-analyzed, or broken down into a sequence of steps. The TS then systematically provided training for John by using behavioral role playing and developing cooperative strategies with the employer. The TS ensured that John had an opportunity to practice social conversation skills with his co-workers. The data collected enabled the TS to determine specific problem areas that he should address in preparing John for work and to pinpoint the areas in which the classroom teacher could provide additional instructional support.

Placement at Multiple Sites

To prepare students fully for successful employment after leaving the educational program, it is important that they be given training in various vocational areas, as well as experiencing all three management styles (i.e., independent, supervisor-directed, and co-worker–directed). For students with minimal job-related social skills, it is helpful to build a progressive program that begins with placement at an independent worksite, advances to a supervisor-directed site, and then progresses to a co-worker–directed site. Movement between work settings will allow students to build viable job-related social skills progressively and to practice generic work adjustment behaviors in a variety of work settings. At the end of training this exposure will provide students with insights as to the type(s) of vocational areas and management styles they feel most comfortable with as employees. The training is further enhanced if the TS replicates the interaction style used at the worksite during on-the-job training sessions. In this way, the TS can encourage job skill acquisition and help students build social skills functional for the particular worksite.

CHAPTER 9

Vocational Support Groups

Vicki Nishioka

Students with emotional and behavioral disorders (EBD) are placed in a variety of paid and unpaid jobs through community-based vocational training. These jobs challenge students to maintain socially acceptable behaviors while at the same time dealing with social situations and interactions they have never experienced before. What do you do if your boss criticizes you harshly? How should you go about getting along with a co-worker you don't like? What should you do if you hate your boring job and want to quit but have worked there only a week? What can you do if the boss rushes you all the time, making you so nervous that you work even slower?

Obviously, it would be impossible to predict all the problems a student may experience or for the transition specialist (TS) to ensure successful resolution of problems as they occur. Complicating this issue is the reality that the TS cannot be on site to coach the student in dealing with each problem at the time it happens. Even if the TS were able to provide this level of supervision, the student could become so embarrassed at having the specialist "help out" that the situation might become even worse. Likewise, it would be impossible to teach students to deal with all potential problems before allowing them to work. It is also unlikely that employers will report every problem the student has at work even if they know them all—which is usually not the case. So, what happens to a student at work when a problem arises? All too often, especially during the early phases of an individual's placement and training, he or she will mishandle the situation, creating more problems.

One solution to this dilemma is first to teach the students appropriate social skills for the workplace and then to provide sufficient support to ensure that they will apply these skills to actual problems they encounter at work. (See chapter 8 for information regarding job-related socials skill training strategies for application in classroom and work settings.) However, an obvious barrier to teaching job-specific social skills to students individually is the time requirement. Another difficulty is that an employer or a TS does not always identify problems perceived by the student or perceive those problems in the same way as the student.

One problem Mike reported in a group meeting was having to arrive 10 minutes early to work because of the bus schedule. He said he was uncomfortable because he didn't know anyone at work and didn't know what to do with his time. The TS had not identified this scheduling issue as a problem; in fact, he perceived the 10 minutes as a bonus break. The incident was not perceived as a problem by the employer or the TS. When Mike was asked why he did not ask for help earlier, he stated that "it wasn't a big deal" and that he "could handle it," when in reality he couldn't, or at least did not know where to begin to address the situation.

Instances such as this have been repeated hundreds of times in our experiences. Try as we might, the problems, frustrations, and perceptions of all of the students with whom we work simply cannot be perceived accurately all of the time—or even much of the time. Further, teaching a set of prescribed skills, of either perceived or empirically derived value, doesn't get to the real problems because in these classes the students become the object of the instruction rather than leaders of the instruction. We should hasten to add that there is a central place for structured social skills instruction, but there also is a clear need for an open group meeting, in which students can voice their personal concerns and then work together and with a teacher or other staff person to resolve these issues. We call such groups Vocational Support Groups (VSGs) and believe that they are an important component of an effective transition program.

This chapter will suggest strategies for organizing and structuring a VSG in a school setting to attain these goals. To ensure that these activities lead to a viable and effective solution that is implemented in the job setting, we also advocate for the use of a pragmatic data collection system to document the impact of these solutions.

STRUCTURE OF THE VOCATIONAL SUPPORT GROUP

A VSG is based on the following assumptions: (a) The TS and the employer cannot always identify situations that the student will perceive as problems; (b) the student will not always ask for help for problems from the TS or employer; (c) the student will be more likely to share problems with peers in a support-group setting and to receive advice on these problems from peers; and (d) the support group provides an arena for the TS to have regular contact with all students under his or her purview.

The VSG consists of 10 to 15 students who meet two to three times each week for 50 to 60 minutes to talk about work-related issues. The meetings are designed to support students in applying job-specific social skills in their work settings. Specifically, the goals of these groups are (a) to provide support to students in the vocational program, (b) to teach students to apply problem-solving skills to the work setting, (c) to teach students to use peers as a natural but extended support system for work situations, and (d) to teach students to give one another honest praise and helpful advice regarding work problems. To achieve these goals, the VSG should be structured in a simple, open, but controlled manner, with the "ownership" of the group placed clearly with the students. It is important to stress that the VSG is *their* group, to address *their* issues and concerns, and not simply "another class." At the same time, it must be recognized that each group will follow a developmental process in which the leader (at the beginning, the teacher, the TS, or both) will need to take an active and central role until participants learn how to conduct the group meetings and teach one another how to solve problems.

A positive and effective VSG involves the use of a simple structure, reasonable rules, and a positive leader. At the beginning of the group and as new students enter the VSG, the leader of the group must teach students to give one another praise for triumphs at work and honest, helpful advice when work problems arise. As the group progresses and the students' skills develop, it also is important for the leader to step away from the leadership role, offering the control and leadership to the students.

Leaders should be skilled in social skills training strategies, the process of social problem solving, leading group discussions, and conducting meaningful role-playing activities with adolescents. In addition, leaders should have a clear understanding of the values and principles that are important to employers and accurate information regarding the demands of each student's current worksite and the status of each student in that site. An ideal instructional team for the VSG consists of the teacher of the job-related social skills class and the TS.

Social skills addressed by the VSG can be taught through consistent modeling and feedback to students, role playing, and systematic support for successful interactions. The rules used to structure the group can also assist the leaders in teaching students to support one another. Rules for a VSG are simple and straightforward; they should be followed closely because sometimes even a small break from the rules can lead the group away from its purpose and allow it to degenerate into a free-for-all discussion unrelated to work issues.

The rules we have established for the VSGs we conduct are simple and clear. Depending upon the group members and their need for structure, it has been our practice to display the rules on a poster, to review the rules at the beginning of each session, or both to ground the upcoming activities firmly within those parameters. The rules are as follows:

- Always use a polite tone of voice.

- Discuss only work-related questions and concerns in the group.

- Listen attentively to others when they are talking.

- Do not interrupt! Wait until others are finished talking before beginning to speak.

- Take turns talking—do not "hog" the discussion or deny others the right to speak.

- Show respect to one another.

- Give honest, helpful, and polite feedback to others.

VOCATIONAL SUPPORT GROUP FUNCTIONS

The VSG can perform two basic functions in facilitating appropriate job-related social skills for students. The first is to provide a forum in which students can share information on job openings and placement possibilities, share their work successes, discuss their work problems and frustrations, and receive and offer social support to one another. Initially it was surprising to us that often the information shared during VSG meetings is the first indication to instructional staff that a student is having a problem that requires assistance. Second, the VSG provides a context for students to apply social problem solving strategies to real problems raised by their peers and themselves and to practice appropriate solutions to those problems by role playing with others in a safe and supportive setting.

Job Possibilities

The VSG provides an excellent forum for making job announcements, and all positions that become available for work experience or paid employment should be shared with the participants. Not only is this an efficient use of time (it is necessary to give the information only once), but disseminating this information at the meetings provides a strong "work" tenor and motivates students to attend to learn of other job possibilities. Typically, jobs that are announced during the VSG have been recruited and developed by the TS. Also by using the VSG to announce job openings, the TS provides opportunities for students to practice decision making about leaving current positions and applying for these new jobs. Obviously, not all jobs should be announced, and not all positions should be open to all members of the group. Still, such announcements, and the question of who will fill those openings, can motivate students to earn the right to future placements. It is not uncommon for such announcements to lead to discussions of why a certain student was placed in the position; such exchanges highlight certain skills and behaviors needed to perform certain types of jobs.

Quentin, a 16-year-old student, had a history of chronic running away, lying, "pseudo-suicide" attempts, aggression, and manipulative behavior. He had previously worked at two job sites. His length of employment varied from 1 day to 2 weeks. Quentin's reasons for leaving the jobs were that they were boring and that all of the other workers' jobs were better than his. Quentin currently was in a work experience placement detailing cars when a restaurant position was announced. Quentin voiced an interest in applying for the position, even though he had been working at the detail shop for only a few days. His peers in the support group helped Quentin analyze this decision. They pointed out that the length of employment at his current job and in previous jobs was an important factor to consider when changing jobs. They told Quentin that employers often place great value on applicants who have demonstrated stable work histories. By assisting Quentin in analyzing the validity of his reasons for making a job change, the VSG prevented him from making his decision too hastily but still communicated to Quentin that he had a "choice" as an active participant in his vocational growth. Quentin decided not to apply for the position.

Job Success

The VSG is a natural arena for encouraging students to report successes or positive changes at their job sites. These events may include advancement to more desirable job duties, raises, advances within the Vocational Phase System (see chapter 5), compliments by the employer, growing friendships with co-workers, increases in hours, and so forth. Special attention to these achievements, celebrated by peers and staff within the VSG, enables students to increase self-esteem and build positive self-concepts. These successes also serve as a model to other students and allow those other students to practice giving compliments and encouragement for a "job well done."

Michelle was an 18-year-old student who had worked hard to build vocational skills in two work placements. As a result, she was hired as a dishwasher for a local restaurant. This achievement was presented at the VSG, and Michelle was awarded a special certificate for her accomplishment. Michelle appeared deeply moved by the praise. She later confided that this was one of the few times in her life that she had received positive reinforcement for her behavior, and she was excited to continue to work hard.

Andrew had been hired at a local pizza parlor to do janitorial work as a part of the morning crew. He was an active member of the worksite, attending staff meetings and staff parties. Reports from the supervisor indicated that Andrew was performing well in his position. These positive reports were discussed at the VSG so Andrew could be recognized. Andrew was asked to discuss his behaviors and his work attitude as an example for other students. Several students asked him about specific problems they had encountered at work and how he would resolve the issues. Andrew provided appropriate suggestions and advice, which instructed the students and reinforced him for his work performance.

Information Gathering

Another important function of the VSG is to assist the TS in keeping current with changes in students' job satisfaction and attitudes toward their placements. It has been our experience that in many cases seemingly small changes at work (e.g., changes in scheduling or supervisors) result in increasing job dissatisfaction or discontent that the TS cannot detect through visits to the worksite or reports from supervisors. In fact, students sometimes view these changes, which seem meaningless from our frame of reference, as personal attacks.

The VSG is also the forum in which students are likely to be the most honest in sharing work problems. It is not uncommon, unfortunately, for students to react in a manner disproportionate to the incident (e.g., "blowing up" over being asked to perform a slightly different job). The VSG, then, provides a safe and appropriate context in which feelings of this type can be shared—often the first time these feelings are heard by staff.

Bob worked part-time at two jobs, janitorial work at one restaurant and dishwashing at another. He was a fast worker, and both employers were very pleased with his performance and often praised him. Following 2 days in which he failed to attend work, Bob shared in the VSG that he had been "goofing off" at the job for a long time because he thought the employer "didn't like him anymore" and had called him a thief. The incident had not been reported by the employer or Bob to the TS, and Bob's comment in the group was the first time any such problem had been mentioned. The next day the TS asked the employer about the situation. About a month previously a coat had turned up missing, and Bob had been asked whether he had seen it. The coat was found later, and the employer forgot about the incident because it seemed unimportant. The TS spoke to Bob to assure him that he was not thought to be a thief but that his work performance could get him into trouble. Over the next week Bob's work performance improved, and the incident seemed to be forgotten.

STAFF ROLE

Although staff should take a secondary, supportive role in the VSG, it must be recognized that the TS is an excellent resource for information regarding students' recent problems, promotions, and job announcements—issues that can and should be discussed by the group. If the TS is not able to co-facilitate or attend group meetings, information of this type should be shared with staff who will participate in the meetings. This input can forewarn the staff person about potential problems and topics of discussion, as well as identify factors to be weighed in reaching solutions. In addition, the TS can provide valuable insight regarding the employer's perspective and goals for students.

Pete was a 20-year-old with a long history of work problems. He had been placed successfully at an above-minimum-wage position in a state government office. After 8 months on the job, Pete began to have attendance problems, complaining of being tired or sick, but he clearly stated he wanted his job. Several interventions were tried unsuccessfully, so this situation was brought to the group by the teacher, who learned of it through the TS. Pete stated that he was bored with the job and wanted another job but wasn't sure what to do, so he had decided to perform in ways that would force the employer to fire him. The group discussed the issue and worked with Pete to come to the conclusion that he should either talk to the supervisor about changing jobs or quit before he was fired. Pete agreed with the suggestion and talked with his TS about meeting with the employer. They talked through how such a meeting would take place and then scheduled a time to talk to the employer. Both the employer's views and Pete's were shared in the meeting, and it was jointly decided that Pete should quit before he was fired. The employer stated that he would be glad to give Pete a good recommendation for other jobs and would even be willing to hire him back in another job.

Vocational staff need to investigate all seemingly minor changes in vocational performance to determine whether these changes indicate growing job dissatisfaction. Early detection of these problems can forestall major infractions at work. However, asking students why they no longer like their jobs usually results in a reply of "I don't know" or explanations that may or may not reflect the real problems. Often students and employers simply do not know why students feel differently about their jobs—they just do.

WORK STRESSORS

It is helpful to look for significant work stressors that students might raise that could affect their work performance in a negative manner. Some of the more common stressors we have encountered are discussed next.

Changes in the Work Supervisor's Schedule

Changes in the amount of contact a student has with a supervisor or co-worker to whom the student feels an attachment may have a negative impact on the student's comfort at the workplace.

Ann worked over 10 consecutive months at a part-time paid job with only one work infraction reported. During this time, Ann maintained her job despite significant problems at home. Then the employer changed her work shift, resulting in the employer's having less contact time with Ann. Almost immediately, Ann began to smoke in unauthorized areas, stole cigarettes, demonstrated poor work skills, and exhibited sporadic attendance. These behaviors resulted in her termination from the job.

Embarrassment at Work

Being embarrassed at the worksite can be very stressful for anyone. Usually compounding the problem is the unavoidable teasing from co-workers or the boss that accompanies these situations. Circumstances such as these can cause students to be uncomfortable at work and may prompt them to exhibit behaviors that would cause them to be fired.

Steve worked hard on his job and appeared to enjoy the work placement. However, the boss and the TS learned from Steve's co-workers that he occasionally masturbated in the bathroom while at work. The boss discreetly told Steve that this behavior was unacceptable. The boss tried to ease Steve's embarrassment by praising his work performance. The TS also attempted to support Steve by debriefing with him after the boss's reprimand and assuring him that the reprimand was confidential. The TS then spent the next 2 weeks with Steve at the worksite to lend support.

Problems With the Work Supervisor

Difficulties with the employer might cause the student to experience problems at work and lose interest in the job.

Tim worked at a restaurant and had a difficult time accepting criticism from authority figures, but especially reacted to criticism from a new female supervisor. He usually reacted to her criticism by loudly complaining and banging equipment. His responses to the previous male supervisor were much more subdued. Tim's antagonism toward his female boss resulted in a very strained relationship, which made it difficult for him to enjoy work. He began to exhibit sporadic attendance and was fired.

Problems With Co-Workers

Problems with co-workers can seriously affect the student's comfort level at work.

John had previously lived on the streets and had a long history of theft and drug involvement. John really enjoyed his paid job at a restaurant. He made steady gains at this job and exhibited no major problems until a co-worker asked him to buy drugs. John refused and reported the co-worker to his boss. Consequently, the co-worker threatened John. The boss chose not to intervene because the co-worker was an excellent worker and would have been difficult to replace. These events caused

John's work performance to suffer and created attendance problems. John also began to have arguments with other co-workers and his supervisor. Fortunately, the co-worker's hours were changed so that John did not have to work directly with him, resolving the situation. If this schedule change had not occurred, the TS would probably have advocated for John to leave the worksite and find a different job.

Boring or Unpleasant Tasks

Job dissatisfaction because the student dislikes the job is a common occurrence. If a student dislikes the job, it is difficult to maintain high-quality work and a pleasant attitude. Likewise, a student who dislikes the working conditions of the job—such as a strict dress code, a high noise level, or dirty conditions—will probably lose interest in the job quickly.

Dennis was generally a great worker who learned jobs very quickly. He was placed at a store stocking and dusting shelves. Dennis learned the routine the first day and soon became bored with the job. Dennis appeared to dislike the job, displaying a sluggish work rate, unhappy facial expressions, and a bored attitude. When asked if he wanted to quit, Dennis was unable to make a decision. He finally agreed to stay but still appeared to dislike his job, despite increased TS support. Shortly afterward, Dennis stole some adult magazines from the store and was fired.

Home or School Problems

The presence of serious problems at home or school may cause anyone—especially adolescents with EBD—to exhibit a decrease in work quality, creating problems at work. Many students find it difficult to separate home problems from work.

Dean was experiencing significant problems with his family. When he was home, he destroyed many of his family's belongings and exhibited extreme verbal aggression toward his parents. During the time the home problems were particularly stressful, Dean would fail to report to work. When questioned by the TS, he reported that he was "afraid he would have problems at work because of stress and so just went home instead."

PROBLEM SOLVING IN THE GROUP

The VSG helps students deal with the stress of everyday work problems by providing a forum to discuss these problems. We strongly believe that these discussions should be structured around the problem-solving approach described in chapter 8 (see pp. 149–151).

Stan was a 16-year-old student with a history of theft, lying, and running away. He was working as a busboy in a local restaurant. During a VSG meeting, he told about a recent incident in which he dropped a tray of cups and saucers. Stan told the group about his embarrassment. He was offered suggestions and support in returning to work and dealing with this situation.

This group also provides a context in which the students can learn to apply problem-solving skills to work-related problems and to *practice* socially acceptable solutions on the job, receiving honest feedback about their performance.

Donna requested work at a beauty parlor, but she soon learned the work was work and not as much fun as she had anticipated. The group questioned Donna about her relationship with her boss and asked her what duties she was assigned. Donna bragged that the boss really liked her and stated that she made coffee, cleaned, and swept. She then stated that she was goofing off, slow to comply to the supervisor's directions, and was beginning to be disrespectful. When confronted by the group about this behavior, Donna simply replied that she would talk the boss into letting her have her job back if she were fired. Tony, another worker, had this reply for Donna: "I thought I could talk my boss into letting me keep my job, too. Remember when I was taking too many breaks and not listening to my boss? But it didn't work. I was fired, and she wouldn't let me have my job back." This example resulted in an improvement in Donna's work performance and was a more effective teaching intervention than any advice the TS could have given.

If students are reluctant to volunteer problems that should, or could, be discussed, the group leader should take the initiative and tactfully introduce the issue. A helpful technique to ease student embarrassment is to ask other students to relate their experiences with a particular problem identified by the TS, tell how this experience made them feel, and explain how they dealt with the problem. The group should then help the student apply problem-solving skills to the work problem to determine an effective solution.

Figure 9.1 presents a data recording form we use in the VSGs to document this process and its results. This form records the problem discussed; the goal, or what the student wants to have happen; and all possible solutions to the problem. Whether or not the student has tried each is indicated in the column headed "tried." Group members then evaluate each solution, first individually and then as a group, determining whether or not the solution will be helpful. If so, this is indicated in the column headed "helpful."

When the problem is reviewed at the next session, follow-up information can be recorded on this form in the "date/result" column. This

Figure 9.1
Problem-Solving Data Recording Form

Student ___Stan___   Worksite ___Bud's Diner___   Date ___12/3/01___

Problem	Goal	Alternative solutions	Tried?	Helpful?	Date/result
1. Stan has trouble with his boss and thinks his boss hates him.	To have boss stop yelling at him first thing in the morning To keep his job	1. Always work hard to impress the boss.	Yes	No	12/10 Stan tried solution #4. Boss told Stan he would not yell and was pleased afterwards. Boss also told TS Stan may need thicker skin to work in real world.
		2. Be polite at all times.	Yes	No	
		3. Ignore the boss's rude comments.	Yes	No	
		4. Ask the boss politely to stop being rude.	No	Yes	
		5. Complain to the boss's supervisor.	No	No	
		6. Yell back at boss.	No	No	
		7. Hit the boss next time he is rude.	No	No	
		8. Complain to co-workers about the problem.	No	No	
		9. Screw up on the job to get back at the boss.	No	No	

documentation should include the date of the review, solution number reviewed, comments regarding the use of this solution, and, finally, a brief explanation of the effectiveness of the solution in resolving the problem. This form helps the TS document problems that have been addressed during the VSG; it also helps ensure that the solutions to job-specific problems are implemented at the worksite.

CASE EXAMPLE

The following paragraphs describe how the VSG helped Stan address the problems he was having getting along with his work supervisor.

Step 1: Defining and Formulating the Problem

Stan was having trouble with his boss and told the group his boss hated him, but he could not, or at least did not, offer any concrete examples of the problem. To assist Stan in clearly defining the problem, group members asked questions that helped Stan state the problem in observable terms. Some of the questions Stan was asked were "What does your boss do?"; "When does he act this way?"; "Are you doing things that would cause the problem?"; "Does he act this way to others?"; and "How do you react when he does this?" To define the problem completely, the group members assisted Stan in discussing and clarifying the exact behaviors that were troubling, the people involved, the conditions present when the problems occurred, and possible reasons the problem occurred.

Step 2: Setting a Goal for the Interaction

To accomplish this step, it was necessary to have Stan decide on and state *exactly* what he wanted to have occur and achieve in his relationship with his work supervisor. In response to a boss who treats a worker rudely, Stan's goal could be to keep the job, to have the boss stop being rude, or to get out of the situation. The solution for each of these goals would be very different, ranging from ignoring the boss's rudeness and establishing more support with co-workers, talking to the boss in a more polite manner, confronting the boss, or quitting the job. After some discussion, Stan admitted that his supervisor was brusque and yelled at him first thing in the morning, when the supervisor might be tired and Stan might not be working at his peak efficiency. Stan still felt that the abuse was unnecessary and wanted it to stop, but he also wanted to keep the job. By setting this goal, Stan was then able to work with the group on ways to solve the problem and achieve this goal.

Step 3: Brainstorming Alternative Solutions

The group helped Stan think of possible solutions to the problem, while the group leader outlined all the ideas offered by Stan or group members on the chalkboard for the group to see. Possible solutions included working hard at all times to impress the boss; being polite to the boss at all times; ignoring the boss's rude comments; telling the boss to stop being rude; and complaining to the boss's supervisor. Other solutions included yelling and hitting the boss, complaining to co-workers, and "screwing up" on the job to get back at the boss. Both "good" and "bad" solutions were analyzed to determine their likely effectiveness in dealing with the problem and to predict the possible consequences they might have. Students often choose inappropriate solutions without thinking of the consequences, creating more problems for themselves. Analyzing inappropriate solutions in a neutral setting may help students stop and think when confronted with the problem in the work setting.

Step 4: Selecting the Best Alternative

The group then worked toward selecting a solution, basing their decision on the potential consequences that would result from performing each alternative. For example, if Stan chose to complain to the boss's supervisor, the group needed to predict what might happen in response to the confrontation. From what they knew of Stan's worksite, they concluded that this would be a mistake—the next level of supervisor was his boss's father! All of the alternatives on the board were evaluated in this manner. As the process continued, it became clear that Stan would have to confront his boss directly, but politely, to resolve the issue. At this point the group began to discuss ways in which Stan could perform this act successfully. After some discussion, Stan agreed that the best way to do this was to talk with his boss as soon as possible, immediately before work began and with no one else around. He said he needed to tell his boss about his discomfort at being yelled at and to ask him to stop, but he also said that he needed to say these things in a calm and nonconfrontational manner. The next step involved practicing the way in which Stan would conduct the interaction.

Step 5: Role Playing the Alternative

Of course, deciding what to do in this situation was only the first step in the VSG's responsibility and role in helping Stan talk with the boss. In order to practice the interaction before it took place, one member was assigned to role play Stan's boss. Prior to the role play, the group leader coached the member privately on what to say and do to be as much like Stan's boss and to present the situation as realistically as possible. At the same time, the VSG talked with Stan about how he might start the conversation and what he might say. Special attention was paid to the way in which Stan should talk because several students felt that if Stan acted angry or upset he could make the boss mad. These suggestions were written on the chalkboard to serve as a visual guide for Stan. Specifically, the suggestions concerned eye contact, facial expression, tone of voice, body posture, clarity in giving the message, and positive closure of the interaction. Stan was then coached regarding possible reactions the boss might have to his solution and what course of action he might and should take.

Stan enacted the role play several times. At the end of each, the group members provided Stan with feedback about his performance and offered suggestions for improvement as well as positive encouragement and praise. Once Stan felt he was "ready," he talked through the pros and cons of having his TS accompany him to the interaction. Both he and the group decided that it would be best if the TS was not involved in the interaction but that it would be positive if the TS would check with Stan and the boss later that day.

Step 6: Evaluating the Effects of the Alternative

At the next VSG meeting, Stan was asked to report on the interaction. Stan stated that the boss was understanding, said he would try not to yell as much, and smiled when they finished. Stan thought that the interaction had gone as well as he had expected. The TS also reported that the boss thought Stan had handled himself well but that the boss had added that Stan just might have to get a "thicker skin" to work in the "real world."

CHAPTER 10

Providing Consultation and Technical Assistance

Julia Bulen

Although millions of dollars have been allocated and hundreds of secondary transition projects have been implemented at the federal, state, and local levels, this effort has not usually taken adolescents with emotional and behavioral disorders (EBD) into consideration (Bullis & Gaylord-Ross, 1991; Knitzer, Steinberg, & Fleisch, 1990). These students, perhaps because of their high dropout rate, poor attendance, or negative social behaviors, are not being involved in transition programs at the same rate or in the same manner as are peers with other disabilities.

Few school districts possess the funding to tailor new secondary transition programs specifically for adolescents with EBD, so it is both logical and pragmatic to adapt existing transition programs to address the unique and very real needs of this population. In order to achieve this end, secondary transition staff most probably will need to be retrained and ongoing support provided to meet the unique demands of this population. Such training and change in program focus are, however, complex and difficult. Even though effective procedures (such as those presented in this book) exist for use with this population, changing the prevailing service delivery system within the school setting is a difficult and slow process. Moreover, the tedious task of developing and implementing such a model is varied and ever-evolving because of the unique characteristics, structure, resources, and needs of individual school systems. Thus, there is no single service delivery model or template of services for every setting. Instead, careful development and implementation of new procedures and program components should be guided through ongoing consultation and technical assistance. Through our work on the secondary transition projects for adolescents with EBD and through various development and inservice projects, we have operated in this specific area and have gained valuable experience in providing such consultation and assistance.

The purpose of this chapter is to review and discuss the process of developing and implementing an effective secondary transition program for adolescents with EBD within existing educational systems. The first section of the chapter summarizes key components for providing consultation and technical assistance within currently operating and established systems. The second part reviews the activities and processes we followed in one project designed specifically to change and improve secondary transition programs for adolescents with EBD.

KEY COMPONENTS FOR PROVIDING CONSULTATION

As demonstrated in the previous chapters, implementing and operating an effective secondary transition program for students with EBD requires a change in the operation of traditional transition programs, including revisions to personnel roles and responsibilities. With these changes come questions regarding who performs these seemingly new responsibilities and what skills are required to fulfill these roles. Administrators and teachers in existing programs may sometimes resist expending the extra effort needed to restructure the core of their system to address new objectives and participants. If there is a lack of enthusiasm, it is likely that program changes will be introduced and maintained as "add-ons" to the service system rather than as integrated system components.

Additional opposition to system change sometimes occurs when attempts to restructure a program are imposed from the "top down," through edicts from administrators to service delivery staff, without involving those who are affected by these changes (Friend & Bauwens, 1988; Smith, Edelen-Smith, & Stodden, 1995). These mandates may lead to an illusion of compliance through changes in schedules or activities but may not be successful without a sense of ownership or commitment to the new program on the part of direct-line staff. Thus it is therefore imperative that all affected personnel and administrators be involved in the design and implementation of any new system structure.

We have found the following four consultation and technical assistance components essential to the process of program change: (a) transition teams, (b) administrative support, (c) teacher buy-in, and (d) schoolwide support.

Transition Teams

The creation of collaborative transition teams has been effective in the development and implementation of transition programs (Stodden & Leake, 1994). These teams should have broad representation, including special education staff, regular educators, school administrators, counselors, parents, business owners, and community-agency representatives (e.g., vocational rehabilitation, mental health, and employment office personnel). Input from this array of individuals and services encourages the development of a wide spectrum of program components found inside and outside the school, and such components are critical to program and student success. Team members should be given the autonomy and responsibility to determine their own direction and vision for structuring the program, thus fostering their personal commitment and motivation to contribute to the program's ultimate success (Kaufman & Herman, 1991; Romanish, 1991).

The transition team must examine the existing program and determine what is valuable to transition outcomes and what needs to be reorganized. A team coordinator should be designated to oversee this process. The most appropriate coordinator is a neutral figure who has the flexibility to coordinate and attend weekly transition team meetings, locate resources, and observe and encourage the different aspects of the transition program implementation process. The coordinator should be skilled in the collaborative consultation process and adept at developing a collaborative team effort (Sileo, Rude, & Luckner, 1988), as well as knowledgeable in the components of a transition program for students with disabilities.

At the outset of one of our projects, none of the schools with which we worked had regularly scheduled departmental meetings involving the classroom and vocational staff. Although instructional assistants provided a large portion of the classroom instruction and most schools had a vocational assistant, these staff members were functioning in isolation. Student information was shared primarily when a crisis occurred, and there was little or no coordination between vocational and educational instruction. To address this situation, we helped the schools establish transition teams that encouraged and valued input from all classroom and vocational staff. Vocational referral processes were established, prevocational skills were taught, and vocational skills were reinforced in the regular academic classroom. Instructional and vocational assistants began contributing to Individual Education Programs (IEPs) and transition plans, and they provided valuable input into both educational and vocational programming. Many previously untapped resources existing both inside the schools and in the community were explored and integrated into the programs. These program additions solidified service delivery by making use of available services and carefully placing them within the transition program. Later, when budget reductions occurred, these additions were spared because of their history and their integration into the system.

Administrative Support

For every system, regardless of its size or level of complexity, administrative support and commitment are crucial to system change and professional development efforts. Administrators must be presented with a clear vision of the proposed secondary transition program, its function and staffing, and their particular role in facilitating implementation.

Unfortunately, although high-level administrators at both the district and school levels often share the vision of transition program development, their hectic schedules make the necessary support and daily involvement nearly impossible. Once approval for program development has been secured, a middle management administrator becomes valuable as an active participant in the transition team and as the key person who can guide program design and implementation.

For example, in one project, we secured the support and commitment of the director of student services at the district level to work with the district staff on secondary transition program changes. Because of other commitments, this administrator could attend only the introductory inservice training. The assistant principals designated to supervise the special services personnel at each of the five large high schools in the district were assigned to attend inservices and become part of each school's transition team, but only three of these five middle-level administrators chose to participate. At the other end of the involvement spectrum was a program director who set out to establish the very type of secondary transition program described in this book. She was extremely active in program development and in the inservice process, and she relied heavily on project staff for assistance and advice. The service model that was implemented included a student screening process and a year-long commitment requirement, as well as a functional academic focus, prevocational and social skills training, and a system of community-based vocational placements in competitive worksites.

Teacher Buy-In

Perhaps the most critical component of any transition program is the special education teacher. Teachers must be reassured that any changes implemented are not simply additions to their workloads but are instead efforts that will improve the work they do and the results their students achieve. With resources and personnel stretched thin, program transformation often must be achieved through creative and innovative restructuring of traditional special education staff roles, responsibilities, and schedules. Therefore, it is important to meet with teachers and secure their commitment and input before starting any actual restructuring. This commitment may be predicated on receiving additional pay, release time, or assistance to complete their existing jobs. Such negotiations may be outside the authority of a consultant and, in these instances, should be relayed to administrative staff and resolved before program development work begins.

Our experiences in providing this type of program-change training suggest that attempting to change an existing program while maintaining the traditional remedial schedule, staff, and staffing patterns is difficult, if not impossible. We have found that the work involved in staff training and program restructuring is more effective and complete when the existing program can be closed for a period of time or when the restructuring can be conducted during summer break. This schedule allows for a total change of program design and focus in a relatively unhurried manner and permits service implementation in its entirety when the program resumes operation.

Schoolwide Support

Although a major focus of transition programs is on community-based vocational placements, the program is anchored in the school setting. The students involved are served and educated within mainstream classrooms by staff who may not be aware of their unique needs or challenges. Thus, to augment and enhance the transition it is essential to provide inservice training and a system of consultative support to the school's general education staff. General education personnel must be presented with a clear picture of the secondary transition program and their role in educating these students. They must also be informed about resources available to assist them in their work and given adequate training in how to educate students with EBD. Such training should cover behavior management techniques, effective teaching practices, and instructional accommodations and modifications. Of course, merely learning about these practices is seldom sufficient to promote and support long-term changes. Sufficient time must be provided for practice, team building, and ongoing support and consultation as these inclusion procedures are integrated into the fabric of the school system and the general education classroom. Providing these resources will help ensure the support of the entire school for the restructuring.

PROJECT IMPLEMENTATION

In 1992, our group was funded by the federal government to provide services and support to several school districts to improve their secondary transition programs, specifically for adolescents with EBD (Bullis, 1992a). We chose to work toward the implementation of a vocational program at each of these sites, in a way similar to that described in this book. We provided ongoing inservice training, staff support, and consultation to ensure that the skills and procedures were fully and appropriately implemented in each program. Each site developed a plan for program change, and a small amount of project money was used to fund necessary program changes and to purchase necessary materials. In this way, each site developed a tailored secondary program for adolescents with EBD that was supported by project staff and resources. Finally, we evaluated the effect of these interventions on the program, staff, and students at each site. The following sections describe our activities during this work.

Needs Assessment

We found that school personnel with little or no transition program experience were unsure of their specific implementation needs. All of the administrators acknowledged the need to infuse a transition focus into their special education programs, but many classroom staff lacked understanding of just what such a program would "look like."

A formal transition program evaluation form such as Halpern's Transition Program Effectiveness Index (TPEI; Halpern, 1988) can provide classroom staff with a detailed description of desired program components, and it can help them identify the areas of their program that are in need of improvement. The TPEI consists of 130 items distributed across six content areas determined to be critical to an effective transition program: curriculum and instruction, coordination and mainstreaming, transition, documentation, administrative support, and adult services. Each item is given a value ranging from zero (not important) to 3 (critical) and is rated on the degree of implementation ranging from zero (achieved) to 3 (not achieved). Figure 10.1 gives sample items from this instrument.

All school staff and administrators, as well as our staff, completed this in-depth program rating at the outset of grant involvement and then yearly to focus and guide continuing program change efforts. An analysis of these ratings identified specific areas of transition programming that were rated as highly desirable yet inadequately implemented. These areas then became the focus of program change efforts.

Additional and specific inservice needs for each site were determined through the use of a training needs survey (Figure 10.2). All classroom and administrative staff completed this survey each spring to identify training needs and inservice format for the following year.

Inservice

Finding room in busy schedules and making inservice programs "high-quality time" for participants require that inservice planners make the benefits of such programs clear to participants (Petrie, 1976), tying training efforts to specific and pressing issues of new program and policy implementation (McCarty, Sitlington, & Asselin, 1991). Inservices about transition should encourage participants to interact and develop collaborative plans for the implementation of the various components of a transition program throughout the school system. The development of training that includes this cross-disciplinary emphasis is a consistent theme throughout the literature about transition personnel training (deFur, 1990; Renzaglia, 1986; Sitlington, 1986; Szymanski, Hanley-Maxwell, & Asselin, 1990).

A national survey of transition specialists in the fields of rehabilitation, vocational education, and special education (deFur, 1990) identified 12 domains of essential competencies required for transition professionals (see Figure 10.3). Inservice training for educators and support personnel should include these components of secondary transition programs. Participants must be presented with a clear rationale for and picture of the functioning of a transition program, as well as achieve competence in the daily instruction of prevocational skills, living skills, social skills, and work experience. As participants gain knowledge of the skills required of them and develop a vision of their

Figure 10.1
Sample Items From the Transition Program Effectiveness Index

Instruction

Students with disabilities have complete access to the regular academic curriculum.

Community-based instruction is available as one option within the secondary curriculum for disabled students.

One component of community-based instruction in the vocational curriculum is actual job experience.

Coordination and mainstreaming

Teachers of regular academic courses are provided with assistance in adapting their instruction in order to meet the needs and entry skills of students with disabilities.

Negative attitudes of regular academic and vocational education teachers toward students with disabilities are acknowledged, when such attitudes exist, and specific activities are undertaken to change such attitudes.

One or more people are specifically designated to coordinate the relationships between special education and the regular academic program for each student with disabilities.

Transition

Transition goals are addressed as part of the planning process for students with disabilities.

Collaborations between special education and relevant adult agencies, for the purpose of transition services, are formalized in a written agreement for students with disabilities.

Procedures exist for securing parent involvement in the transition implementation process for their son or daughter with disabilities.

Documentation

Demographic information (age, gender, ethnicity, and type of disability) is available for students with disabilities currently enrolled in regular (academic and vocational) and special education programs.

Well-defined criteria exist for determining who may receive a regular diploma, a modified diploma, and/or a certificate of achievement.

Procedures exist for conducting systematic follow-up evaluations on the community adjustment of students with disabilities who leave school either by graduation, by dropping out, or by aging out.

Administrative support

The school special education coordinator, the school principal, and the district special education administrator are all supportive of secondary special education programs.

Workload assignments to teachers include adequate time to prepare lessons.

There is a discrete secondary advisory board—consisting of school staff, community agency representatives, parents, students, and former students and employers—that meets regularly to monitor, evaluate, and recommend improvements for the secondary special education program.

Adult services

High-quality services and opportunities are available that address the employment needs of school leavers with disabilities.

High-quality services and opportunities are available that address the social support needs of school leavers with disabilities.

Referral and eligibility determination procedures are adequate and timely for employment services that are available to school leavers with disabilities.

Note. From "Characteristics of a Quality Program" by A. S. Halpern, in *Secondary Special Education: A Guide to Promising Public School Programs,* edited by C. Warger and B. Weiner, 1988, Reston, VA: Council on Exceptional Children. Reprinted by permission.

Figure 10.2
Training Needs Survey

Name _____Jane Doe_____   **Date** _____9/14/01_____

In order to best meet the individual training needs of each project site, we would like your input on training preferences. Please indicate your choices below.

Which areas of transition programs would you like additional information on?

_____ Positive behavior management

__✓__ Social skills training

_____ Independent living and leisure

_____ Functional academics

_____ Creating a phase system for transitioning back to high school

_____ Including students in regular high-school academics

_____ Functional vocational skills assessment

_____ Prevocational skills—notebooks—portfolios

__✓__ Coordinating with/services offered by community service agencies

_____ Developing a variety of vocational placements

_____ Other _____

From whom would you like to receive more information?

__✓__ Project staff

__✓__ Community services personnel

_____ High school programs in state

_____ Vocational specialists

__✓__ Behavioral specialists

_____ Other _____

When would you be available for paid inservice days?

❑ _Aug. 20–24_   ☑ _Aug. 27–31_   Days of week ____M–F_____

How much large-group training (all grant sites) would you prefer?

(*Circle.*)   1   ②   3   4   5   ✓ Full days   ___ Half days

How much training/work time at your individual site would you prefer?

(*Circle.*)   1   ②   3   4   5   ___ Full days   ✓ Half days

Figure 10.3
Transition Personnel Competency Domains

Rank	Domain
1	Knowledge of agencies and systems change
2	Development and management of individualized plans
3	Working with others
4	Vocational assessment and job development
5	Professionalism, advocacy, and legal issues
6	Job training and support
7	Assessment (general)
8	Administrative functions
9	Philosophical and historical considerations
10	Career counseling and vocational theory
11	Program evaluation and research
12	Curriculum, instruction, and learning theory

school transition program, they should become active participants in the design and composition of ongoing inservice training to ensure competence and confidence in all aspects of the transition process.

Administrators, counselors, special and regular educators, instructional assistants, and vocational assistants all require various levels of training in a wide variety of issues specific to EBD (e.g., drug abuse) and effective service components (e.g., job placement in the community). Inservice programs should then be carefully aligned with school system initiatives (Renzaglia, 1986) and with the perceived needs of transition staff.

We held inservice training for the program staff involved in our project on a yearly basis. The first day of the 3-day inservice provided participants with background information on transition programs and services specifically for adolescents with EBD and featured presentations from three area vocational transition programs. The second day consisted of extensive training in functional curriculum, behavioral interventions, and social skills instruction. The final day focused on community transition issues. Local experts on transition planning shared their systems, and representatives from the state vocational rehabilitation and mental health departments discussed ways in which school programs could access local services.

The second inservice was for 2 days and was held shortly before the beginning of the second grant year (just before the school year began). The following areas had been identified in the needs assessment and were addressed in the training: behavior management, job support groups, prevocational classes, and program design. The first day included specialists who discussed behavior management at the worksite, the function and format of in-class job support groups, and the components of prevocational training. The second day consisted of in-depth instruction and guided practice in the design and implementation of vocational program components.

The third inservice, held at the beginning of the third year, was also 2 days in length and addressed six areas. On the first day, staff in the project received information on secondary academic requirements, writing Individual Educational Programs (IEPs) for functional skills, and assisting students in obtaining a general educational development (GED) certificate as an alternative to returning to high school. On the second day, vocational and instructional assistants were trained separately on behavior management techniques, while teachers and administrators received information on the implementation of a vocational support group. This training included input from students with EBD who were in a successful and widely known vocational training program.

A series of inservice trainings for general educators, administrators, and counselors was the focus of the fourth and final inservice training. Regular education staff expressed an overwhelming need for assistance in teaching students with EBD, and a large number of administrators and counselors acknowledged their need for additional training in dealing effectively with these students throughout school settings. Noting increased inclusion of students with EBD into academic and vocational education courses, teachers expressed a pressing need to receive training in ways to support and accommodate students with EBD in regular classroom settings. Special educators involved in the project also requested guidance and training in providing consultative support to these general educators.

On the first day, all participants were provided with an in-depth description and definition of students with EBD, ways to manage student behaviors, and ways to promote cooperation among school staff. Two half-day follow-up sessions were then provided for each of two groups of participants: (a) regular educators and (b) administrators, counselors, and special educators. Regular educators were provided with a follow-up session that discussed methods and materials for students with EBD, curriculum modifications, and program structure for behavior control. Participants were provided suggestions for working with specific students in their classes. The second follow-up session for this group consisted of a discussion of instructional and behavior modification techniques.

Administrators, counselors, and special educators were provided with follow-up training in behavior management, designing and implementing behavioral interventions, and talking with students in crisis. Participants were then provided with assistance in designing interventions for specific students. In the second follow-up session, participants discussed the results of their implementation of behavioral interventions and received instruction on teaching self-regulation strategies and social skills to students with EBD.

Site Consultation and Support

Many special education teachers express feelings of isolation and a lack of understanding and support from the school staff as a whole. Special education staff attempting to implement major changes in their programs, roles, and responsibilities are particularly susceptible to these feelings and need the nonjudgmental support and encouragement of knowledgeable observers such as the staff in this project. We found that project staff could quickly gain common ground with site teachers and their assistants by becoming participants in classroom activities. Project staff became frequent visitors to the various programs in which we worked and provided assistance to students and local staff in conducting lessons and activities. It was crucial that the staff come to be viewed as program advocates—never as administrators checking on progress and work.

The degree of support and service we offered each school involved in the project varied at each site and within each site from year to year. For example, our initial involvement with one site required a very intensive approach that included project staff's teaching prevocational and social skills classes at the site. We hired a program specialist to conduct a technical assistance visit and evaluation of this site, and we also hired a specialist to provide staff training in behavior management and intervention techniques. We also arranged for the classroom teachers to visit a model demonstration vocational program specifically for students with EBD. Support and training at that site in the program's second year focused on vocational placements and the establishment of a classroom-based business. In the third year, training was provided to classroom teachers in the form of tuition for a collaborative consultation course. Additional support and assistance were provided in the second and third years in the selection and purchase of a prevocational and functional skills curriculum and software.

All three sites were provided with opportunities and funding for classroom and vocational staff to visit vocational programs throughout the locale and to attend conferences and inservices. Educators at all sites expressed interest in establishing school-based businesses; therefore, additional support and training were provided toward this goal.

Supplemental Funds

Although the grant was able to fund the major expense of inservice training, as well as ongoing consultation, we were acutely aware of each site's need for additional funding for the purchase of the curriculum and materials necessary to establish the new program. Accordingly, based on individual program requests, we provided each program with a portion of our yearly grant funds, ranging from 1,500 to 3,500 dollars per year per site. Generally, these funds were spent each fall for curriculum materials, software, supplies, or support services. All of the programs involved chose to spend a portion of their funds on the purchase of equipment in order to establish a classroom-based student business. These businesses included selling helium balloons, baking cookies, printing greeting cards, and running a landscaping business. Additional funds were spent on a wide variety of items, including a computerized record-keeping system, curriculum materials, software, staff training, student work clothes, and field trips. Participants at all of the sites felt that the availability of these funds and the guidance in designating them were critical to the establishment of their programs.

Results

The most immediate change at all three sites was the addition and development of community-based work experiences for their students. The easiest job placements for new vocational programs to secure were unpaid, low-level service industry jobs. However, as students and vocational assistants gained knowledge and experience, we assisted all three programs in obtaining more meaningful, higher level paying jobs. All three programs also developed a system of in-class businesses, job shadowing, and work experience advancement culminating in paid work experience for older students nearing school completion. These experiences were supported by classroom instruction in prevocational skills, functional living skills, and social skills. By the end of the project, significant changes had been made at all three sites, with a positive impact on the programs, staff, and students. We are optimistic that the sites will continue to offer vocational and transition services and that the students will benefit from these efforts.

CHAPTER 11

Gathering Longitudinal Information on Transition Adjustment

Michael Bullis

A common misperception is that, once a program participant leaves the transition program for any reason (e.g., graduation, moving, dropping out, incarceration), services to and contact with that person cease immediately. This belief is incorrect: Follow-up monitoring of program participants after they leave the transition program is a crucial service component. Unfortunately, these activities are infrequently included or considered part of services.

Adolescents with emotional and behavioral disorders (EBD) present very real and persistent personal, emotional, and social problems. Although these problems can be brought under control and although many youths can achieve fairly high levels of transition success, a number will need some type of ongoing support and/or service.

For some, this intervention may be minimal (e.g., talking to a transition specialist or learning about other job openings). For others, though, the intervention may require the full complement of program services through program reentry or through services provided by other agencies (e.g., drug and alcohol treatment, job retraining). No one will become aware of these former students' needs, however, unless efforts are made to gather the necessary data over a period of time after they leave the transition program. Moreover, in this era of fiscal accountability, one of the ways in which the effectiveness of a program can be evaluated is by quantifying its long-term impact on the transition success of its former students. Stated differently, one way to gauge the quality of a program is through the success its "graduates" have after leaving. This criterion is applied to many educational programs (e.g., for high schools, the percentage of their graduates who complete college) and social programs (e.g., for correctional programs, the percentage of leavers who are employed after 1 year). Although it usually is possible to locate a small number of program graduates and secure testimonials from these persons regarding program effectiveness, solicited comments may not be representative of all individuals who received services through the program under evaluation, and such responses may paint an inaccurate picture of the long-term impact of the program on its participants.

Longitudinal investigations of program leavers are important for both service delivery and program delivery, but most transition programs with which we are familiar make little attempt to monitor program participants after they move beyond the project's umbrella. The logic behind this lack of follow-up is based on three points.

First, given the time and resource demands of direct service, there is no shortage of things to do in a transition program. Accordingly, participants who leave the program do not receive attention because they are not directly receiving services.

Second, most participants tend to be categorized by staff into two groups: those who are successful and those who are not. Participants who leave a program successfully are doing well (at least at that point in time) and are not in need of services. Conversely, persons who leave a program unsuccessfully may well have been uncooperative or difficult to work with, so there may be reluctance on the part of staff to reinitiate contact and/or services.

Third, conducting a long-term study of persons outside of a program's direct purview is time consuming, resource demanding, and difficult. In our experience, it is the rare service delivery practitioner who is trained to conduct this type of follow-up evaluation.

The first two points can be addressed by making a commitment to develop, implement, and conduct follow-up contacts with program leavers. Of course, merely making a decision to collect longitudinal data about program leavers does not guarantee that staff will have the know-how to conduct such a study. The purpose of this chapter is to provide an overview of how to conduct a longitudinal investigation of program leavers as efficiently—and as pragmatically—as possible. To present this information in an understandable and useable form, we have chosen to present questions routinely asked by professionals with whom we have worked and questions with which we have grappled as we have sought to conduct this sort of data collection. We also suggest that the reader consult other references that describe such procedures in order to gain more detail than it is possible to present in this brief chapter (e.g., Blackorby & Edgar, 1992; DeStefano & Wagner, 1992; Dillman, 1978; Edgar, 1985; Fairweather 1984; Halpern, 1990; Menhard, 1990).

WHAT WILL A LONGITUDINAL DATA COLLECTION SYSTEM LOOK LIKE?

There are two general approaches to gathering longitudinal data on the transition experiences of program leavers: the follow-up method and the follow-along method (Halpern, 1990). In the *follow-up method,* data are collected at specified intervals from persons who leave the program during the time period of the study. For example, every 2 years an effort would be made to track down and study those who left the program during the previous 2 years. Data to be gathered would focus on the time period since the individual had left the program, which for some might be 2 years and for others much less time.

In the *follow-along method,* data are gathered routinely at regular intervals from program leavers. For example, data would be gathered on a participant on exit from the program and then every 4 months for the next 3 years. Data to be gathered in each interview would focus on the individual's experiences during the preceding 4-month period.

The follow-up approach may at first seem simpler and less cumbersome than the follow-along method, but the former approach has a number of shortcomings.

1. If one puts off collecting data until a designated time after students exit from a program, it is easy to lose track of them. Frankly, locating some of these individuals is a difficult task, and participants who cannot be located do not provide information on their transition experiences.

2. Even when former participants can be located, it has been our experience that there may be a reluctance on their part and on the part of their families to respond to inquiries about their lives at single and irregular points in time. We believe that this reluctance is probably due to the length of time of separation from the program and its staff.

3. Probably related to the first two items, the follow-up approach tends to suffer from low response or contact rates, a fact that limits the validity and generalizability of the results. Because of difficulties locating former participants and gathering data about them, that information may be inaccurate and not representative of all program leavers.

4. It is difficult for program leavers to reconstruct periods of their lives, and it is hard to design useable questionnaires to gather data retrospectively. The numerous choices in one's life over a lengthy period of time (e.g., 1 or 2 years) are not easily captured in a questionnaire, and an individual's recollection of past events tends to diminish over time. Because participants are asked to respond to questions covering relatively long periods of time, data collection usually takes longer.

5. Because it is difficult to sequentially order retrospective data (e.g., Did *A* come before *B*?), certain relevant analyses (e.g., Did our services at exit result in greater job success 6 months after you left the program?) are weakened or precluded.

Follow-along studies of program leavers' transition experiences, in contrast, offer a number of advantages over the follow-up approach.

1. Data collection becomes a regular and central part of the service delivery milieu. Staff expect to engage in data collection activities, at least in some form, on a routine basis. Because of regularity of data collection, the amount of time required for data gathering is minimized. Former program participants expect to be in contact with a representative of the program, and the staff member's questions about their lives and postproject experiences seem routine. These facts work together to improve longitudinal data collection efficiency, accuracy, and response rates from respondents, when compared with the follow-up approach.

2. Data routinely are gathered, summarized, and examined by program staff; thus, they can be used to refine and improve the program on an ongoing basis rather than at single points, as would be the case with a follow-up approach. Further, should there be an unforeseen need to present data on program leavers (e.g., the school board asks for a presentation of the project and its effects), it is possible to respond to that request quickly and with a minimum of additional effort.

3. When contact is made with former program participants at regular intervals, program staff gain a much earlier awareness of problems and other issues of importance. As a result, longitudinal data collection actually becomes a crucial ingredient of long-term support and intervention.

4. A participant's response is more accurate because the follow-along method minimizes the need for the respondent to recall and reconstruct particular experiences over a period of time. Also, the technique of gathering data at shorter, more regular intervals makes it possible to time and identify key events precisely, to identify interrelationships among variables, and to describe fluctuations in participant behaviors over time and across areas of the respondent's life (e.g., independent living, vocational experiences, postsecondary education).

In our opinion, the advantages of the follow-along method are clear. This is not to say that there is no place for a follow-up investigation, but as a general rule the follow-along method is simpler, more efficient, and of more practical use in service delivery and program improvement.

WHO SHOULD GATHER THE DATA?

A question invariably raised concerns who should be responsible for collecting data on program leavers. There are two basic ways to staff a longitudinal data collection system for transition program leavers. The first way is to designate one staff member or a small number of staff members to assume responsibility for tracking program leavers. The second way is to make transition specialists (TSs) responsible for tracking those participants with whom they worked.

The major advantage of assigning responsibility to a single person or a small number of staff is that this method underscores the importance of gathering these data and allows those individual(s) to become skilled in the application of data collection procedures. Their growing expertise will lend more objectivity and scientific credibility to the results of their investigations. This is especially true if participants are asked their opinions of the project and/or services they received (e.g., Would you recommend the program to others? What was the worst thing about your experience?) because respondents generally tend to be more honest with persons they do not know. Finally, an individual whose sole program responsibility is the collection of longitudinal data will presumably be more invested in regular and accurate data collection than would staff members with other multiple responsibilities.

On the other hand, a person who is not familiar with a participant may not be accepted by that participant, rendering interviews awkward, with the potential for poor or inaccurate responses. Also, if data collection efforts are to be used as support or to provide interventions and services to meet current needs of respondents, an individual unknown to the participant may lack the awareness to assess what is going on with the individual and thus may be unable to respond appropriately to presenting problems.

The major advantage of making service staff, such as TSs, responsible for the data collection is that the activities become ingrained in service delivery. That is, if TSs are assigned to track the individuals with whom they work after those participants leave the program, there should be close connection between the staff and participants. This connection should foster awareness of participants' locations (or at least of how or where to find them) and better rapport during the exchange. Also, if the goals of longitudinal data collection include providing long-term support and structuring services to address current participant needs, then TSs are the most logical people to perform these functions. Furthermore, when TSs are involved in these activities, they gain an appreciation for the importance of these data and what the results mean for program and service improvements. However, TSs may balk at collecting data on persons who are not receiving services and fail to see the value of gathering such data. There is also the potential that by assigning these tasks to TSs or other program staff some time formerly devoted to *direct* service delivery will be taken away.

There really is no one clear choice between these two options. For some programs, the first alternative will be best, whereas for others the second will be preferable. In either case, it is necessary to assign these responsibilities to someone and to be sure that these data collection tasks are completed on a regular basis. Whoever is chosen to conduct the data collection should be trained in data collection procedures.

WHICH PROGRAM LEAVERS SHOULD BE INCLUDED?

A fundamental assumption in providing transition services is that individuals who receive the services will do better—that is, will demonstrate better transition outcomes—than individuals who do not receive the services. A variation on this premise is that individuals who receive more services or who receive services for a longer period of time should do better than participants who receive fewer services or those who are served for a shorter time.

In our experience, four groups of adolescents are typically referred to vocational transition programs. The first group consists of individuals who are referred to the program but who are ineligible to receive services because they do not meet the eligibility criteria. The second group consists of individuals who are referred to the program and who are eligible to receive services by virtue of their presenting emotional or behavioral characteristics but who, for one reason or another, do not enter the program or who only go through the intake process and do not receive a full complement of services. The third group consists of participants who will be taken into the program and receive services for some period of time, perhaps a few months, but who will then leave the program. The fourth group will enter the program and receive services for a relatively lengthy period of time—at least 1 year.

It is important to include the last three groups in the longitudinal data collection process and to compare the transition experiences of the three groups. Of course, different programs may choose to define the groups somewhat differently. For example, participants could be grouped by those who never received services, those who received services for less than the average length of the stay in the program, those who received services for the average length of stay in the program, and those who received services for longer than the average length of stay in the program. Other options certainly are possible, and some may make more sense or be of more interest to particular schools and locales. For example, to examine the issue of program effectiveness, it may make sense to identify those participants who were "successful" in the program (e.g., completed school, worked without being fired) and those who were unsuccessful, then compare the transition experiences of these two groups. One question that program staff, administrators, and third-party observers may raise relates to how participants with certain demographic characteristics do after leaving the program or how well they do relative to persons with different demographic characteristics (e.g., gender, type of special education or psychiatric disability, cultural/ethnic background, gang involvement).

It is important to consider the issues that are of interest—or that later may be of interest—and to structure meaningful descriptions of program participants in light of those issues prior to data collection. It is always possible to describe participants in different ways and then to examine only a "slice" of those variables. An example of this would be comparing successful program completers versus unsuccessful completers by sex. The point to remember is to be as flexible and as comprehensive as possible in describing the participants and their characteristics because the decisions made at this point will have implications for the ways in which these data can be analyzed later.

HOW SHOULD DATA BE GATHERED?

There are three basic approaches to gathering longitudinal data: mailed paper-and-pencil surveys to be completed by the respondent, personal interviews, and phone interviews. For three reasons, we do not recommend using mailed paper-and-pencil forms to gather longitudinal data. First, it is difficult to construct survey forms that are brief, easily understood, and easy to follow and that accurately reflect the numerous possibilities in an individual's life. Second, it has been our experience that because of low reading abilities paper-and-pencil surveys with this population yield low and unacceptable response rates, as well as questionable results. This is the case because the reading ability of many of these adolescents is low. They will either disregard a written form or complete the survey inaccurately. Third, if one of the primary reasons for collecting data is to provide long-term support and intervention for participants' current problems, questions on a form may not address those issues adequately.

The personal interview, in which the data collector meets face-to-face with a program leaver and asks questions about the leaver's transition experiences is probably the most effective approach in terms of gathering accurate and complete data because in the personal exchange the interviewer can clarify questions and responses. However, personal interviews (a) are time consuming (it usually is necessary for the interviewer to meet the leaver at some acceptable place in the community); (b) may be difficult or impossible to schedule due to the highly transitory nature of the living arrangements of many past program participants (i.e., they tend to move frequently); or (c) may be difficult to schedule because leavers may only be able to be contacted in the evenings or on weekends. Further, personal interviews with some program leavers may actually be treacherous, both because they may have a history of aggressive or assaultive behaviors and/or because the interviews must be conducted in high-risk locales.

Phone interviews with program leavers have some of the advantages of the personal interview as well as others. As in face-to-face interviews, the interviewer can query a respondent to clarify questions and responses. Moreover, phone interviews are cheaper, safer, and easier to schedule and conduct because they can be completed by the staff in the safety of the office or home and at various times (e.g., in the evening, on weekends).

In the longitudinal data collection we have conducted to evaluate our own vocational transition projects, we have used telephone interviews. Only rarely have we conducted in-person interviews—for example, when a former program participant happened to stop in to see project staff or made personal contact in some other way. Phone interviews have been minimally disruptive and have been accepted by our staff. We have found phone interviews consistent with our dual goals of gathering evaluative data and monitoring our leavers over the long term.

Any type of interview should always be preceded by a letter telling the respondent that he or she will be contacted at a certain time. Return of the letter as undeliverable warns staff that the leaver is not at the last known address and triggers a search to find the missing individual's whereabouts by contacting family and friends.

As a general rule, we try to contact past participants 15 times before placing them in the nonrespondent category. Figure 11.1 is the telephone log we maintain to document the time and date of each contact or attempted contact, as well as to specify times at which others at the number (e.g., parents, roommates) tell us the leaver may be available to be interviewed. This information should be carefully monitored: It may be that calling on the same day of the week or at the same time of day will continue to yield a nonresponse because the former program participant is working or committed at those times. It has been our experience that the best time to complete phone interviews is in the late afternoon or early evening (4:00 P.M. to 7:00 P.M.) and on the weekends, particularly in the late mornings (9:00 A.M. to noon).

WHAT SHOULD PROGRAM LEAVERS BE ASKED?

Language in the Individuals with Disabilities Education Act (IDEA) establishes that transition consists of several outcome domains: employment, education (including postsecondary education), independent living, and social experiences (e.g., personal happiness, mental health status). In addition, because a major focus of the service delivery effort for this population is to develop and provide a comprehensive support system from multiple social agencies, it is important to document the number and type of services participants receive after leaving the school-based vocational transition program.

Consideration must be given to the length of time the interview will take. As a rule, we have found that the interviews we have developed and administered take between 15 and 30 minutes to complete, a time commitment that has been reasonable in the vast majority of the hundreds of interviews we have conducted. In fact, it has been interesting that most of the longer interviews have been completed with leavers who wanted to talk and who said that they enjoyed the contact and hearing from staff.

An interview protocol we have developed and used for several years is given as Appendix C. This script can be adapted to the characteristics of a particular program, or it can serve as a guide for developing an interview for a specific program or purpose.

Structure

As shown in the script, there is a distinct structure to the questions and the way in which they are asked. At the same time there is a casualness in the administration that makes the questioning almost like an informal conversation. It is important to maintain a balance between

Figure 11.1
Interviewer Telephone Log

Student _Maurice_   **Interviewer** _Mike Brown_

Phone number	Comments
123-4567	Number was disconnected, call alternate contact number.
555-7654	New number for Maurice—has several roommates.

Date	Day of week	Time	A.M./P.M.	Call-back information
1/4/01	Thursday	6	P.M.	No answer.
1/5/01	Friday	noon		No answer.
1/8/01	Monday	10	A.M.	Phone disconnected.
1/8/01	Monday	11	A.M.	Contacted alternate number—secured new number.
1/9/01	Tuesday	4	P.M.	Spoke with roommate—call back later.
1/11/01	Thursday	6	P.M.	Maurice not home.
1/12/01	Friday	8	A.M.	No answer—no message machine.
1/12/01	Friday	noon		Maurice not home.
1/15/01	Monday	11	A.M.	Contact with Maurice—interview completed.

structure and personal contact because this format yields the most positive results.

Skip Patterns

Skip patterns are apparent in the interview and are important because they reflect real-life experiences. To illustrate, if an individual is not working, it is important to ask a *queuing question* immediately to ascertain whether subsequent questions regarding current employment are needed. For example, if the response to the question about current employment is that the respondent is not currently working, then it is appropriate to skip to the next logical question. This aspect of interview development is difficult to perfect and takes some effort to word correctly.

Fixed-Response Categories

Questions can be asked in an open-ended manner but have fixed-response categories that are coded based on the respondent's answer to a particular question. This feature reduces the awkwardness of the interview process. For example, the leaver will be asked about the type of school he or she is attending. The interviewer codes the response according to the response options listed below the question. We have found that response options for specific questions must sometimes be changed when we work in different locales. For example, certain social service agencies may have one name in one community and another in a different community, and it is necessary to revise or expand response options to ensure the accuracy of the response.

Open-Ended Questions

A few questions at the end of the interview are truly open-ended questions. We have found that these questions are critical because sometimes leavers tell us things that are totally unexpected or revealing. Also, by asking their opinions, we send a message that what they think is valued. We believe that this feature fosters their cooperation and future involvement in data collection.

Future Data Collection

We end the interview by telling the leaver that he or she will be contacted again in a specified time period and by asking about his or her planned whereabouts at that time. This feature orients the leaver to the importance of the interview and, we believe, promotes future cooperation.

We also address a point that may come up at some time in the data collection effort. Specifically, if it is not possible to interview a leaver, is it appropriate to interview a substitute respondent (e.g., a parent) and use those responses in place of the leaver's? Research on this topic suggests that parents are accurate respondents when answering questions on their son's or daughter's work, school, and living experiences (Levine & Edgar, 1994) but that they are poor respondents on antisocial behavior and on mental health issues, tending to underreport such matters (Janes, Hesselbrock, Myers, & Penniman, 1979). If you do substitute parent responses for direct interviews with leavers, you should be aware of this shortcoming and report your results with some caution for this particular set of variables.

HOW OFTEN SHOULD PROGRAM LEAVERS BE CONTACTED?

Most studies of the longitudinal transition adjustment of adolescents with special needs gather data at 6-month intervals (DeStefano & Wagner, 1992; Halpern, 1990). Thus, a person who leaves a transition program on January 1 would be interviewed again on or about June 1, January 1 of the following year, and so on.

In the transition projects we have operated, in which we have collected data to evaluate the long-term impact of our services, we have adopted this 6-month cycle for data collection. We interview leavers as they exit the program and then at subsequent 6-month intervals. Our choice of a 6-month period was made based on our past experiences in conducting research studies and on the fact that we thought that our service delivery staff would rebel if we asked them to contact leavers more frequently. The wisdom of this choice has been borne out as evidenced by the facts that (a) our staff continue to perform these functions without complaining and actually look forward to contacting the persons with whom they have worked and (b) we have been able to develop interview protocols that allow us to gather data about the 6-month time span without being too cumbersome or lengthy.

We have had contact with some vocational transition programs where staff have chosen to contact leavers more often (e.g., every 3 months) because of the nature of their program (e.g., parole work programs where it is important to gather data frequently on the transition experiences of the participants). If there is some debate over the frequency of contact, we suggest that the choice be to contact leavers more frequently (e.g., every 2 or 3 months) rather than less frequently (e.g., every 12 months). If the decision is made to lengthen the contact period, leavers will be lost, and when they are contacted, it will be difficult for them to describe the totality of their experiences in a structured interview protocol.

A related issue is the question of over how long a period of time leavers should be tracked. Again, reviews of transition studies suggest that 1 to 2 years is typical, and we try to keep track of leavers for at least 2 full years. However, we find that it is possible to keep track of the majority (more than 60 percent) of the leavers only over a 1-year period, although we have tracked some leavers for much longer. This means that we typically complete three interviews with the majority of the leavers from our programs (on exit from services and at 6 months and 12 months after leaving).

Of course, data on leavers who can be tracked longer than the typical time period may shed light on the longer term effects of this group's transition experiences. For example, we have been able to track a small number of leavers for more than 10 years. While these persons are not representative of the larger group, their unique experiences have provided us with an interesting and highly insightful perspective on the continuing nature of emotional and behavioral disorders and on the way in which these persons struggle to address such issues into their adult years. Description of these isolated cases provides a useful and powerful complement to quantitative summaries of data.

HOW SHOULD THE DATA BE KEPT?

Our sense is that typical program leavers will be interviewed over the phone by project staff who record responses on paper forms. The issue is what to do with these forms and data. This decision should be made before beginning data collection. Waiting until after the interviewing process begins to develop a system for data entry and management will complicate matters greatly.

It is fairly simple and straightforward to enter these data into an "off-the-shelf" computer database management program. It will be important to secure the services of a data analyst to set up the database into which the data will be entered because such a system allows for far easier data entry monitoring and analysis.

The best choice is to develop a dedicated data collection system, such as a Computer-Assisted Telephone Interviewing (CATI) system. This software-based system is easily adaptable to different interview questions and skip patterns, and it allows for reduction in data entry errors and quick data analysis. Such systems are often used by marketing firms that conduct large-scale surveys. Although these systems can be expensive (i.e., 3,000 to 5,000 dollars), the cost may be more than offset if the sample size to be tracked is large and if there are important reporting requirements for the project. In a CATI system, the respondent is contacted via telephone by a trained interviewer who administers the interview protocol. The interviewer talks to the respondent while reading the survey questions from the screen of a computer terminal. CATI can check instantly to make sure the coded response is an answer within the parameters of possible answers. For example, the computer will not allow a coded response of "3" to be entered if the response options are "1" and "2." The computer can also skip questions that are not applicable to a particular respondent.

Decisions on this important matter should be predicated on such factors as the number of leavers to be tracked, staff computer skills, and program reporting requirements. Whatever the choice regarding the way in which the data will be entered and stored, it is critical to seek the assistance of an expert before starting in order to minimize the number of problems that could be encountered later.

WHAT DO WE DO WITH THE RESULTS?

It is far beyond the purpose of this chapter to discuss the many different ways longitudinal data can be analyzed. Generally, data on leavers' transition experiences are analyzed for program staff, who will use the results to guide program changes. Results also may be provided to administrators, who must examine the program's effectiveness (e.g., end of the fiscal year) or make budgetary decisions regarding the project.

If the data are to be summarized for the purpose of review by service delivery staff, it is probably not necessary to go to great lengths to produce complicated reports. What we have done on past projects is to produce a yearly report for the staff, which is usually a printout of the findings. We present and review the findings in an orientation meeting to ensure that everyone understands the printout and ask staff to review the outcomes so they can be discussed at a second meeting. In that second meeting, we review the findings and discuss what we believe to be the strengths and weaknesses revealed by the findings. Based on these judgments, we identify necessary program changes and begin to explore the best ways to make those changes.

Reports for administrators are somewhat different. Typically, reporting to administrators is based on the requirement for regular evaluation of the program or for budgetary justification. These reports usually are more formal and may be presented in an oral presentation. The majority of people who will review the program results will not be researchers and will have neither the time nor inclination to read extensive and complicated reports. Thus, we believe that summaries of the longitudinal transition experiences of leavers should be short (four to five pages); be based on simple descriptive statistics relating to key variables; use a bare minimum of text; and use bulleted statements, figures, and tables to highlight key findings. The saying that "a picture is worth a thousand words" holds true in these situations, so it is critical to develop clear and precise figures and tables to portray important findings. Many off-the-shelf database software packages have data analysis features that allow the program to summarize data and display it in tabular and graphic form. Reports are enhanced with descriptions of real people, illustrating specific transition experiences and program results. A powerful effect can be achieved in presentations by coupling the presentation of quantitative results with testimonials from leavers who comment on their own experiences and perceptions.

Longitudinal data collection is an important and necessary part of the service delivery effort in transition programs for adolescents with EBD. The ideas presented in this chapter should provide basic guidance in setting up such data collection systems and ensure that these data will be beneficial for the program, its staff, and the young people who are served.

APPENDIX A

Program Forms

Intake Interview Form

Student _____ **TS/interviewer** _____ **Date** _____

Address _____ **Social security no.** _____ **D.O.B.** _____

_____ **Phone** _____ **Parent/guardian** _____

Does student have a work permit? _____ Yes _____ No   Work permit no. _____

Student long-range goals

Vocational

_____ Competitive employment

_____ Supported work

Education

_____ High school diploma

_____ Community college career classes

_____ College

_____ Other (_Explain._) _____

_____

Previous vocational training

_____ Application

_____ Interview

_____ Career awareness

School information

1. After-school activities _____

2. Favorite classes/activities _____

3. School/work dislikes _____

4. Any physical barriers _____

5. Hobbies, interests/other skills _____

Interests

What type of job(s) is the student interested in? Rate preference 1 (high) to 4 (low):

_____ Art/graphics/photo

_____ Health care

_____ Hotel support services

_____ Auto body/mechanics

_____ Computers

_____ Other _____

_____ Custodial

_____ Grounds maintenance

_____ Farm work

_____ Construction

_____ Restaurant work

_____ Office/clerical

_____ Manufacturing

_____ Work with animals

_____ Work with children

_____ Retail

Intake Interview Form (continued)

Student _____   Date _____

Previous work experience

Worksite	Dates of employment	Supervisor	Wage	Duties	Reason for termination/comments

Job-Related Social Skills Checklist

Student _____ TS/interviewer _____ Worksite _____ Date _____

	Has skill	Needs training	Item no./comments
Work-related behavior			
1. Checks own work..........	☐	☐	
2. Corrects mistakes	☐	☐	
3. Works alone without distruptions for specified periods with no contact from supervisor/teacher	☐	☐	
4. Works continuously at a job station for specified amount of time........	☐	☐	
5. Safety			
a. uses appropriate safety gear	☐	☐	
b. responds appropriately during fire drill	☐	☐	
c. follows safety procedures specific to classroom/shop	☐	☐	
d. wears safe work clothing	☐	☐	
e. cleans work area........	☐	☐	
f. identifies and avoids dangerous areas	☐	☐	
g. responds appropriately to emergency situation (sickness, injury, etc.)	☐	☐	
6. Participates in work environment for specified periods of time	☐	☐	
7. Works in group situation without being distracted	☐	☐	
8. Works faster when asked to do so	☐	☐	
9. Completes work by specified time when told to do so	☐	☐	

Job-Related Social Skills Checklist (continued)

Student _____   Date _____

	Has skill	Needs training	Item no./comments

Work-related behavior (continued)

10. Time management

   a. comes to class/work for designated number of times per week .... □ □

   b. arrives at class/work on time .... □ □

   c. recognizes appropriate time to take break or lunch .... □ □

   d. recognizes appropriate time to change task □ □

   e. returns promptly from

     (1) break .... □ □

     (2) restroom .... □ □

     (3) lunch .... □ □

11. Observes classroom/shop rules .... □ □

12. Does not leave works tation without permission □ □

Mobility/transportation

1. Takes appropriate transportation to and from school/work .... □ □

2. Moves about class/work environment independently .... □ □

Self-help/grooming

Does independently

1. Dresses appropriately for school/work .... □ □

2. Cleans self before coming to school/work .... □ □

3. Cleans self after using restroom .... □ □

4. Cleans self after eating .... □ □

5. Shaves regularly .... □ □

6. Keeps hair combed .... □ □

7. Keeps nails clean .... □ □

204

Job-Related Social Skills Checklist (continued)

Student _____   Date _____

	Has skill	Needs training	Item no./comments

Self-help/grooming (continued)

	Has skill	Needs training
8. Keeps teeth clean	☐	☐
9. Uses deodorant	☐	☐
10. Bathes regularly	☐	☐
11. Cares for menstrual needs (if applicable)	☐	☐
12. Cares for toileting needs	☐	☐
13. Eats lunch and takes breaks	☐	☐
14. Washes before eating	☐	☐
15. Brings lunch/snack	☐	☐
16. Uses napkin	☐	☐
17. Displays appropriate table manners	☐	☐

Social communication

	Has skill	Needs training
1. Does not engage in		
a. self-stimulatory or abusive behavior	☐	☐
b. aggressive/destructive behavior	☐	☐
c. self-indulgent (attention-getting) behavior	☐	☐
2. Engages in relevant, appropriate conversation	☐	☐
3. Responds calmly to emotional outbursts of others	☐	☐
4. Talks about personal problems at appropriate times	☐	☐
5. Refrains from exhibiting inappropriate emotions at school/work	☐	☐
6. Refrains from bringing inappropriate items to school/work	☐	☐
7. Refrains from tampering with or stealing others' property	☐	☐

Job-Related Social Skills Checklist (continued)

Student _____

	Has skill	Needs training	Item no/comments

Social communication (continued)

	Has skill	Needs training
8. Responds appropriately to changes in supervisors/teachers	☐	☐
9. Interacts with co-workers/students at appropriate times	☐	☐
10. Responds appropriate to social contacts such as "Hello" or "Good morning"	☐	☐
11. Initiates greetings appropriately	☐	☐
12. Ignores inappropriate behaviors/comments of co-workers/students	☐	☐
13. Refrains from inappropriate sexual activity at school/work	☐	☐
14. Laughs, jokes, and teases at appropriate times	☐	☐
15. Responds appropriately to strangers	☐	☐
16. Approaches supervisor/teacher appropriately when		
a. needs more work	☐	☐
b. makes a mistake he/she cannot correct	☐	☐
c. tools or materials are defective	☐	☐
d. does not understand task	☐	☐
e. is sick...........................	☐	☐
17. Complies with supervisor's/teacher's requests in specified period of time............	☐	☐
18. Responds appropriately to corrective feedback from supervisor/teacher	☐	☐
19. Responds appropriately to changes in routine	☐	☐
20. Follows instructions	☐	☐

206

IEP Vocational Goals Form

Student _____   School _____

D.O.B. _____   Review date _____

Present performance level
Long-term goal

Objective(s)	Provider	Criteria	Evaluation

Integrated Service Plan

Student _____ D.O.B. _____ Date of plan _____

Present	Placement date	Stable
Residential		yes no
Vocational		yes no

Future	Projected date	Comments
Residential		
Vocational		

FINANCIAL

Long-term goal			
Action	Agency	Timeline	Completed

VOCATIONAL TRAINING

Long-term goal			
Action	Agency	Timeline	Completed

Integrated Service Plan (continued)

Student _____ Date of plan _____

EDUCATION

Long-term goal			
Action	**Agency**	**Timeline**	**Completed**

TRANSPORTATION

Long-term goal			
Action	**Agency**	**Timeline**	**Completed**

MEDICAL ISSUES

Long-term goal			
Action	**Agency**	**Timeline**	**Completed**

Integrated Service Plan (continued)

Student _____   Date of plan _____

Long-term goal			
Action	**Agency**	**Timeline**	**Completed**

SOCIAL SUPPORT SYSTEM

Long-term goal			
Action	**Agency**	**Timeline**	**Completed**

SOCIAL SKILLS TRAINING

Long-term goal			
Action	**Agency**	**Timeline**	**Completed**

Integrated Service Plan (continued)

Student _____   Date of plan _____

SERVICE INTEGRATION

Contact person	Agency	Reason	Timeline	Completed

Work Policy Form

Worksite _____

We agree to the following points:

[empty box]

I, _____, have read and understand the above policies. I agree to follow the policies as set forth.

I, _____, have clarified the above policies as set forth.

_____
(Signature of employee)   (Date)

_____
(Signature of transition specialist)   (Date)

Total Task Data Form

Student _____ TS _____ Program _____

Terminal objective _____ Date _____

Total no. of Xs																						
Total no. of steps																						
% independence																						
Dates/baseline _____																						

Task Program Cover Sheet

Student _____ TS _____ Program _____

Terminal objective _____ Date _____

Materials	Nonverbal cues (setup)
Instructional cues	**Criterion**
Reinforcement procedure	
Correction	**Teaching notes**

Task Checklist

Student _____   TS _____

Worksite _____   Date _____

Task	Description	Date begun	Date mastered

Work Data Form

Student _____ TS _____

Date initiated _____ Date terminated _____

Worksite _____

Week of	Vocational phase	Phone/visit		Late	No show/ no call	Theft	Work quality	Aggressive	Noncompliant	Inappropriate dress		Staff change	TS change	Task change	Boss problem	Co-worker problem	Boredom	Personal/ nonwork		Volunteer extra time	Positive interaction/ boss	Positive interaction/ co-worker	Initiative	Time management	Follow worksite policies

(Column group headers: **Work infraction** — Late, No show/no call, Theft, Work quality, Aggressive, Noncompliant, Inappropriate dress; **Client stressors** — Staff change, TS change, Task change, Boss problem, Co-worker problem, Boredom, Personal/nonwork; **Positive performance** — Volunteer extra time, Positive interaction/boss, Positive interaction/co-worker, Initiative, Time management, Follow worksite policies)

Work Data Form (continued)

Student _____   Worksite _____

Week of	Comments	Follow-up	Date complete

Behavior Data Form

Student _____

Worksite _____ TS _____

Date initiated _____ Date terminated _____

Behavior	Date								Total

Note: Use for multiple weeks.

218

Behavior Data Form

Student _____ Worksite _____ TS _____

Date initiated _____ Date terminated _____

Behavior	Date							Total

Note: Use for multiple behaviors.

Functional Behavioral Assessment Form

Student _____   TS _____

Worksite _____   Date _____

Target behavior

1. Do prescribed medication or medical conditions influence the occurrence of the target behavior? If so, explain.

2. Is the behavior used to get something and/or to avoid or escape something? Explain.

3. What are common triggers for the behavior?

Events/situations	Behavior most likely to occur	Behavior least likely to occur
Time of day		
Settings		
Persons		
Activities		
Other		

Page 1 of 2

Student _____   **Date** _____

4. What are warning signs or precursor behaviors that the individual may exhibit prior to the target behavior?

5. What reinforcers may be maintaining the behavior?

6. What punishers or conditions may help remediate the behavior?

7. What has worked in the past to treat this behavior?

8. What skills could be taught to replace this behavior?

9. What is the hypothesis for why this behavior is occurring?

10. What intervention(s) does the staff recommend? Number the choices 1–4, with 1 being the intervention to initiate first, 2 second, and so forth.
    _____ Behavior does not warrant intervention
    _____ Schedule change
    _____ Staff change/training
    _____ Medical treatment
    _____ Skills training program
    _____ Referral for intervention (e.g., counseling, drug/alcohol treatment)
    _____ Environmental change
    _____ Behavior program change or other modification

Behavioral Intervention Program Cover Sheet

Student _____   TS _____

Date initiated: _____   Date terminated _____

Program: Home ❑ School ❑ Vocational *(specify worksite)* _____

Program objective

Collection procedure

Date	Baseline data	Comments and treatment

Program summary

Date	Weekly total	Treatment no.	Date	Weekly total	Treatment no.

Posttreatment follow-up

If program terminated, state reason _____

Behavioral Intervention Treatment Form

Student _____ TS _____

Worksite _____ Date _____

Behavior to increase

Behavior to decrease

Treatment no. and date	When behavior to increase occurs, do this	When behavior to decrease occurs, do this

Behavior Contract

I, _____ , understand that I am expected to maintain acceptable work habits

and courteous social skills at _____ . I understand that if I perform

the work expectations at a satisfactory level I will be entitled to the work incentives described.

Work expectations

Work incentives

I, _____ , agree with this contract and will cooperate with the expectations

listed.

_____	_____
Student	Date

_____	_____
Parent/guardian	Date

_____	_____
Transition specialist	Date

_____	_____
Employer	Date

Worksite Record Form

Student _____   Placement date _____

TS _____   Worksite _____

Supervisor _____   Address _____

Alternate supervisor _____   _____

Transportation _____   Phone _____

Program objective

Social/behavioral objective

Comments

Worksite Record Form (continued)

Student _____

Worksite _____

Week of	Mon	Tu	Wed	Th	Fri	Total time	Comments

Vocational Phase Form

Student _____ Worksite _____ TS _____

Intake date _____ Placement date _____ Expected termination date _____

Reason for termination _____

Phase I _____ Phase II _____ Phase III _____ Phase IV _____ Phase V _____
Learning Responsibility Transition Independence Employability

Date	Infraction	Consequence

Vocational Log

Student _____   TS _____

Worksite _____   Placement date _____

Date	TS initials	Program	Comments

Skills-Training Program Data Form

Student _____   Date program started _____

TS _____   Date program completed _____

Worksite _____

```
┌─────────────────────────────────────────────────────────────┐
│ Program objective                                            │
│                                                              │
│                                                              │
│                                                              │
│                                                              │
│                                                              │
└─────────────────────────────────────────────────────────────┘
```

```
┌─────────────────────────────────────────────────────────────┐
│ Reinforcement schedule                                       │
│                                                              │
│                                                              │
│                                                              │
│                                                              │
│                                                              │
└─────────────────────────────────────────────────────────────┘
```

```
┌─────────────────────────────────────────────────────────────┐
│ Correction procedure                                         │
│                                                              │
│                                                              │
│                                                              │
│                                                              │
│                                                              │
└─────────────────────────────────────────────────────────────┘
```

```
┌─────────────────────────────────────────────────────────────┐
│ Teaching notes                                               │
│                                                              │
│                                                              │
│                                                              │
│                                                              │
│                                                              │
└─────────────────────────────────────────────────────────────┘
```

Page 1 of 2

Skills-Training Program Data Form (continued)

Student _____   Worksite _____

Job description/task analysis	Date																	
Total no. of Xs / Total no. of steps																		
% independent																		
TS initials																		

Skills-Training Program Log

Student _____   TS _____

Worksite _____   Placement date _____

Date	Comments	TS initials

Employer/Co-Worker Contact Form

Student _____ TS _____ Placement date _____

Worksite _____ Supervisor _____ Alternate supervisor _____

Date	Name of contact	Time	Type of interaction				Comments
			Discipline	Training	Praise	Admin.	

Student Progress Report

Student _____ **TS** _____

Worksite _____ **Evaluation period** _____

	(lowest)				(highest)
1. Gets to work regularly and on time.	1	2	3	4	5
2. Reports if unable to work.	1	2	3	4	5
3. Completes tasks to best ability.	1	2	3	4	5
4. Uses work time efficiently.	1	2	3	4	5
5. Works at reasonable speed.	1	2	3	4	5
6. Uses equipment properly and safely.	1	2	3	4	5
7. Works independently.	1	2	3	4	5
8. Dresses appropriately.	1	2	3	4	5
9. Has good grooming habits.	1	2	3	4	5
10. Complies with standards and rules of job.	1	2	3	4	5
11. Gets along well with others.	1	2	3	4	5
12. Is willing to take criticism.	1	2	3	4	5
13. Exhibits appropriate behaviors.	1	2	3	4	5
14. Exhibits appropriate attitudes.	1	2	3	4	5
15. Works at same rate/quality as regular worker.	1	2	3	4	5

Would you hire this student? At minimum or submininimum wage? Why or why not?

What problem areas do you identify?

Additional comments

Date _____ **Evaluated by** _____

Please contact _____ at _____ if you have any questions or concerns.
If you need more space, please continue on the reverse.

Problem-Solving Data Recording Form

Student _____ Worksite _____ Date _____

Problem	Goal	Alternative solutions	Tried?	Helpful?	Date/result
			|	|	
			|	|	
			|	|	
			|	|	
			|	|	
			|	|	
			|	|	
			|	|	
			|	|	

Training Needs Survey

Name _____ **Date** _____

In order to best meet the individual training needs of each project site, we would like your input on training preferences. Please indicate your choices below.

Which areas of transition programs would you like additional information on?

_____ Positive behavior management

_____ Social skills training

_____ Independent living and leisure

_____ Functional academics

_____ Creating a phase system for transitioning back to high school

_____ Including students in regular high-school academics

_____ Functional vocational skills assessment

_____ Prevocational skills—notebooks—portfolios

_____ Coordinating with/services offered by community service agencies

_____ Developing a variety of vocational placements

_____ Other _____

From whom would you like to receive more information?

_____ Project staff

_____ Community services personnel

_____ High school programs in state

_____ Vocational specialists

_____ Behavioral specialists

_____ Other _____

When would you be available for paid inservice days?

❑ _____ ❑ _____ Days of week _____

How much large-group training (all grant sites) would you prefer?

(*Circle.*)   1   2   3   4   5   ___ Full days   ___ Half days

How much training/work time at your individual site would you prefer?

(*Circle.*)   1   2   3   4   5   ___ Full days   ___ Half days

Interviewer Telephone Log

Student _____   Interviewer _____

Phone number	Comments

Date	Day of week	Time	A.M./P.M.	Call-back information

APPENDIX B

Various Indicators of Criminal and Conduct Involvement

The purpose of this questionnaire is to quantify a youth's criminal activities and gang involvement. In many cases the youth will not admit these activities to authority figures, so the referral information that is given will not be complete. In order to develop a suitable service plan and to describe the youth as fully as possible, it is essential that as much information as possible be gathered. Accordingly, this form should be administered at the intake, along with the other instruments required in the project, for this express purpose. Given the personal nature of the questions and content and the student's reluctance to disclose information, it is advisable to administer this questionnaire last, after a degree of rapport has been established. Use discretion in the way questions are asked.

Responses to the questions will be recorded three ways. First, after each question is a series of closed-ended response categories. Mark the category (or categories) that best describes the particular question. If none of the categories "fits" the response, summarize the response as clearly and succinctly as possible in the space near the question. Second, after the interview is completed, you will answer a series of general questions about your impression of the subject. These responses will be scored using a 4-point Likert scale: 1—*disagree strongly* with the statement; 2—*disagree* with the statement; 3—*agree* with the statement; or 4—*agree strongly* with the statement. Third, you will code a list of antisocial behaviors relating to the student. Code each behavior using a three-point scale: 1—there is *no evidence* or you are *not sure* from the intake interview or referral information that the student performs this behavior; 2—there is sufficient reason from the intake interview and the referral information to *suspect* that the student performs this behavior; or 3—there is *reasonable certainty* from the intake interview and the referral information that the student performs this behavior.

Various Indicators of Criminal and Conduct Involvement

Student _____

Interviewer _____ **Date** _____

Questions

1. What do you want to do with your life? Check only one.
   _____ Clear, realistic plan for work and life
   _____ Vague, realistic plan for work and life
   _____ Unrealistic plan for work and life
   _____ No plan for work and life

2. How do you usually spend your free time? Check only one.
   _____ Alone (e.g., watches TV, stays home)
   _____ Around others but unattached to a group (e.g., goes to a dance alone)
   _____ With a few close friends
   _____ With family members
   _____ With a large group of peers

3. Are you close to your family?
   a. _____ YES _____ NO
   If yes, ask b. If no, go to Question 4.
   b. Whom in your family are you close to? Check each that applies.
   _____ Father
   _____ Mother
   _____ Brother/sister
   _____ Grandparent
   _____ Other family member

4. Do you have close friends?
   a. _____ YES _____ NO
   If yes, ask b. If no, go to Question 5.
   b. How many?
   _____ 1
   _____ 2 or 3
   _____ 4 or more

5. Have any of your friends ever been in trouble with the police?
   a. _____ YES _____NO
   If yes, ask b. If no, go to Question 6.
   b. What for? Check either or both *status offense* or *index offense*. If no, probe with additional questions before going to Question 6.
   _____ Status offense (underage driving, breaking curfew)
   _____ Index offense (criminal activity)

6. Have you ever gotten into trouble at school? By this I mean have you ever been referred to the principal for discipline problems or been suspended?
   a. _____ YES _____NO
   If yes, ask b, c, and d. If no, go to Question 7.

(Item 6, continued)

b. What for? Check all that apply. If no, probe with additional questions before going to Question 7.

_____ Minor property offense (e.g., broke a locker)
_____ Major property offense (e.g., destroyed school property)
_____ Minor personal offense (e.g., harassed a student, disagreed with staff)
_____ Major personal offense (e.g., assaulted a student)

c. How many times in the past year have you been in trouble at school? Check only one.

_____ Only 1–2 times
_____ A few times (3–5)
_____ A lot (over 5)

d. In general, was this problem (were these problems) your responsibility?

_____ Yes, it was completely my fault.
_____ It was partly my fault.
_____ It wasn't my fault at all.

7. Have you ever been drunk?

a. _____ YES _____ NO

If yes, ask b. If no, go to Question 8.

b. How many times in the past year have you been drunk?

_____ 1–2/year
_____ 1–2/month
_____ 1–2/week
_____ Almost daily

8. Have you ever used illegal drugs, such as marijuana, LSD, or cocaine?

a. _____ YES _____ NO

If yes, ask b. If no, go to Question 9.

b. How many times in the past year have you used?

_____ 1–2/year
_____ 1–2/month
_____ 1–2/week
_____ Almost daily

9. What do you think about gangs? Check only the one that best represents the response.

_____ Gangs are stupid—I want no part of them.
_____ Some gangs are OK—I hang out with them sometimes.
_____ Gangs are neat—I want to be involved.
_____ I am in a gang.
_____ No or conflicting response.

10. Have you ever gotten into trouble with the police? By this I mean have you ever been suspected of, charged with, or arrested for a crime?

a. _____ YES _____ NO

If yes, ask b, c, and d. If no, go to Question 11.

b. What for? Check either or both *status offense* or *index offense*. If no, probe with additional questions before going to Question 11.

_____ Status offense (e.g., underage driving, breaking curfew)
_____ Index offense (criminal activity)

(Item 10, continued)

  c. How many times in the past year have you been in trouble with the police? Check only one.

    _____ Only 1–2 times

    _____ A few times (3–5)

    _____ A lot (over 5)

  d. In general, was this problem (were these problems) your responsibility?

    _____ Yes, it was completely my fault.

    _____ It was partly my fault.

    _____ It wasn't my fault at all.

11. Last question: How truthful were you answering these questions?

  _____ Very truthful

  _____ Truthful

  _____ Dishonest

  _____ Very dishonest

Impressions

Use the following scale for these questions: 1—*disagree strongly* with the statement, 2—*disagree* with the statement, 3—*agree* with the statement, or 4—*agree strongly* with the statement.

1. The student was honest about his or her own antisocial behaviors.	1 2 3 4
2. The student was honest about his or her affiliation with other antisocial peers.	1 2 3 4
3. The student seems motivated to work.	1 2 3 4
4. The student seems motivated to be involved in the program.	1 2 3 4
5. The student's family will be supportive of the program.	1 2 3 4
6. The student indicated a genuine interest to change.	1 2 3 4
7. The student answered questions in a clear and responsive way.	1 2 3 4
8. The student's answers appeared truthful and were not contradictory.	1 2 3 4
9. The student dressed appropriately for the interview.	1 2 3 4
10. The student used appropriate language responding to the questions.	1 2 3 4
11. The student exhibited clear and logical thinking in answering the questions.	1 2 3 4
12. The student took responsibility for antisocial behaviors.	1 2 3 4
13. The student is an excellent candidate for this program.	1 2 3 4

Antisocial behaviors

Use the following scale for each behavior: 1—there is *no evidence* or you are *not sure* from the intake interview or referral information that the student performs this behavior; 2—there is sufficient reason from the intake interview and the referral information to *suspect* that the student performs this behavior; or 3—there is *reasonable certainty* from the intake interview and the referral information that the student performs this behavior.

1. Purposely damaged or destroyed property belonging to parents or other family members?	1 2 3
2. Purposely damaged or destroyed property belonging to a school or teacher?	1 2 3

3. Purposely damaged or destroyed property, not including family, school, or teacher property?   1 2 3

4. Lied about age to gain entrance or to purchase something? For example, lying about age to buy liquor or get into a movie.   1 2 3

5. Stolen or tried to steal a motor vehicle (e.g., car, truck, motorcycle)?   1 2 3

6. Carried a nonregistered, hidden weapon?   1 2 3

7. Stolen or tried to steal things worth less than 10 dollars?   1 2 3

8. Stolen or tried to steal things worth 10 dollars or more?   1 2 3

9. Knowingly bought, sold, or held stolen goods or tried to do any of these things?   1 2 3

10. Purposely set fire to a building, a car, or other property or tried to do so?   1 2 3

11. Been involved with gang fights or other illegal gang-related activities?   1 2 3

12. Used checks illegally or used counterfeit money to pay for something? (Includes intentional overdrafts.)   1 2 3

13. Sold *any* illegal drugs (e.g., pot, hash, crack, etc.)?   1 2 3

14. Threatened, hit, or attacked someone, such as another student, parent, teacher, employer, roommate, and so on?   1 2 3

15. Stolen money or things from parents or other family members?   1 2 3

16. Been exceptionally loud, rowdy, or unruly in a public place—disorderly conduct?   1 2 3

17. Avoided paying for such things as movies, bus rides, or food?   1 2 3

18. Been drunk or high on drugs in a public place?   1 2 3

19. Drunk beer, wine, or hard liquor?   1 2 3

20. Used marijuana or illegal drugs?   1 2 3

21. Tried to cheat someone by selling them something that was worthless or not what it was claimed to be?   1 2 3

22. Bought or provided liquor for a minor?   1 2 3

23. Broken or tried to break into a building, house, apartment, store, warehouse, or vehicle to steal something or just look around?   1 2 3

24. Begged money or things from strangers?   1 2 3

25. Used or tried to use credit cards without the owner's permission?   1 2 3

26. Made obscene telephone calls?   1 2 3

27. Used force or threat of force to rob a person, store, bank, or other business establishment?   1 2 3

APPENDIX C

Telephone Interview Protocol

Program year (*circle*) 1 / 2 / 3   **Interview no.** (*circle*) 1 / 2 / 3 / 4 / 5

Student _____ **Student no.** _____

D. O. B. _____ **Sex   M   /   F**

Interview date _____   **Interviewer** _____

(*After reaching student*)

Hello, my name is _____, and I'm calling to conduct the follow-up survey sponsored by _____. The interview is quick and easy, and I'd like to interview you now if possible. Is that convenient?

<IF NO> When would be a good time? (*Write on telephone log and call back.*)

<IF YES> Great . . .

. . . before we begin, I'd like you to know all your answers will be kept confidential. Second, you can choose not to answer any question or stop the interview at any time. Finally, we will contact you again _____ (*specify date*).

Ready?

Respondent: [   ]

    (1) student

    (2) foster parent

    (3) mother

    (4) father

    (5) sibling

    (6) grandparent

    (55) OTHER _____

    _____

1. EDUCATION

1a. [   ] In the past 6 months, how many schools have you been enrolled in?

    (0) none   *<IF NONE, GO TO 1j>* ●

1b. [   ] Are you currently enrolled in any type of school?

    (0) no *<IF NO, GO TO 1j>* ●   (55) OTHER _____

    (1) yes   _____

1c. [   ] What type of school are you enrolled in?

    *(1) residential high school   (4) apprenticeship/technical

    *(2) public high school   (5) community college

    *(3) work adjustment/rehab/OJT   (6) 4-year college

                                      (7) military

    <IF 1, 2, OR 3, GO TO 1d> ▲   (55) OTHER _____

                                        _____

                                        (99) DON'T KNOW

                                        <IF 4, 5, 6, 7, 55, OR 99, GO TO 1h> ◆

▲ 1d. [   ] Have you received any help from any school or program personnel in planning your transition from the school or program to your next placement?

    (0) no   (99) DON'T KNOW

    (1) yes

1e. [   ] Has a written plan been drawn up to guide your movement to the next placement?

    (0) no   (99) DON'T KNOW

    (1) yes

1f. [   ] Are you planning to move or transition from your current program or placement in the next 6 months?

    (0) no *<IF NO, GO TO 1i>* ■   (99) DON'T KNOW

    (1) yes

1g. [   ] Have firm plans been made by any service personnel to provide contact and follow-up with you in this new placement?

(0) no <GO TO 1i> ■   (99) DON'T KNOW

(1) yes <GO TO 1i> ■

◆ 1h. [   ] What is the major reason you are going to this school?

(1) proximity/location   (9) future/program indecision

(2) scholarship/funding   (10) size

(3) availability of major   (11) direct referral/placement

(4) reputation of school   (12) self-growth

(5) family history/friends   (13) no choice

(6) acceptance   (55) OTHER _____

(7) social/extracurricular   _____

(8) special services   (99) DON'T KNOW

■ 1i. [   ] How happy are you with your current school and educational program on a scale of 1 to 4, with 1 being "very unhappy," 2 being "unhappy," 3 "happy," and 4 "very happy?"

(1) very unhappy   (3) happy

(2) unhappy   (4) very happy

                                       (99) DON'T KNOW

● 1j. [   ] Six months from now, do you plan to be enrolled in school?

(0) no   (55) OTHER _____

(1) yes <IF YES, GO TO 1l> ■   (99) DON'T KNOW/MAYBE

1k. [   ] Do you plan to be enrolled in school any time in the future?

(0) no <IF NO, GO TO 2a> ▲   (55) OTHER _____

(1) yes   (99) DON'T KNOW/MAYBE

■ 1l. [   ] What type of school will it be?

*(1) residential high school   (4) apprenticeship/technical

*(2) public high school   (5) community college

*(3) work adjustment/rehab/OJT   (6) 4-year college

                                       (7) military

*<IF 1, 2, OR 3, GO TO 2a> ▲   (55) OTHER _____

                                       _____

                                       (99) DON'T KNOW

1m. [   ] What will your major focus of study be?

COLLEGE MAJORS (1–6)

(1) education

(2) liberal arts

(3) social sciences

(4) hard sciences/agriculture/engineering

(5) computer science

(6) business/economics

(7) voc/tech/work experience

(8) college prep/undeclared

(9) GED

(10) finish high school

(55) OTHER _____

_____

(99) DON'T KNOW

1n. [   ] What was the major reason you chose this particular school?

(1) proximity/location

(2) scholarship/funding

(3) availability of major

(4) reputation of school

(5) family history/friends

(6) acceptance

(7) social/extracurricular activities

(8) special services

(9) future/program indecision

(10) size

(11) direct referral/placement

(12) self-growth

(13) no choice

(55) OTHER _____

_____

(99) DON'T KNOW

2. EMPLOYMENT HISTORY AND PLANS

▲ 2a. [   ] In the past 6 months, how many jobs have you had?

(0) none <IF NONE, GO TO 2j> ◆

(55) OTHER _____

_____

(99) DON'T KNOW

2b. [   ] Have you been fired from any job(s) in the last 6 months?

(0) no

(1) yes   Why? _____

_____

2c. [   ] Are you currently employed in a paid job?

(0) no <IF NO, GO TO 2j> ◆

(55) OTHER _____

(1) yes

2d. [   ] What is the primary type of work you do?

(1) professional, technical, managerial

(8) structural work

(2) clerical and sales

(55) OTHER _____

(3) service

_____

(4) agricultural, fishery, forestry

(Include job description.)

(5) processing

_____

(6) machine trades

_____

(7) benchwork

_____

2e. [   ] How did you find this job?

(1) self/family/friend

(6) employment services (community, state, or private)

(2) Department of Vocational Rehabilitation

(7) military

(3) mental health division

(55) OTHER _____

(4) developmental disabilities division

_____

(5) through school/work study

(99) DON'T KNOW

2f. [   ] On the average, how many hours a week do you usually work? *(Combine if more than one job.)*

(99) DON'T KNOW

2g. [   ] About how much do you usually make a week before anything is taken out of the check? *(Or ask about pay rate. Combine if more than one job.)*

(99) DON'T KNOW

2h. [   ] How many months have you worked in this job? *(Inquire about primary job.)*

(99) DON'T KNOW

2i. [   ] How happy are you with your current job(s)?

(1) very unhappy

(3) happy

(2) unhappy

(4) very happy

(99) DON'T KNOW

◆ 2j. [   ] Six months from now, do you plan to be working?

    (0) no *<IF NO, GO TO 3a>* ■   (55) OTHER _____

    (1) yes   (99) DON'T KNOW

2k. [   ] What kind of work are you planning to do then?

    (1) professional, technical, managerial   (8) structural work

    (2) clerical and sales   (55) OTHER _____

    (3) service   _____

    (4) agricultural, fishery, forestry   *(Include job description.)*

    (5) processing   _____

    (6) machine trades   _____

    (7) benchwork   _____

2l. [   ] Do you have this job?

    (0) no   (99) DON'T KNOW

    (1) yes

2m. [   ] How many months do you plan to work there?

    (00) always   (99) DON'T KNOW

2n. [   ] On average, how many hours a week do you plan to work in 6 months?

    (99) DON'T KNOW

2o. [   ] And, in 6 months, about how much do you plan to make a week before anything is taken out of the check? *(Or ask about pay rate. Combine if more than one job.)*

    (99) DON'T KNOW

2p. [   ] How did/will you find this job?

    (1) self/family/friend   (6) employment services (community, state, or private)

    (2) Department of Vocational Rehabilitation   (7) military

    (3) mental health division   (55) OTHER _____

    (4) developmental disabilities division   _____

    (5) through school/work study   (99) DON'T KNOW

3. LIVING PLANS

■ 3a. [   ] In the past 6 months, how many places have you lived?

    (0) none   (99) DON'T KNOW

3b. [   ] Where do you currently live?

    (0) supported   (1) unsupported

    _____ with parents   _____ community rental

    _____ supervised living/group home   _____ school dorm (fraternity/sorority)

    _____ incarcerated/prison   _____ military housing

    _____ with other family members (*Ask with whom.*)

    _____ foster home   (55) OTHER _____

    _____ community shelter   _____

    _____ institution

3c. [   ] How long have you lived there? (*Convert to months.*)

    (00) always   (99) DON'T KNOW

3d. [   ] How happy are you with this current living situation?

    (1) very unhappy   (3) happy

    (2) unhappy   (4) very happy

                                       (99) DON'T KNOW

3e. [   ] Thinking about the future again, in 6 months, what kind of place do you plan to live in?

    (0) supported   (1) unsupported

    _____ with parents   _____ community rental

    _____ supervised living/group home   _____ school dorm (fraternity/sorority)

    _____ incarcerated/prison   _____ military housing

    _____ with other family members (*Ask with whom.*)

    _____ foster home   (55) OTHER _____

    _____ community shelter   _____

    _____ institution   (99) DON'T KNOW

4. COMMUNITY SERVICE AGENCY HISTORY

I'm now going to ask some questions about your experiences with community service agencies.

(Record codes for generic questions in the table at the bottom of this page.)

4a. Since we last interviewed you have you *received services* from (*AGENCY*)?

    (0) no *<Skip to next AGENCY>*   (99) DON'T KNOW

    (1) yes *<Ask Question 4b for AGENCY>*

4b. How satisfied were you with that agency and its service?

    (1) very unhappy *<Ask Question 4c for AGENCY>*   (3) happy *<Skip to next AGENCY>*

    (2) unhappy *<Ask Question 4c for AGENCY>*   (4) very happy *<Skip to next AGENCY>*

                                                   (99) DON'T KNOW

4c. What was the ONE main reason you were UNHAPPY with that agency?

    (1) not helpful or responsive   (6) inadequate personnel

    (2) little or no financial help   (7) removed work motivation

    (3) too much bureaucracy   (55) OTHER _____

    (4) poor or no job placement   _____

    (5) poor or no communication   (99) DON'T KNOW

AGENCY	Question 4a — Received services? NO	Question 4a — Received services? YES	Question 4b — How satisfied were you with the agency?	Question 4c — If 1 or 2, what was the main reason you were unhappy?
1. Vocational rehabilitation				
2. Mental health division				
3. Social Security: Supplemental security or Social Security disability				
4. Public welfare				
5. Public employment office				
6. Other				

5. INVOLVEMENT WITH THE CRIMINAL JUSTICE SYSTEM

I'm now going to ask you some personal questions and want to remind you that you can choose not to answer these questions if you wish.

5a. [   ] Since we last interviewed you, have you been arrested?

    (0) no *<IF NO, GO TO 6a.>* ▲   (2) POSSIBLE/MAYBE

    (1) yes   (99) REFUSE/DON'T KNOW

5b. What were all the offenses you were arrested and/or charged with in the last 6 months? (*List offense and frequency—for example, "Assault 3 times."*)

_____

_____

_____

6. CONCLUSION

▲ 6a. [   ] Two final questions. First, in general, how happy are you on the 4-point scale we've been using?

    (1) very unhappy   (3) happy

    (2) unhappy   (4) very happy

                    (99) REFUSE/DON'T KNOW

6b. [   ] And the final question: How truthfully did you answer the questions I've just asked, on a 4-point scale, with 4 being totally honest and 1 being almost everything was made up?

    (1) almost everything was made up   (3) almost totally honest

    (2) quite a bit was made up   (4) totally honest

                    (99) REFUSE/DON'T KNOW

As I mentioned, we will contact you about every 6 months to ask similar questions about your school, work, and living experiences. Where can I call you next _____ (*specify date*)?

You must get contact information, including at least one address and phone number for next contact. Many students do not know where they will be, but get addresses and phone numbers of family and friends who can help locate them. Phone numbers are most important!

Student _____

Address _____

_____

Phone no. _____

Other person (family or friend?) _____

Address _____

_____

Phone no. _____

Other person (family or friend?) _____

Address _____

_____

Phone no. _____

Thank you for this interview. Your input will be helpful to our project. We look forward to talking

with you in _____ (*specify date*). Thanks again. Bye.

References

American Psychiatric Association. (1994). *Diagnostic and statistical manual of mental disorders* (4th ed.). Washington, DC: Author.

Benz, M. R., Lindstrom, L., & Halpern, A. S. (1995). Mobilizing local communities to improve transition services. *Career Development for Exceptional Individuals, 18,* 21–32.

Blackorby, J., & Edgar, E. (1992). Longitudinal studies in the post-school adjustment of students with disabilities. In F. Rusch, L. DeStefano, J. Chadsey-Rusch, L. Phelps, & E. Szymanski (Eds.), *Transition from school to adult life.* Champaign, IL: Sycamore Publishing.

Blalock, G., & Benz, M. R. (1999). *Using community transition teams to improve transition services.* Austin, TX: PRO-ED.

Bower, E. M. (1982). Defining emotional disturbance: Public policy and research. *Psychology in Schools, 19,* 55–60.

Bullis, M. (1992a). *Enhancing professionals' skills to improve services to adolescents with serious emotional disturbances.* (Office of Special Education Programs, Directed Competition on Improving the Capacity of Education to Serve Students with Serious Emotional Disturbance). Monmouth: Western Oregon State College, Division of Teaching Research.

Bullis, M. (1992b). *Project SERVE: Support for the emotional, residential, vocational, and educational needs of young adults with emotional disorders.* (Rehabilitation Services Administration, Non-directed Special Projects). Monmouth: Western Oregon State College, Division of Teaching Research.

Bullis, M., & Cheney, D. (1999). Vocational and transition interventions for adolescents and young adults with emotional or behavioral disorders. *Focus on Exceptional Children, 31*(7), 1–24.

Bullis, M., & Davis, C. (1996). Further examination of job-related social skills measures for adolescents and young adults with emotional and behavioral disorders. *Behavioral Disorders, 21,* 161–172.

Bullis, M., Fredericks, H. D., Lehman, C., Paris, K., & Corbitt, J., & Johnson, B. (1994). Description and evaluation of the Job Designs program for adolescents with emotional or behavioral disorders. *Behavioral Disorders, 19,* 254–268.

Bullis, M., & Gaylord-Ross, R. (1991). *Moving on: Transitions for youth with behavioral disorders.* Reston, VA: Council for Exceptional Children.

Bullis, M., Nishioka-Evans, V., Fredericks, H. D., & Davis, C. (1993). Identifying and assessing the job-related social skills of adolescents and young adults with emotional and behavioral disorders. *Journal of Emotional and Behavioral Disorders, 1,* 236–250.

Bullis, M., Nishioka-Evans, V., Fredericks, H. D., & Davis, C. (1998). *Scale of Job-Related Social Behavior for Adolescents and Young Adults With Emotional and Behavioral Disorders.* Santa Barbara: James Stanfield Company.

Burchard, J. D., Burchard, S. N., Sewell, R., & VanDenberg, J. (1993). *One kid at a time: Evaluative case studies and description of the Alaska Youth Initiative Demonstration Project.* Washington, DC: Child and Adolescent Service System Program, Technical Assistance Center, Georgetown University.

Chandler, M. (1973). Egocentrism and antisocial behavior: The assessment and training of social perspective training skills. *Developmental Psychology, 9,* 326–332.

Cook, J. A., Solomon, M. L., & Mock, L. O. (1988). *What happens after the first job placement: Vocational transition among severely emotionally disturbed and behavior disordered adolescents.* Chicago, IL: Thresholds Research Institute.

Council for Children With Behavioral Disorders. (1989). Position paper on the provision of service to children with conduct disorders. *Behavioral Disorders, 15,* 180–189.

Covey, S. R. (1989). *The 7 habits of highly effective people: Restoring the character ethic.* New York: Simon and Schuster.

deFur, S. H. (1990). *A validation study of competencies needed for transition specialists in vocational rehabilitation, vocational education, and special education.* Ann Arbor: University Microfilms.

Delbecq, A. L., Van de Ven, A. H., & Gustafson, D. H. (1975). *Group techniques for program planning: A guide to nominal group and Delphi processes.* Glenview, IL: Scott, Foresman.

DeStefano, L., & Wagner, M. (1992). Outcome assessment in special education: What lessons have we learned? In F. Rusch, L. DeStefano, J. Chadsey-Rusch, L. Phelps, & E. Szymanski (Eds.), *Transition from school to adult life.* Champaign, IL: Sycamore Publishing.

Dilley, J. S. (1965). Decision-making ability and vocational maturity. *Personnel and Guidance Journal, 44,* 423–427.

Dillman, D. (1978). *Mail and telephone surveys.* New York: Wiley.

Dishion, T., Loeber, R., Strouthamer-Loeber, M., & Patterson, G. (1984). Skills deficits and male adolescent delinquency. *Journal of Abnormal Child Psychology, 12,* 37–54.

Dodge, K. (1980). Social cognition and children's aggressive behavior. *Child Development, 51,* 162–170.

D'Zurilla, T. J. (1986). *Problem solving therapy: A social competence approach to clinical intervention.* New York: Springer.

D'Zurilla, T. J., & Goldfried, M. (1971). Problem solving and behavior modification. *Journal of Abnormal Psychology, 78,* 107–126.

Edgar, E. B. (1985). How do special education students fare after they leave school? *Exceptional Children, 51,* 470–473.

Fairweather, J. (1984). *Alternative study designs and revised conceptual framework for the longitudinal study of handicapped youth in transition.* Menlo Park, CA: SRI International.

Farrington, D. P. (1987). Early precursors of frequent offending. In J. Q. Wilson & G. C. Loury (Eds.), *From children to citizens: Vol. 3. Families, schools, and delinquency prevention.* New York: Springer-Verlag.

Field, S., & Hoffman, A. (1996). *Steps to self-determination: A curriculum to help adolescents learn to achieve their goals.* Austin, TX: PRO-ED.

Forness, S. (1988). Planning for the needs of children with serious emotional disturbance: The National Special Education and Mental Health Coalition. *Behavioral Disorders, 13,* 127–133.

Forness, S., Kavale, K., & Lopez, M. (1993). Conduct disorders in school: Special education eligibility and comorbidity. *Journal of Emotional and Behavioral Disorders, 1,* 101–108.

Forness, S., & Knitzer, J. (1992). A new proposed definition and terminology to replace "serious emotional disturbance" in the Individuals With Disabilities Education Act. *School Psychology Review, 21,* 12–20.

Fredericks, H. D., & Bullis, M. (1989). *A community-based supported work program for SED adolescents* (Funded grant proposal, Rehabilitative Services Administration). Monmouth: Western Oregon State College, Division of Teaching Research.

Fredericks, H. D., & Nishioka-Evans, V. (1987). Functional curriculum. In C. M. Nelson, R. B. Rutherford, & B. I. Wolford (Eds.), *Special education in the juvenile justice system.* Columbus, OH: Merrill.

Freedman, B. J., Donahoe, C. P., Rosenthal, L., Schlundt, D. G., & McFall, R. M. (1978). A social-behavioral analysis of skill deficits in delinquent and nondelinquent boys. *Journal of Consulting and Clinical Psychology, 46,* 1448–1462.

Friend, M., & Bauwens, J. (1988). Managing resistance: An essential consulting skill for learning disabilities teachers. *Journal of Learning Disabilities, 21,* 556–561.

Gaffney, L. R., & McFall, R. M. (1981). A comparison of social skills in delinquent and nondelinquent adolescent girls using a behavioral role-playing inventory. *Journal of Consulting and Clinical Psychology, 49,* 959–967.

Gelatt, A. B. (1962). Decision-making: A conceptual frame of reference for counseling. *Journal of Counseling Psychology, 9,* 240–245.

Goldstein, A. P., & Glick, B. (1987). *Aggression Replacement Training: A comprehensive intervention for aggressive youth.* Champaign, IL: Research Press.

Halpern, A. S. (1988). Characteristics of a quality program. In C. Warger & B. Weiner (Eds.), *Secondary special education: A guide to promising public school programs.* Reston, VA: Council on Exceptional Children.

Halpern, A. S. (1990). A methodological review of follow-up and follow-along studies tracking school leavers from special education. *Career Development for Exceptional Individuals, 13,* 13–27.

Halpern, A. S., Benz, M. R., & Lindstrom, L. E. (1992). A systems change approach to improving secondary special education and transition programs at the community level. *Career Development for Exceptional Individuals, 15,* 109–120.

Halpern, A. S., Herr, C. M., Doren, B., & Wolf, N. K. (2000). *Next S.T.E.P.: Student transition and educational planning.* Austin, TX: PRO-ED.

Hazel, J. S., Schumaker, J. B., Sherman, J., & Sheldon-Wildgen, J. (1982). Group social skills training: A program for court-adjudicated probationary youth. *Criminal Justice and Behavior, 9,* 35–53.

Hess, A. (1986). Educational triage in an urban school. *Metropolitan Education, 1,* 39–52.

Illback, R. (1993). *Evaluation of the Kentucky IMPACT program for children with severe emotional disabilities: Year two.* Frankfort, KY: Cabinet for Human Resources, Division of Mental Health, Children and Youth Services Branch.

Institute of Medicine (1989). *Research on children and adolescents with mental, behavioral, and developmental disorders.* Washington, DC: National Academy Press.

Izzo, M. V. (1994, Spring). Ohio wins systems change grant to improve transition services. *The Bridge,* p. 2.

Janes, C., Hesselbrock, V., Myers, D. G., & Penniman, J. (1979). Problem boys in young adulthood: Teachers' ratings and twelve-year follow-up. *Journal of Youth and Adolescence, 8,* 453–472.

Johnson, J. R., & Rusch, F. R. (1993). Secondary special education and transition services: Identification and recommendations for future research and demonstration. *Career Development for Exceptional Individuals, 16,* 1–18.

Joint Commission on the Mental Health of Children. (1969). *Crisis in child mental health*. New York: Harper and Row.

Jordan, D. D., & Ichinose, C. (1992). *Children's services report*. Ventura, CA: Ventura County Mental Health Services.

Kauffman, J. M. (1989). *Characteristics of behavior disorders of children and youth* (4th ed.). Columbus, OH: Merrill.

Kaufman, R., & Herman, J. (1991). Strategic planning for a better society. *Educational Leadership, 48,* 4–8.

Kavale, K., Forness, S., & Alper, A. (1986). Research in behavioral disorders/emotional disturbance: A survey of subject identification criteria. *Behavioral Disorders, 11,* 159–167.

Kelly, J. (1982). *Social skills training*. New York: Springer.

Kendall, P. C., Deardorff, P., & Finch, A. J. (1977). Empathy and socialization in first and repeat offenders and normals. *Journal of Abnormal Psychology, 5,* 93–97.

Knitzer, J. (1982). *Unclaimed children: The failure of public responsibility to children and adolescents in need of mental health services*. Washington, DC: Children's Defense Fund.

Knitzer, J., Steinberg, Z., & Fleisch, B. (1990). *At the schoolhouse door*. New York: Bank Street College of Education.

Kortering, L. J., & Edgar, E. B. (1988). Vocational rehabilitation and special education: A need for cooperation. *Rehabilitation Counseling Bulletin, 31,* 178–184.

Kunisawa, B. (1988). A nation in crisis: The dropout dilemma. *National Education Association Today, 6*(6), 61–65.

Lehman, C. M. (1996). *Families with children who have emotional or behavioral disorders: An examination of the nature and extent of the informal and formal support families receive and parent perceptions of how helpful these supports are in meeting the needs of their children and families*. Unpublished doctoral dissertation, University of Oregon, Eugene.

Levin, H. (1982). *The cost to the nation of inadequate education* (Report to the Select Committee on Equal Opportunity). Washington, DC: U. S. Government Printing Office.

Levine, P., & Edgar, E. B. (1994). An analysis of respondent agreement in follow-up studies of graduates of special and regular education programs. *Exceptional Children, 60,* 334–343.

Levinson, M., & Neuninger, C. (1971). Problem-solving behavior in suicidal adolescents. *Journal of Consulting and Clinical Psychology, 37,* 433–436.

Lindsey, P., & Blalock, G. (1993). Transition to work programs in rural areas: Developing collaborative ethics. *Career Development for Exceptional Individuals, 16,* 159–170.

Loeber, R. (1991). Antisocial behavior: More enduring than changeable? *Child and Adolescent Psychology, 30,* 393–397.

Marder, C. (1992). *Secondary students classified as seriously emotionally disturbed: How are they being served?* Menlo Park, CA: SRI International.

Martin, J., Huber-Marshall, L., Maxson, L., & Jerman, P. (1996). *Self-directed IEP*. Colorado Springs: Sopris West.

McCarty, T., Sitlington, P. L., & Asselin, S. (1991). Preparing personnel to educate and employ individuals at risk: A look into the 21st century. *The Journal for Vocational Special Needs Education, 14*(1) 17–20.

Menhard, S. (1990). *Longitudinal research*. Newbury Park, CA: Sage.

Naglieri, J. A., LeBuffe, P. A, & Pfeiffer, S. I. (1993). *Devereux Behavior Rating Scale–School Form.* San Antonio: The Psychological Corporation.

National Transition Network. (1996–1997, Winter). Transition systems change and school-to-work: Emerging areas of collaboration. *Network News,* pp. 1, 3, 6.

Neel, R. S., Meadows, N., Levine, P., & Edgar, E. B. (1988). What happens after special education: A statewide follow-up study of secondary students who have behavioral disorders. *Behavioral Disorders, 13,* 209–216.

Nelson, C. M., & Pearson, C. A. (1991). *Integrating services for children and youth with emotional and behavioral disorders.* Reston, VA: Council for Exceptional Children.

Nishioka-Evans, V. (1987). The Sprague High School Project for severely emotionally disturbed youth. *Teaching Research Newsletter, 15*(5).

Parker, J., & Asher, S. (1987). Peer relations and later personal adjustment: Are low-accepted children at risk? *Psychological Bulletin, 102,* 357–389.

Petrie, H. G. (1976). Do you see what I see? The epistemology of interdisciplinary inquiry. *Educational Researcher, 5,* 9–15.

Platt, J., Scura, W., & Hannon, J. (1973). Problem-solving thinking of youthful incarcerated heroin addicts. *Journal of Community Psychology, 43,* 278–281.

Platt, J., Spivack, G., Altman, N., & Altman, D. (1974). Adolescent problem-solving thinking. *Journal of Consulting and Clinical Psychology, 42,* 787–793.

President's Commission on Mental Health. (1978). *Report of the Subtask Panel on Infants, Children and Adolescents.* Washington, DC: U. S. Government Printing Office.

Renzaglia, A. (1986). Preparing personnel to support and guide emerging contemporary service alternatives. In F. R. Rusch (Ed.), *Competitive employment issues and strategies.* Baltimore: Paul H. Brookes.

Romanish, B. (1991). *Empowering teachers: Restructuring schools for the 21st century.* Lanham, MD: University Press of America.

Rumberger, R. W. (1987). High school dropouts: A review of issues and evidence. *Review of Educational Research, 57*(2), 101–121.

Sailor, W., & Guess, D. (1983). *Severely handicapped students: An instructional design.* Boston: Houghton Mifflin.

Sileo, T. W., Rude, H. A., & Luckner, J. L. (1988). Collaborative consultation: A model for transition planning for handicapped youth. *Education and Training in Mental Retardation, 23,* 333–339.

Sitlington, P. (1986). *Transition, special needs and vocational education.* Columbus, OH: National Center for Research in Vocational Education. (ERIC Document Reproduction Services No. 272 769)

Slaby, R., & Guerra, N. (1988). Cognitive mediators of aggression in adolescent offenders: Assessment. *Developmental Psychology, 24,* 580–588.

Smith, G. J., Edelen-Smith, P. J., & Stodden, R. A. (1995). How to avoid the seven pitfalls of systemic planning: A school and community plan for transition. *Teaching Exceptional Children, 27,* 42–47.

Stodden, R. A., & Leake, D. W. (1994). Getting to the core of transition: A re-assessment of old wine in new bottles. *Career Development for Exceptional Individuals, 17,* 65–76.

Stroul, B. A., & Friedman, R. M. (1986). *A system of care for severely disturbed children and youth*. Washington, DC: (Child and Adolescent Service System Program, Technical Assistance Center, Georgetown University Child Development Center.

Szymanski, E. M. (1994). Transition: Life-span and life-space considerations for empowerment. *Exceptional Children, 60,* 402–410.

Szymanski, E. M., Hanley-Maxwell, C., & Asselin, S. (1990). Rehabilitation counseling, special education, and vocational education: Three transition disciplines. *Career Development for Exceptional Individuals, 1,* 29–38.

United States Congress, Office of Technology Assessment. (1986). *Children's mental health: Problems and services* (OTA–BP–H–33). Washington, DC: U. S. Government Printing Office.

Valdes, K., Williamson, C., & Wagner, M. (1990). *The National Longitudinal Transition Study of Special Education Students: Volume 3. Youth categorized as emotionally disturbed.* Palo Alto, CA: SRI International.

Wagner, M. (1991). *Drop outs: What do we know? What can we do?* Menlo Park, CA: SRI International.

Wagner, M., & Shaver, D. (1989). *Educational programs and achievements of secondary special education students: Findings from the National Longitudinal Transition Study.* Menlo Park, CA: SRI International.

Walker, H. M., & Rankin, R. (1983). Assessing the behavioral expectations and demands of less restrictive settings. *School Psychology Review, 12,* 274–284.

Weber, J. (1987). *Strengthening vocational education's role in decreasing the dropout rate.* Columbus: Ohio State University, Center for Research in Vocational Education.

Nochajski, Susan M - University at Buffalo
Dept. of O.T.
515 Kimball Tower
Buffalo NY 14214
Phone (716) 829-3141
nochajsk@buffalo.edu

About the Editors

From 1984 through 1995, Dr. Michael Bullis worked in the Teaching Research Division of what was then Western Oregon State College and is now Western Oregon University. During this time he collaborated with Dr. H. D. Fredericks on model demonstration and research projects for adolescents with emotional and behavioral disorders, as well as other high-risk behaviors. In 1995, Dr. Bullis took a position at the University of Oregon, where he currently is a professor in the College of Education, Area of Special Education, and is continuing work with high-risk adolescents.

Dr. H. D. ("Bud") Fredericks worked in the Teaching Research Division of Western Oregon State College, now Western Oregon University, from 1968 until his retirement in 1995. He is a nationally recognized expert in service provision for children and adolescents with extreme behavioral challenges. Since his retirement he has maintained active involvement in Work Unlimited, a supported work agency he established, and he is the chairperson of Benton County, Oregon's, Commission on Children and Families. In 2001, the College of Education at the University of Oregon selected Dr. Fredericks as its Outstanding Alumnus.

About the Contributors

Job Designs and the Sprague High School Program are programs developed by the Teaching Research Division of Western Oregon State College, now Western Oregon University.

Dr. Constance Lehman coordinated the Job Designs project from 1989 through 1991. She earned her PhD from the University of Oregon in special education in 1996. Dr. Lehman currently works at Portland State University in the School of Social Work.

Dr. Michael R. Benz is a professor in the College of Education at the University of Oregon and is head of the Area on Special Education. He is a nationally recognized expert on the development of transition programs.

Ms. Janet Corbitt worked in the Job Designs project from 1989 through 1994. She currently is at home full-time, raising three children.

Ms. Kathleen Paris began work in the Job Designs project in 1989 and coordinated the project from 1992 through 1995. She currently is director of the Benton County, Oregon, Court Appointed Special Advocates Program for children and adolescents.

Dr. Vicki Nishioka worked in and coordinated the Sprague High School Program from 1984 through 1996. She earned her doctorate from the University of Oregon in special education in 2001. She currently is a research associate in the University of Oregon's Institute on Violence and Destructive Behavior, working on a project for at-risk middle school students.

Ms. Julia Bulen worked with Dr. Michael Bullis at Teaching Research from 1989 through 1995 on projects focusing on the development of transition programs in high schools. She is an instructor at Teaching Research.